The Sophoclean Chorus

Cynthia P. Gardiner

The Sophoclean Chorus

A STUDY OF CHARACTER AND FUNCTION

UNIVERSITY OF IOWA PRESS
IOWA CITY

University of Iowa Press, Iowa City 52242
Copyright © 1987 by the University of Iowa
Printed in the United States of America
First edition, 1987

Jacket and book design by Dariel Mayer
Typesetting by G & S Typesetters, Inc., Austin, Texas
Printing and binding by Edwards Brothers, Inc., Ann Arbor, Michigan

Library of Congress Cataloging-in-Publication Data

Gardiner, Cynthia P., 1942–
  The Sophoclean chorus.

  Bibliography: p.
  Includes index.
    1. Sophocles—Technique. 2. Sophocles—Characters.
3. Drama—Chorus (Greek drama). 4. Characters and
characteristics in literature. I. Title.
PA4417.G35   1986   882'.01   86-16008
ISBN 0-87745-155-9

To R. E. G.

Contents

Preface

When I began working on this book, many years ago, the critical literature on Sophocles was already so vast that it seemed almost impertinent to want to add to it; but I had perceived what I believed was a small niche, nearly empty but still important, that needed to be filled. Shortly after the first draft was completed, Burton's book on the chorus was published. But our approaches, as the reader will soon discover, are so different that the niche, far from being crowded, has now expanded, and much more work will, I hope, be done on the chorus in years to come.

This book is about dramatic technique, about methods of characterization and the function of character in drama. It is written chiefly for classicists, but I hope it will also offer something to less specialized readers; to this end, I have attempted to confine the most technical discussions to the footnotes. My coverage of the scholarship has necessarily been selective rather than comprehensive, especially in the case of material that appeared after I completed the final draft. I apologize to any whose work I may have neglected.

I owe a great deal to Gordon Kirkwood for his invaluable advice and support and to two superb teachers, Richmond Lattimore and Robert Murray, who are alive now only—but always—in memory. I am also deeply grateful to the many teachers, friends, and colleagues who, over the years, have helped me with their comments and encouragement, especially Sam Atkins, Ruth and Harold Cherniss, Richard DePuma, Phyllis and David Furley, Mabel Lang, and Bill Scott; to my father, James B. Gardiner; to Jean Greenwood, Jean Peterson, and Jane Davis, who labored over the preparation of the manuscript. And to both the reader for the Press and the editorial staff, whose careful attention and expertise have rescued me from many embarrassments.

There are two persons whom I will never be able to thank adequately: my husband, Clifton Scott, whose love and champagne have kept me going; and Ralph Giesey, a dear friend and a great scholar, to whom this book is respectfully dedicated.

CHAPTER I

Introduction

Sophocles, according to the *Suda,* wrote "a prose work on the chorus." Even if we should believe the testimony of that often unreliable tenth-century encyclopaedia, the work may only have covered technical and musical matters (such as dance, costume, types of voices) and not the larger question of the chorus' dramatic character and function. Still, it is a tantalizing piece of information when considered in light of Aristotle's opinion that Sophocles' choruses participate more actively in the structure of the play than do Euripides'.[1] But despite these suggestions that Sophocles paid particular attention to the chorus' place in the drama, his choruses are usually lumped together with those of the other two poets and treated as manifestations of a general phenomenon, "The Greek Chorus." It must indeed be granted that certain obvious features immediately distinguish the chorus from the other participants in the drama. The chorus of a play are a group of persons, "they" rather than "it," speaking or singing in unison; although occasionally represented by an individual who speaks in iambic trimeters, as a group they speak almost exclusively in lyric or anapestic meters, never making a speech in iambics. So great are these differences, so readily perceptible to both ear and eye, that at first it seems rea-

---

1. *Poetics* 1456a25–32. The exact meaning of the passage is still disputed; cf. Else (*Aristotle's Poetics: The Argument* [Cambridge (Mass.), 1963], 551–558), who holds that Aristotle only means that the chorus' songs must be connected with the plot and not be entirely unrelated interludes. But the statement that the chorus must be one of the actors and contend (συναγωνίζεσθαι) as in Sophocles' plays rather than as in Euripides' could easily include the notion that the chorus, like the actors, must have a character consistent with their utterances, since Euripides' choral odes are seldom less connected to the plot than, say, the first stasimon of *Antigone,* although his choruses' characters are sometimes less than fully believable. Jürgen Rode ("Das Chorlied," 115n100) tries to eliminate the contrast between the poets by saying that Aristotle is referring only to the late plays of Euripides in which the songs may be considered "pre-embolima."

sonable to consider the chorus a discrete phenomenon, especially since the chorus' function, according again to Aristotle, was already beginning to atrophy in the fifth century. Consequently, the choruses of all Greek tragedies were for too long ignored entirely, or their utterances were regarded as the poet's own views and their function deemed that of an "ideal spectator."[2]

Yet such a view ignores not only the authority of Aristotle but the testimony of Aristophanes, who may serve as a reliable eyewitness if his words are interpreted with care and a sense of humor. When Dicaeopolis in *Acharnians* explains why he wants to borrow a ragged costume from Euripides, he says (440–444):

> For today I must seem to be a beggar, I must be who I am and yet not seem to be him. The spectators must know me for what I am, but the chorusmen must be there as dupes, so that I may make fools of them with my wisecracks.

Although it may be argued that the comic chorus differed from the tragic, Euripides' immediate approval of Dicaeopolis' scheme (445) would surely remind the audience of similar deceptions of the chorus in tragedy. If the chorus could be deceived by a disguise, they can hardly have been commonly accepted as an "ideal spectator." In fact, the nineteenth-century concept of the chorus as an ideal spectator, an interpreter for the audience of the dramatic events, probably derives from the only other ancient testimony that survives, Horace's admonition to Roman playwrights that the chorus should be a friend and advisor of the good and should be modest, just, and pious (*Epistles* 2.3.196–201).

Nowadays, largely owing to Kirkwood's pioneering work, it is no longer a matter of dispute whether Sophocles has to some degree endowed his extant choruses with recognizable dramatic characters.[3] The principle of the choral character is commonly invoked to assist critics in interpreting particular odes or choral comments. When, however, as often happens, the meaning of the passage in question still remains obscure, critics tend to modify the principle freely. One common modification is the assumption

2. Schlegel's famous dictum, that the chorus represent the *idealisierte Zuschauer*, was maintained, with variations and adaptations, for nearly a century and a half by German scholarship (cf. Kranz, *Stasimon*, 225) until Müller followed the lead of English scholars in refuting it with the evidence of the plays themselves (cf. "Chor und Handlung," 212–213).

3. In *Sophoclean Drama*, chapter 4: "The Role of the Chorus," Kirkwood demonstrates that Sophocles has given an individual and consistent character to each of his choruses, although he considers the chorus' iambic contributions to have only slight dramatic value (188–189).

that the chorus may slip in and out of character as the poet requires.[4] This slippage seems to occur because the choral characters are so broadly and vaguely sketched in comparison with the principals' characters that the chorus' identity easily blurs during the play, and they become "the chorus" rather than this particular chorus.[5] Horace's remark may have influenced a similar view, that the chorus always play essentially the same character and role in every drama, such as that of ordinary persons whose limited and often mistaken perceptions contrast with and thus magnify the greatness of the heroic individuals in the play.[6]

Because the chorus' character seems inadequately delineated in comparison with the personae of the principals, critics usually find that the chorus' dramatic function in the play is likewise limited. The chorus tend to be viewed much more as singers of odes than as characters in the drama.

4. Kitto, for example, maintains that the poet deliberately abandoned the choral character upon occasion, most noticeably at the second stasimon of *Oed. Tyr.* (*Poiesis*, 223–224; *Greek Tragedy*, 167–168). Even Ronnet, who insists that the chorus always have a character (*Sophocle*, 167), finds that occasionally a chorus may "lose its character" for a moment, appear to intrude unrealistically on a private conversation, or sing songs that are almost mere interludes between episodes (135, 157–158). Burton, in his extensive monograph on Sophocles' choruses, pays much more heed to the chorus' character. He maintains, however, that although the chorus never say anything that is not dramatically relevant—that is, they never sing mere musical interludes—their "group personality" does not require the same degree of characterization as a principal's, and so they sometimes speak inconsistently (*The Chorus*, esp. 3, 35, 170, 238). Only Errandonea defends the unbroken integrity of every choral character in Sophocles, but his work (*Sófocles* [1958]) is not an organized study of the chorus, and many of his conclusions are dubious in the extreme.

5. Such was Kranz's assessment of the choral character (*Stasimon*, 220–222), and his view, variously adapted, of its relatively tenuous construction is common. Cf. Winnington-Ingram (*Sophocles*, 137, 241n77), and Burton's statement that "it is a convention in Greek Tragedy that a group of people whose sympathies are known to be wholly devoted to one contestant should step out of character for a moment and make a detached, even censorious reflection on both" (*The Chorus*, 35).

6. Müller ("Chor und Handlung," esp. 217) accepts the proposition that all Sophoclean choral utterances proceed from a dramatic character but maintains that this character is essentially the same in every play: average mortals who cannot comprehend the hero and are usually mistaken. So also Ronnet, who finds that the chorus, although speaking as a dramatic character, never entirely "approve of the hero" but always in the end embody "la commune médiocrité" (*Sophocle*, 168). Kaimio (*Chorus of Greek Drama*, 243–244), observing the regular use of the first person singular by Sophoclean choruses, believes that this usage reflects Sophocles' practice of always making the chorus fail to understand and share the sufferings of the hero. Others give the chorus an even more bland and generalized character; see, for example, Whitman (*Sophocles*, 31), or Webster's view (*Introduction*, 81) that the chorus are "sympathetic and helpful friends of the characters with the sanity and religion of the ordinary man." Cf. the statement at [Aristotle] *Problemata* 922b26, that the chorus' only role is that of an inactive watcher who displays a friendly attitude to those onstage.

The odes are certainly the chorus' longest and most impressive utterances, and critical attention is therefore concentrated upon them, while the iambic and lesser anapestic passages are ignored entirely or dismissed as banal and mechanical. The songs of all the Greek tragedians, especially of Sophocles, have been extensively examined by scholars and critics, who generally take one or both of the following approaches: first, the classification of the songs into various types—such as lament, hyporcheme, meditative interlude—and the study of the function of these types in the structure of the plays; second, the analysis of the poetic composition of each ode—its imagery, themes, lyric structure, meter, symbolism—and the relation of these elements to the moods and themes of both the surrounding scenes and the play as a whole. The information gained from these studies is then used to determine both the immediate emotional responses that the individual odes evoke from the audience and the cumulative effect of these emotional responses on the audience's perception of the actions and issues of the play.[7]

Such thorough study of the chorus' lyric function has, of course, played an important part in our understanding and appreciation of Greek tragedy. The splendid poetry of many of these songs contributes not merely to the spectacle of performance but also to the continuity of theme and the emotional effects of the play. In Sophocles' dramas especially, the odes are a rich source of his famous dramatic irony, filled with images and references that signify far more to the audience than to the characters onstage. Yet in these examinations of the lyrics the chorus' character has been largely neglected, to such an extent that the odes often seem to take on an existence apart from the choruses that sing them. In discussing the interpretation and function of an ode, critics frequently speak of the song itself, rather than the chorus, as performing a dramatic role. The ode becomes the actor: it "offers a commentary on the previous scene," or "examines the king's behavior," or "looks forward to coming events." Seldom indeed do critics attempt any comparable disembodiment of the actors' speeches; it is almost always the character, not the speech, who "says" or "comments" or "reminds us of" something.

7. The title of Parry's book, *The Lyric Poems of Greek Tragedy* (Toronto, 1978), exemplifies this tendency to concentrate attention upon the odes and ignore other choral utterances. Many do not bother to distinguish among the three poets' treatment of character (cf., e.g., Rode, "Das Chorlied," 113–115). Even Burton dismisses most of the chorus' iambic lines as commonplace or conventional and concentrates upon the odes' poetic construction and textual problems.

As a result of concentrating on the content of the odes while neglecting the singers, scholarship has tended to lose sight of the chorus as a character in the drama, and to define the chorus' dramatic function by simply inferring from the plays the existence of certain conventions that severely limited choral behavior. One critic, for example, observing that the chorus do not make long speeches, claims it is "an unbroken law" that the chorus can never give descriptive pieces, prove contentions, or engage in logical debate, and they are therefore excluded from the rhetorical element of tragedy.[8] Another insists that the chorus' participation in the actions always occurs early in the play (if at all), before the principals "have set to work."[9] Another, and even more important, result of the neglect of the choral character is the loss of the significant dramatic effects that an individual ode had as the utterance of a particular character. Since there are many important speeches by the principals that could admit of very different interpretations, and dramatic functions, if they were uttered by different characters, it is surely reasonable to ask whether the chorus' utterances were likewise interpreted by the audience according to its perception of the chorus' character. Certainly we must not continue to assume without further proof that the odes superseded the singers, that the ancient audience was always inclined to ignore the chorus' dramatic function in favor of the lyric one.

This investigation therefore attempts to redress the existing imbalance between the study of poetry and the study of character by analyzing the roles of the chorus in each of Sophocles' extant tragedies and determining the extent to which he meant the audience to perceive the chorus as a character in the play. We shall examine each choral utterance within its specific context and in its dramatic sequence, bringing to bear on the problem all the analytic processes and standards that are used to study the characters of the principals. In taking this new approach to the study of the chorus, we are not contributing to the neglect of the poetry of the odes and their lyric effects, for they have been often and thoroughly examined elsewhere. Here we shall examine the poet's methods of characterization, trying to see beneath the splendor of the poetry the technical dramatic foundation that sustains it.

The very act of concentrating on a single element of a play is a deviation from the logical approach to drama, which is to view it as a spectator in the

---

8. A. M. Dale, "The Chorus in the Action of Greek Tragedy," *Collected Papers*, 211.
9. Kitto, *Greek Tragedy*, 162.

context of fifth-century Athens. We must not rove back and forth through the play searching for clues and hidden meanings, as many do, but must examine the play as the original audience did: from the beginning, watching as the poet progressively discloses the actions and characters.[10] Since these plays were composed chiefly for a single performance, upon which the honor of a first prize depended, we may presume that the passages which confuse modern critics did not confuse the original audience. The performance of a play includes no pauses for deep and subtle analysis of motive; one may ponder afterward the themes and general truth of the whole work, but the course of the action must be immediately comprehensible. An audience which does not understand what is happening in a play does not award its author the first prize.

The problem of considering a play as a performance is of course greatly magnified when the visual aspect of production is missing. But we cannot merely exclaim what a pity it is that we have lost the music and dance of a Greek tragedy, and then, perhaps rather thankfully, return to a careful analysis of the written text. The movement of the players and the delivery of the lines were presumably orchestrated by the poet-producer as a part of the entire dramatic effect. Movement especially is exceedingly difficult to reconstruct, but its importance in criticism of ancient drama is coming to be more and more widely recognized.[11] We must at least decide whether to accept the traditional "conventions," largely scholiastic, about choral movement that have grown up over the centuries.

Prominent among these traditions is the notion that the chorus were an essentially rectangular formation, arranged in neatly labeled ranks and files. It is based chiefly on Pollux, and there is no evidence that such a convention obtained for the chorus of fifth-century tragedy. Nor is the assumption that the chorus danced odes in a circular pattern—strophe clockwise, antistrophe counterclockwise—accepted by modern scholarship.[12] There remains, however, the broader question of when and how often the chorus did dance. From the Aristotelian term for a post-parodos choral ode, *stasimon*, was inferred the now discredited notion that the chorus stood still during the odes. But this notion in turn generated the

10. As does Kitto in *Form and Meaning*, where his success in dealing with the so-called Sophoclean inconsistencies testifies to the validity of his method.

11. Cf. Taplin's introductory remarks on "Visual Meaning," *Stagecraft*, 12–28.

12. See, in general, Lawler (*Dance*, esp. 11–12) and Pickard-Cambridge (*Dramatic Festivals*, 246–257).

likewise erroneous term *hyporcheme*, to designate songs so "lively" that they must surely have been danced.[13] Perhaps the desire for more dance from the chorus was responsible for the further assumption, again scholiastic in origin, that the chorus sometimes accompanied an actor's speech with mimetic gestures and even dancing.[14]

The reaction to these old errors, however, may be responsible for the currently widespread belief that the chorus danced during every song.[15] Dance does indeed seem to have been an important part of Greek celebration, particularly in religious ceremonies and festivals, and the dramatists apparently choreographed their own lyrics. But no matter how common dancing may be in a culture, there are numerous occasions which are hardly suitable for dancing. The old would seldom dance except for religious reasons, and even then people might laugh at them or scorn their impropriety; in Euripides' *Bacchae*, Teiresias and Cadmus admit that they may appear foolish (204–205, cf. 251–252). And it is most unlikely that the Council of Thebes would dance while pondering weighty problems of state. The proposition that tragic choral lyrics were nearly always danced rests on the presumption that the chorus could drop out of character and do things that would be wholly contrary to the practices of "real life." We must assume that the chorus are dancing when they say they are, and also during odes with a generally religious or celebratory tone, such as hymns of thanksgiving. Otherwise, however, we must assume they behaved in a manner consistent with the character they display in the song. That manner would naturally include the use of expressive gestures such as the actors used, but there is no evidence whatever to confirm the notion that a choral ode was an independent performance, always accompanied by dance even when dancing would be wholly inappropriate to the dramatic situation. Finally, the nature of the dances that the chorus did perform is still hypothetical. Much work has been done on the figures of the dance as

13. Cf. Dale, "Stasimon and Hyporcheme," *Collected Papers*, 34–40. Lawler (*Dance*, 30–31) associates the term with a native Cretan dance and proposes that the word was eventually generalized to mean "merely a lively, joyous dance, with strong mimetic gestures."

14. This convention, propounded by the scholiast on Aristophanes, *Clouds* 1352, would be repellent to any Western actor of the last four hundred years; against it, see Dale (*Lyric Metres*, 213) and Taplin (*Stagecraft*, 20).

15. Cf. Dale, "Words, Music and Dance," *Collected Papers*, 156–169, esp. 163–164. It is hard to believe that the audience needed the dance as "a pictorial clarification" of the song. For the meagre ancient testimony on tragic dance, see Pickard-Cambridge, *Dramatic Festivals*, 249–252.

represented in art, but the various attempts to associate certain dance steps with specified metrical patterns are still quite unproven.[16]

Although the music is lost, the modes of delivery of the choral utterances may be subjected to inquiry in the hope of obtaining at least a working hypothesis. The attempts to show in fine detail a direct relation between meter and content are still purely speculative.[17] We can only draw reasonable inferences about general types of utterances. Iambic trimeter lines assigned to the chorus in dialogue scenes were probably delivered by the chorus-leader alone, in the usual tragic "speech" mode, since groups of persons do not normally converse as a whole with individuals. As for choral iambic trimeters in lyric passages, if there is a change of speaker before and after the choral trimeters (that is, the trimeters are part of an "epirrhematic" sequence),[18] it is reasonable to suppose they were delivered in the speech mode by the chorus-leader alone, thereby contrasting with the lyric utterances of the other speaker. But the real problem is the single iambic trimeter that is directly preceded or followed by lyric without a change of speaker; such lines not infrequently occur at the beginning or middle of a lyric stanza, as in the parodos of *Philoctetes*. It is quite possible that these lines were delivered in a manner other than purely lyric, thereby effecting a perceptible contrast with the surrounding lyric.[19] The same may apply to other stichic or "spoken" meters, such as dactylic; we shall examine the probable dramatic effects at each passage within the contexts.

16. See Prudhommeau (*Danse grecque*, 495–524), who choreographs various phrases from tragedy with much imagination and little evidence. Cf. Fitton (*CQ* 23 [1973], 254ff.) and Webster (*Greek Chorus*). The latter draws a great many inferences from poetry and vase paintings about the dancing "tempi" and hence about the particular dance-steps associated with different meters. But interesting as they may be, they are still only conjectures. See, for example, his hypothesis of the existence of "walking time" (long "lines" of poetry), "striding time" (shorter "lines"), and "excited time" (still shorter "lines"), which is proposed (54) and assumed as fact (200), but never proven.

17. For examples of the type (besides Webster's "tempi"), see Korzeniewski (e.g., *RhM* 105 [1962], 142ff.) and Fowler (*C&M* 28 [1967], 143–171). The judgments tend to be subjective—"sprightly dactyls," "rising choriambic," and so forth—whereas we can as yet properly say only that sequences of long syllables probably sounded heavy and solemn and sequences of short syllables, light and rapid.

18. Some distinguish tragic "epirrheme" from "kommos," restricting the latter term to the purely lyric dialogue (cf. Popp, "Das Amoibaion," 222–223, 230–235); Taplin (*Stagecraft*, 474) would limit it even further, allowing it to apply only to dirges. Since the various distinctions are not consistently applied, and since the mode of delivery of anapests is uncertain, we shall simply use the term "kommos" as a convenience, to identify all passages of dialogue in which the chorus participate and which contain at least some lyrics.

19. Cf. Dale, *Lyric Metres*, 86, 207–208.

The problem of the passages of anapestic dimeters is even more difficult. The alleged distinction between "recitative" and "melic" (or sung)
anapestic systems is based largely on whether they are written in the Attic
of the speeches or the "literary Doric" of the lyrics, a distinction that often
depends on the judgment of the scribe.[20] Again, we can only examine the
possible contrastive effects in particular passages and offer appropriate hy-
potheses. There seems to be a tendency in Sophocles for both actors and
chorus to deliver facts in anapests rather than lyrics, so that the systems
may not always have been sung. But elsewhere the content of anapestic
passages sometimes suggests a more agitated or emotional delivery than
that of iambic trimeters, so that there may have been some "intermediate
mode" of delivery. Nor can we tell whether the anapestic systems assigned
to the chorus were uttered by the group as a whole or the chorus-leader
alone. It is possible, for example, that the occurrence of anapestic systems
in iambic scenes might indicate delivery by the group in contrast to the
chorus-leader's iambic trimeters.

The absence of vital factual information gives rise to one last problem
that must be considered before beginning the analysis of the chorus, and
that is the order in which the plays should be examined. The most obvious
approach is to study them in chronological order of composition, but only
two of the seven extant plays are securely dated. There being, therefore, no
sure way of using chronology to determine the development of the treatment of the chorus, we might instead search for some apparent progression in the characterization of the chorus and use it to postulate a relative
chronology of the plays. Yet although this method may have a certain validity when applied to technical matters of style, such as meter and diction, in
the larger area of characterization and plot construction statements about
chronological development can hardly have much accuracy when they are
based on fewer than eight percent of Sophocles' tragic production (assuming that at least three-quarters of the 123 plays ascribed to him by the *Suda*
were tragedies). With such a small statistical base, it seems unlikely that

20. See Pickard-Cambridge (*Dramatic Festivals*, 156–164) for the evidence on the "recitative" mode, although his assumptions about the delivery of specific passages are largely
speculative. On the difficulties of distinguishing the two kinds of anapests by dialect or
meter, see the appendix to Jebb's commentary on *Antigone*, 248, *ad Ant.* 110ff., and below,
chapter 3, on the parodos of *Ajax*. Sylvia Brown's study of all the anapestic passages in the
extant tragedies is concerned with categorizing the content of the passages according to types
of ritual—prayer, lament, procession, "mimesis"; she accepts the technical distinctions of
"melic" and "recitative" without further investigation ("The Anapest," 49).

we can accurately determine whether the use or absence of a particular dramatic device is the result of artistic development or of the exigencies of particular plots and themes.

Instead of the chronological approach, therefore, we shall take the comparative one. Since the question at hand is characterization, we shall compare what appear to be similar choral characters, to see whether Sophocles distinguishes their individual identities or uses more general types. The choruses of the seven extant plays readily fall into three groups according to their basic personae: there are two choruses of men under the command of a military leader, three of civilian counselors to a king, and two of women. All are free, and all are Greek. Of the two reliably datable choruses, the men of *Philoctetes* have been chosen as the starting point, the model for analysis, and the remaining choruses then fall into a natural order of comparison according to their character-groups: men at war, men at home, and women.

Despite, or perhaps because of, the lack of detailed factual information in so many technical areas, it is tempting to indulge in speculative generalizations about the customary practices of "the Greek theatre." But without thorough comparative studies, especially of movement and delivery, in all of Greek drama, we cannot yet make any certain comprehensive statements about these problems in Sophocles. In numerous questions of performance and interpretation, the investigation must be restricted for now to a careful analysis of the context of each utterance. We may compare passages with earlier ones in the play, but if we are to sustain the role of audience we cannot go forward in the play in search of evidence except under certain limited circumstances. It is also essential to bear in mind the historical context of the chorus' statements and the audience's perception of them. It is all too easy to presume that because a particular interpretation or mode of performance would be more impressive, more "dramatic" than another according to one's own tastes and standards, it was therefore the one that Sophocles also preferred. Although many Sophoclean tragedies have a timeless quality that allows them to be interpreted effectively (but not always accurately) in the theatrical fashion of our era, it is our task here to reconstruct, as much as possible, the original performance as Sophocles produced it, to examine his dramatic techniques and attempt to determine in each instance the dramatic effect at which he was aiming, the particular response that he sought to elicit from his contemporary audience.

PART I

Men at War

CHAPTER 2

Philoctetes

There are several reasons for taking *Philoctetes* as a model for the analysis of Sophocles' dramatic use of the chorus, not the least of which is its well-established date. The play was presented in 409 B.C., late in the poet's long life. If we agree with the tradition that he was far from becoming senile, we may suppose the play to be the product of a formidable dramatic expertise. A poet with such a long history of success in manipulating his audience may fairly be assumed to have eliminated the imperfections of youth and inexperience and so to have made no blatant mistakes in this play, with which, as usual, he took first prize. Although this play, like every other Sophoclean tragedy, is not free from critical controversies, it is not as beleaguered by them as many others, such as *Antigone* or *Trachiniae*. In general, the relations of the principals to each other and to the plot are fairly clear,[1] so that we may examine the chorus' behavior without being too distracted by the principals' difficulties.

The choral parts involve some technical problems, most notably in the only ode of the play, but there is nothing like the interpretive concern that envelops the lyrics of, say, *Oedipus Tyrannus*. The chorus of *Philoctetes* are particularly unusual because they apparently have been assigned the role of a deceitful character. They are required to participate in the subterfuge and utter outright falsehoods. This behavior is hardly appropriate to the voice of the poet, the ideal spectator, or the embodiment of moderation. We shall therefore examine their role in detail, not only to define the chorus of this particular play but also to shed some light on the several

---

1. There are a few exceptions to this view, such as Calder's notion that Neoptolemus is portrayed as a liar throughout the entire play (*GRBS* 12 [1971], 153–174). Even the function of Heracles, once greatly disputed, has now been convincingly explained by Winnington-Ingram (*Sophocles*, 297–301).

problems of choral function and dramatic technique that recur in the other six plays.

It is usually assumed that the chorus enter the scene and begin their parodos after Odysseus' departure at the end of the prologue. But the fact that they know a great deal about Philoctetes' circumstances, about his suspiciousness (136) and hostility (156), seems to indicate that they were present during the prologue, or at least in a position to overhear the conversation. Neoptolemus' use of the plural rather than the dual (92) and Odysseus' use of the plural rather than the singular (126) also suggest the presence of a third party. Several critics have therefore proposed that the chorus enter with the principals at the beginning of the play.[2]

Nowhere else in Sophocles, or indeed in any of the extant tragedies, do the chorus enter silently and remain silent for more than a hundred lines before the parodos. Such entries may, of course, have taken place in lost plays, or this one may be a deliberate innovation. Perhaps the novelty of a silent chorus would combine with the furtiveness of the main characters to create a striking dramatic effect. Tragedy, however, required a firm mastery of dramatic economy. A great deal of information had to be condensed into a space much smaller than that of modern plays; and since the audience had no playbill listing the cast of characters in order of appearance, the task of identifying them devolved upon the author. Thus in every play we find that the first concern is for immediate identification of place, background information, and especially characters. The chorus, too, are never neglected, and both their entrance and their identification are often previously motivated, as, for example, in *Oedipus Tyrannus* (144: "let someone gather together Cadmus' people here") or *Oedipus Coloneus* (78–79: "I will go and tell these things to the local people," and then 111–112: "some old men are coming, looking for you"). Even the silent Pylades is quickly identified, although he may never speak, and thus distinguished from the mute attendants (Aesch., *Choëph.* 20; Soph., *Electra* 15–16; Eurip., *Electra* 82–83).

We must ask what would be the reaction of an audience, accustomed to knowing who is who, to an unidentified group standing about during the conspiratorial conversation between Odysseus and Neoptolemus. Surely the spectators would be wondering whether the men are able to see or hear what is going on. Are they Odysseus' men, or Neoptolemus'? Do they have

---

2. Chiefly Capps (*TAPA* 22 [1891], 24–25), Errandonea (*Sófocles* [1958], 264–265; cf. *Sófocles* [1970], 179–182), and Webster's commentary, 66 and 79.

some connection with the absent Philoctetes? Are they the chorus, or just an unusually large retinue of mutes? All these questions would divert the audience's attention from the important dialogue taking place between the characters, a dialogue which is supplying vital information about plot and action. It seems likely that a continuous distraction during such a critical scene as the prologue, or indeed during any scene at all, would offset any effect that the chorus' silent entrance might have.

The parodos itself (135ff.) justifies the assumption that the chorus were not visible during the prologue. The men of the chorus do indeed display a general knowledge of Philoctetes and his situation. They are aware that he is hostile, diseased, abandoned, and of noble origin, all matters which were discussed during the prologue. But the chorus are clearly unaware of the two important discoveries that have just been made—the nature and location of Philoctetes' dwelling and the fact that he is not now in it (152–158 and 161). If the chorus were in fact on the scene while Neoptolemus was discovering and exploring the cave, then the repetition of his discoveries in the parodos would seem an unnecessary waste of precious time. On the other hand, there is no reason to suppose that the audience would be startled or puzzled by the chorus' awareness of the general dramatic situation; one would assume, without actually stopping to ponder the question, that their awareness has resulted naturally from talk (or gossip) that occurred outside the play.[3]

Similarly, the chorus' apparent knowledge (which we deduce from their later actions) of the plot against Philoctetes is not evidence of their early entrance, but another example of Sophocles' dramatic thrift. An outline of the upcoming action has been accurately sketched in the prologue—the object of taking Philoctetes, the false story, the pseudo-merchant—and the facts are fresh in the audience's mind when the chorus begin their song. To repeat them in the name of realism would be uninstructive and tedious. Instead, Sophocles maneuvers the audience into accepting the chorus' general familiarity with the plot, by avoiding further discussion of specific tricks while throwing out a few general allusions to conspiracy in the chorus' request for instructions (142–143) and Neoptolemus' reply that they should come forward at need (148–149).[4] Since a premature entrance

3. Cf. Taplin, *Stagecraft*, 370. Schmidt (*Philoktet*, 48 and 53) believes that the chorus have been briefed by Odysseus; but if the poet wanted us to know that, he would have made the chorus say so.

4. Especially 143: τί σοι χρεὼν ὑπουργεῖν, echoing the ὑπουργεῖν of line 53, which Odysseus also addressed to Neoptolemus. On Sophocles' ability to manipulate his audience in

by the chorus would thus be irrelevant as well as distracting, and since the plurals used in lines 92 and 126 may easily refer to an escort of mutes that customarily attended important characters, we may presume the chorus enter the scene after Odysseus' departure.[5]

The complete absence of visual evidence, which is responsible for the debate about the timing of the chorus' entrance, also places us at a disadvantage when we try to delineate the chorus' dramatic identity. The costumes and movements would have given the audience some indication of the chorus' age and station, but we must fall back upon the literary evidence. The second argument to *Philoctetes* says that the chorus are old men sailing with Neoptolemus (ἐκ γερόντων τῶν τῷ Νεοπτολέμῳ συμπλεόντων), although this conclusion appears to be based solely on the chorus' habit of addressing Neoptolemus as "son" (παῖ and τέκνον). Nowhere in the play are they described or addressed as old men, and we may assume that elders could not plausibly be presented as sailing off on military missions. Because they are συμπλέοντες they are almost always referred to as Neoptolemus' "sailors," an unfortunate term which conjures up visions of the sailor-hatted, hornpipe-dancing chorus of *Pinafore*. A better rendition would be "shipmates," for according to Homer (our source and Sophocles' for the Trojan War) the ships were manned by warriors; there is never any mention of a distinction between rowers and fighters.[6] Although Philoctetes does later call them φίλοι ναῦται (531), after they have agreed to bring him along, it is clear from the reference in lines 1076–1077 that the duty of preparing the ship to sail belongs not to these men but to other ναῦται. Hence it seems most likely that the members of the chorus were costumed to represent fighting men of military age.

It is commonly said that the chorus are Neoptolemus' loyal and devoted

---

this way, see Kitto's analysis of the construction of the play (*Form and Meaning*, 87–137) and Knox's comments thereon (*Heroic Temper*, 187–190 [note 21]); cf. also Easterling (*ICS* 3 [1978], 27–30).

5. It is one of these mutes who is sent off as a guard and supposedly returns later as the false merchant. Jebb (*ad* 90ff.) suggests that although the chorus have not yet appeared (cf. *ad* 135f., 152ff.), Neoptolemus is alluding to them in line 92. Hinds (*CQ* 17 [1967], 174) cites Odysseus' use of the plural at 126 as proof that he plans to get Philoctetes himself on the ship, not just the bow.

6. See *Il.* 2.719–720, on Philoctetes' contingent at Troy, and Thucydides 1.10. Cf. also *Od.* 9.488–490, 12.193–194, and especially Elpenor's words at 11.74–78. Against Burton's assertions that the choruses of both *Phil.* and *Ajax* are not soldiers (*The Chorus*, 6–7, 226) see below, chapter 3, on the parodos of *Ajax*.

followers, that they support him in his deception, and that here in the parodos their function is to introduce the new theme of pity for Philoctetes.
Although there is a measure of truth in these generalities, we shall see
whether they are not inadequate to explain all of the chorus' utterances.
The chorus' first lines establish their own identity: Neoptolemus is their
master (135: δέσποτ'); alone in a strange land, they require his advice;
they seek his orders, indeed demand them (137: φράζε μοι). Then, in giving the reason (γάρ) why they seek his advice, they further identify Neoptolemus: the skill and judgment of kings is best, and he himself is such, a
Homeric sceptered king.[7] Therefore, they say, let him advise them how
they may help. Hitherto we have seen Neoptolemus in an essentially subordinate position to Odysseus; now the arrival of his men reminds us that the
son of Achilles is a king and commander. But at the same time that they
reaffirm Neoptolemus' status for the audience, they bring out certain aspects of their own position. The phrase ὦ τέκνον implies both that they
are older than their chief and also that a certain familiarity exists between
them and him. They are respectful of, but hardly awed by, their young
commander.

Neoptolemus responds to their request in a military fashion, by issuing
suitable orders: they are to look around now, but when the time comes they
are to be at hand ready to assist him.[8] Thus he quickly draws them into the
plot with him, and the audience can accept the chorus' complicity without
needing any realistic repetition of the scheme. But his vague instructions,
in contrast to Odysseus' earlier explicitness, allow the chorus freedom of
invention, and perhaps imply some dependence upon them. The chorus
appear to pick up this implication at the beginning of the antistrophe.
While continuing to stress Neoptolemus' status (150: ἄναξ), they remind
him, and inform the audience, that they have always been vigilantly mindful of his welfare, and presumably will continue to be so. This statement,
which might sound somewhat patronizing, suggests that they are veterans
in his service, men who consider themselves older and more experienced.
Then, firmly changing the subject (152: νῦν δέ), they turn to the practical
aspects of the situation and ask for information on the task: where is Philoc-

7. For the scepter as the symbol of kingly power, see especially *Il.* 9.97 and *Od.* 11.568 on
the judgmental power of the scepter-holder.
8. Jebb (*ad* 148) and Linforth ("Philoctetes," 110) take πρὸς ἐμὴν αἰεὶ χεῖρα προχωρῶν
literally: "coming forward towards my (beckoning) hand—*i.e.*, at a sign given by me—from
time to time" (Jebb), implying that Neoptolemus will physically signal to the chorus.

tetes' abode, and is he in it? The pattern of questioning in the antistrophe is parallel to that of the strophe: first a request, then the reason for it (156: μὴ προσπεσών με λάθῃ ποθέν), and then the request repeated.

Thus far, all is methodical, even military; Neoptolemus responds succinctly (159–160), and the chorus fire another question at him (161). At this point, Neoptolemus introduces the first tentative note of pity for Philoctetes. The action of the prologue and facts pointed out there (the crude furnishings of the cave, the dirty rags) are obviously designed to affect the audience, but not until now, when Neoptolemus says that hunting is Philoctetes' only means of sustenance (162–168), has anyone mentioned Philoctetes' miserable life. The chorus, having digested this information, respond with their summary of the situation: the man's existence is utterly wretched and unbearable (169–179). They do indeed express pity for Philoctetes, but there is no suggestion whatever that either his misery or their pity should influence their behavior toward him. No doubt the dramatic effect of their words is to increase the audience's sympathy for Philoctetes, but their statement is hardly an emotional commitment. The personal aspect occurs only in the first line of the strophe and is not repeated; the emphasis is on Philoctetes' misery, not on the chorus' own sympathy for that misery. Indeed, their observations are generalized and somewhat puzzled in tone: how does he endure, how do these things happen, that one of noble birth should sink so low?

Neoptolemus' response to the chorus (191–200) has been the object of much psychological analysis by modern critics. He is uncomfortable, some say, and disturbed in his mind by the chorus' remarks; therefore he stifles his scruples and speaks defensively, blaming it all on the gods.[9] This analysis is based largely upon our modern prejudice in favor of the underdog. We feel that the only proper reaction to the chorus' words is one of strong sympathy for Philoctetes. Since Neoptolemus' reaction is coldly puritanical, it is therefore startling and repugnant to us. Yet we perceive that he is not a natural villain, and therefore he must be guiltily covering up his true, warm, human feelings.

This line of reasoning requires the false assumptions that Philoctetes has been depicted as an object of compassion and that Neoptolemus' "theological" explanation is unnatural and out of place. First of all, the audience does not know a great deal about Philoctetes at this point, nor do any of the characters. They do not know that he will be glad to see Greeks,

9. See, for example, Kitto (*Form and Meaning,* 112), Linforth ("Philoctetes," 107), Knox (*Heroic Temper,* 127); and *contra,* Schmidt (*Philoktet,* 51–52).

that he will welcome the son of Achilles and treat him with gentlemanly courtesy, and this despite the terrible wrongs (of which little has as yet been said) that the Greeks have done to him. The audience thus far knows only what Neoptolemus and the chorus know: Philoctetes prevented sacrifice by his animal-like cries (9); if he sees Odysseus he will kill him, and Neoptolemus with him (76); his weapons are dread and unopposable (104–107); he is suspicious (136); and he lives among animals (184–185: μετὰ θηρῶν). The chorus pity him for his physical discomfort, but there is as yet no reason to think of him as other than a savage and dangerous adversary. Perhaps the audience may feel the first faint stirrings of pity for Philoctetes, but they are surely overlaid with apprehensiveness at his approach.[10]

Neoptolemus is also accused of cold-bloodedness and egoism in not responding to the new tone of pity expressed by the chorus, but this pity is only in its primal stage; and it is pity for Philoctetes' situation, not for the man himself. What Neoptolemus does respond to is the tone of questioning: "Isn't it strange how this sort of thing can happen?" To this he answers: "It's not really so strange, the causes are thus and such." Under the circumstances his reply is natural, and it fits into the pattern of the whole exchange, wherein the chorus ask a series of questions to which Neoptolemus replies in his newly displayed capacity of king and leader. The new piece of information is presented not as an excuse but as a logical conclusion based on general knowledge (199: λέγεται). There is no reason for the audience to think that Neoptolemus or the chorus do not believe it; that Philoctetes considers the Atreidae, not Chryse, the source of his suffering is as yet entirely unknown. Furthermore, Sophocles gives the audience no time to ponder upon the significance of Neoptolemus' statement. The chorus suddenly interrupt their leader's reflections and call his attention to the matter at hand. It is his soldiers, and not Neoptolemus, who hear the cry and diagnose it as Philoctetes', who conclude that he must be approaching. While he is thus in the very act of exercising his kingly qualities, Neoptolemus is recalled by his men to the practical necessities of the moment.

In the parodos, then, the chorus have been presented as possessing a moderately well defined character. They are Neoptolemus' soldiers, loyal

10. That the audience had any contrary knowledge of Philoctetes' character derived from "tradition" is most unlikely. Both Aeschylus and Euripides, according to Dion of Prusa (*Orations* 52 and 59), seem to have presented him as angry and violent. Cf. also Avery (*Hermes* 93 [1965], 279–282).

king's men, yet not so much deferential subordinates as patronizing familiars, perhaps comparable to the Paedagogus of *Electra*. Their manner is
practical and businesslike. It is also curiously reminiscent of Odysseus' in
both word and action. We may compare Odysseus' concern for practical
matters (11–12) with theirs (151–210); they follow Odysseus in addressing
Neoptolemus as παῖ and τέκνον; and there are other verbal echoes between Odysseus and the chorus, particularly their almost identical expressions of fear of Philoctetes.[11] Yet although the chorus bear many striking
resemblances to Odysseus, they clearly contrast with him in the humaneness of their consideration of Philoctetes' physical circumstances and their
awareness that his existence must be a miserable one; there has been no
sign of such humaneness in Odysseus. In this reasonably composite, but
hardly intricate, character the chorus perform the function of showing
Neoptolemus as a military leader, in contrast to his subordinate position
vis-à-vis Odysseus in the prologue. At the same time, their behavior continues to stress his youth and inexperience. A careful balance is maintained: each time Neoptolemus asserts his own independence and dignity,
the chorus' advice or exhortations, especially in the final stanzas (201–218),
seem to reassert his reliance upon them.[12]

The structure and the meter of the parodos give it a distinctly conversational tone. It is not technically a kommos, a lyric duet between chorus
and actor, but has more the form of a dialogue, since the anapestic systems
which separate the lyric stanzas were probably delivered in a "recitative"
mode. The moderate use of antilabe (201, 210) and the alternation of
speakers within an anapestic system (159–161) reinforce the question-and-
answer effect. Particularly striking is the meter of the chorus' entrance-
words: the first strophe and antistrophe each begin with an iambic trimeter followed by a phalaecean hendecasyllable. The intrusion of iambic
trimeters in the middle of a lyric passage occurs elsewhere in Sophocles,
and they may have been delivered in such a way as to contrast with the
surrounding lyrics.[13] But the occurrence of an iambic trimeter as the first
line of a choral stanza, and particularly of the parodos, is an unusual phe-

11. Odysseus, 46: μὴ καὶ λάθῃ με προσπεσών. Chorus, 156: μὴ προσπεσών με λάθῃ
ποθέν.

12. The contrary view (see, e.g., Schmidt, *Philoktet*, 53; Burton, *The Chorus*, 228) that
the chorus are only simple men who are utterly devoted to and dependent upon Neoptolemus
ignores the effect of the numerous imperatives and the familiar form of address.

13. See Dale (*Lyric Metres*, 86 and 207–208) on the "mixed delivery" of iambic lines and
phrases within lyrics.

nomenon which would not be likely to escape the audience's notice. Although we cannot determine the mode of delivery of these lines with complete certainty, it seems reasonable to assume that it was closer to ordinary speech than to singing. The essentially iambic phalaecean line that follows could serve as a transition to the fully lyrical measures; and the iambic dimeters catalectic with which the strophe and antistrophe close may serve to connect the chorus' lyric questions with Neoptolemus' anapestic replies. As a result, the parodos seems to take on the qualities of a military conference hastily convened in the field to discuss immediate tactics.

The episode that follows the parodos centers upon Philoctetes the man, and on Neoptolemus' execution of his assigned role. The chorus, however, are not to be ignored; that Philoctetes includes them all in his first address (219–231) could suggest that at the end of the final antistrophe they are grouped around Neoptolemus, who only steps forward from them at line 232. Confronted by the friendly Philoctetes, the son of Achilles haltingly enters upon his deception, with short declarative sentences (232–233, 239–241). He has barely begun when Philoctetes sets forth his version of the past events, at the end of which the chorus-leader speaks (317–318): "I believe that I also pity you as your former visitors did, O son of Poias." The traditional judgment of such lines following long speeches is that they are tedious or platitudinous.[14] It is, in fact, the general practice to lump all choral iambic trimeters together as possessing little, if any, dramatic value. The couplets at the ends of long speeches are especially slighted, often being allowed only the most starkly mechanical functions. The remarks continue the tone of the preceding speech, we are told, and provide a sort of verbal pause during which the audience can digest what has been said. It has even been suggested that they are designed to give the audience a chance to applaud a major speech without missing anything important.[15]

14. They are often said to "mark the end of a major speech," as if the audience might not otherwise recognize the end of a speech (cf. Webster, *ad* 317).

15. Gilbert Norwood, *Greek Tragedy* (4th ed.: London, 1948), 79–80; the possibility is accepted by Kirkwood (*Sophoclean Drama*, 189). This suggestion evidently presupposes that ancient acting technique did not include the modern practice of the "stage freeze," whereby the actors automatically hold the scene during laughter or applause. When the noise dies down, the scene continues; the lines which were drowned out by the applause are repeated. Although this behavior is not instinctive (actors must be trained to stop), it seems far more likely than the assumption that the ancient audience customarily interrupted with applause but the actors disregarded it and continued willy-nilly, so that the poet had to guess when applause would occur (and how long it would last) and insert unimportant lines to cover it. If this were true, we should expect the same choral comments after every joke in comedy.

Others will allow that the couplets usually have a rather generalized function, such as showing the audience "what view a sane man takes of such a speech."[16]

If these generalizations are set aside and the lines examined in their own specific place in the play, it may seem at first that the chorus are genuinely moved by Philoctetes' speech and express their sincere pity for him, a pity which we also feel. But the original audience may have gotten a different impression. It is evident that Philoctetes is meant to understand the chorus' words solely as an expression of pity and sympathy, as indeed he does. Yet surely this is a curious way to express pity, by equating the nature of their feelings with those of earlier visitors. For Philoctetes has just said that, although the others pitied him in words (307–308: λόγοις ἐλεοῦσι μέν), they refused to take him home, and we know that thus far the new visitors' intent is not dissimilar—they pity him, yet they do not plan to take him home; on the contrary, they intend to use him for their own purposes. This ambiguity is intensified by the order in which the words are heard. Of the ten words which the chorus speak, the first six contain the comparison with the previous visitors; only at the seventh does one finally hear the mention of pity. Whether the chorus were understood here as being either genuinely sincere in their pity or deliberately equivocal may have depended upon gesture and intonation. Nevertheless, it seems certain that the listener is meant to note the ambiguity of expression and the resulting irony of the situation.[17] The effect of this ambiguity is to draw the audience's attention, and Neoptolemus', sharply from what Philoctetes has said back to the conspiracy, to prepare for Neoptolemus' plunge into profound deceit.

With the aid of the chorus, who have provided the transition, Neoptolemus again picks up the thread of the deception, and again is briefly deterred by Philoctetes' surprisingly civilized behavior: before Neoptolemus has had a chance to bring out the falsehood which is supposed to win over the man, he utters a truth which deeply affects Philoctetes—the death of Achilles. But Neoptolemus plunges ahead and tells his story, which was dictated to him by Odysseus and which we therefore know to be patently false, but which nonetheless contains some heavily ironic statements (e.g., 386–388). His speech is immediately followed by a brief choral strophe (391–402), sometimes called a hyporcheme, which has oc-

16. Webster, *Introduction*, 91.
17. Cf. Schmidt, *Philoktet*, 79.

casioned some puzzlement. The occurrence of a lyric stanza here is generally considered a typical instance of the "conventional lyric interlude"
used to break up a long episode, and perhaps to replace an expected iambic couplet after a long speech.[18] It is quite true that such songs do occur
during dialogue scenes (e.g., Soph. *Trach.* 205ff.; Aesch. *Prom.* 687ff.;
Eurip. *Suppl.* 918ff.), but they are always astrophic; this one is unusual in
that it represents the first half of a strophe-antistrophe. The audience, however, cannot possibly know that this song will be followed a hundred lines
later by a corresponding antistrophe, and would therefore not at the moment regard it as being intrinsically different from other astrophic choral
interjections.[19]

Although the chorus do speak within the dramatic context, they are
merely echoing Neoptolemus, supporting their chief's lies as they have
been instructed to do. Nevertheless, the intensity of their affirmation
seems a bit excessive in view of its purpose, for they appear to be uttering a
prayer or oath in support of an obvious lie. Would the audience have been
shocked at this, and have regarded the chorus as guilty of a serious impiety? And if so, why does Sophocles raise the issue here, when he could
easily have had them give a more secular confirmation, and then drop it
without following up the question of whether they ought (or ought not) to
suffer the consequences of impiety?

The doubts inherent in these and similar questions have given rise to
some interesting solutions, of which Zielinski's is the most ingenious.[20] He
maintains that the chorus' invocation of Γῆ μήτηρ is not an impious
falsehood but rather a direct reference to an earlier, lost play by Sophocles,
Neoptolemus, in which such a scene actually took place. According to his
reconstruction of the play, Neoptolemus demanded the arms of Achilles
from Odysseus and appealed to the Atreidae, but they decided in favor of
Odysseus. In the following stasimon, the third one of the play, the chorus
of "Neoptolemus' Myrmidons" prayed to the goddess, the "montium
Troianorum patrona," to redress the wrong done to their leader. It is that
stasimon to which he believes the chorus of *Philoctetes* are here referring;

18. Cf. Kitto (*Form and Meaning,* 115), Linforth ("Philoctetes," 111), Burton (*The Chorus,* 232).

19. Unless perhaps it was indicated by some aspect of the dance; but the old theory that
the chorus moved in one direction during the strophe and in the reverse direction during the
antistrophe has been largely discounted (see Lawler, *Dance,* 11–12).

20. *Eos* 27 (1924), 60–61 and 73. Whitman (*Sophocles,* 275) is in agreement with most of
Zielinski's explanation. Calder (*GRBS* 12 [1971], 159n27) also tries to give historical validity
to the chorus' claim that they were present at the award of the arms.

therefore, there is clearly no falsehood, nor does any stain of impiety cling to either the chorus or the poet. Yet even if this conjecture were true—and there is no further evidence for the alleged stasimon beyond the *Philoctetes* passage itself—the association of the earlier scene with this would lead the audience not to understanding but to confusion. For why should the poet now imply that Neoptolemus' story is true, when he made it clear in the prologue that the whole thing is a lie invented by Odysseus?

The introduction of the gods is not in itself surprising; Neoptolemus ends his speech with the ambivalent wish that he who hates the Atreidae may be as dear to the gods as he is to Neoptolemus (390: ἐμοί θ' ὁμοίως καὶ θεοῖς εἴη φίλος). The chorus elaborate this theme in their opening words by naming the goddess Earth, mother of Zeus himself; so far it sounds as if they are about to pray in earnest to a recognized universal deity. But instead, they proceed to qualify the deity by adding a narrow geographical restriction: "you who rule great golden Pactolos" (394). The Lydian river Pactolos, carrying gold dust down from Mount Tmolus, flows through Sardis, where according to Herodotus there was a temple of Cybele (ἐπιχωρίης θεοῦ Κυβήβης).[21] By the end of the fifth century, this goddess appears to have been associated by the poets with the Hellenic Earth-Rhea-Mother-of-the-Gods. It is quite clear, however, that Herodotus regarded her as a strictly local divinity; the only two other foreign gods which he does not identify with Greek ones are also described by him as "native," ἐπιχώριος.[22] Moreover, the worship of Cybele does not seem to have been officially established at Athens, although it was privately practiced in the Piraeus. There is no clear evidence for the public acceptance of the particularly Phrygian cult of the goddess by the Greeks.[23]

We may reasonably conjecture that the Athenian audience would not have been offended at hearing Greeks—their Greekness has been stressed by Philoctetes (223ff., 233ff.)—call an essentially foreign divinity to wit-

21. Herodotus 5.101–102; cf. Bacchylides 3.44–45.

22. Linforth, "Greek Gods and Foreign Gods in Herodotus" (*Univ. of Calif. Publications in Classical Philology* 9 [1926–1929], 1–25), 23–24. The other two are Thracian, Pleistorus (9.119) and Salmoxis (4.94). How and Wells (*A Commentary on Herodotus* [Oxford, 1912], II, 59) agree that Herodotus here considers her a foreign goddess, although they cite the Sophoclean passage as evidence for the worship of Cybele in Athens!

23. M. P. Nilsson (*Geschichte der griechischen Religion* [3d ed.: Munich, 1967], 72–77) believes in the early introduction of oriental cults into Greece, but L. R. Farnell (*The Cults of the Greek States*, III, 302–304) argues persuasively that the Phrygian rites of Cybele were only practiced privately and were probably considered repellent. Haldane (*CQ* 13 [1963], 56) claims that the strophe is one of several hymns that Sophocles deliberately introduces in his plays to "pay a compliment" to cults newly established at Athens.

ness a lie, especially a divinity which was not officially recognized at Athens. Further substance is lent to this assumption by the fact that the chorus deliver the statement of geographic qualification in iambic trimeter (394). Since the iambic trimeter within a lyric passage probably had a somewhat different mode of delivery, it would have carried to the ear the special significance of the foreign reference,[24] and with it the implied stipulation of the alien aspect of the deity.

As the chorus continue, we realize that they are not uttering an oath, or even a prayer. Their words are designed to convince Philoctetes that they were present during the alleged outrage to Neoptolemus, but actually they make no request for divine witness, such as the usual ἴστω Ζεύς,[25] nor do they invoke any curse in case of nonfulfillment. All that they do is address a divinity while stating a falsehood—and the falsehood itself is cleverly confined to the statement that they previously addressed the goddess, not that the things described actually happened. There is no oath, therefore there can be no perjury. Divine punishment has been cleverly avoided by geographical restriction of the divinity and especially by the skillfully worded address.

The earliest approximate precedent for this sort of behavior is found in Autolykos, Odysseus' maternal grandfather, whom Homer describes as one who "excelled in thievery and the oath" (*Od.* 19.395–396: ὃς ἀνθρώπους ἐκέκαστο / κλεπτοσύνῃ θ᾿ ὅρκῳ τε). Here the word ὅρκος is usually taken to mean the art of so wording an oath that it may later be disregarded without actually committing perjury. Although there remain to us no verbatim examples of such devious and skillful oaths, Greek literature abounds with examples of oaths and promises cleverly unfulfilled, of successful lies and trickery which bring no punishment; indeed, Autolykos has the blessing of Hermes himself (*Od.* 19.396–398). There can be no reason, then, to believe that the audience would have been astounded by the chorus' pseudo-prayer, any more than by Odysseus' lies, or would have expected some treatment of this as a religious issue, with the imminent possibility of divine punishment.

That the audience would not have been perplexed by the chorus' words is not to say that it would have cheerfully approved of them. Most fifth-century examples of oaths contrived with the deliberate intention of avoid-

24. Cf. Kranz, *Stasimon*, 108–109.

25. *Il.* 10.329; Soph., *Tr.* 399; cf. *Il.* 15.36: ἴστω Γαῖα, and so forth, and Soph., *Oed. Col.* 522: θεὸς ἴστω. On Webster's suggestion (*ad* 391) that by using two imperfect verbs the chorus "do not quite commit themselves to the lie," see Bers (*Hermes* 109 [1981], 502–503).

ing their conditions concern the grim realities of war, and often end in murder and massacre (e.g., Herodotus 4.201; Thucydides 3.34). Where the successful evasion of an oath's obligations is apparently condoned, or even smiled upon, it is usually the case that the oath was extracted by force or under false pretenses (e.g., Herodotus 4.154).[26] Thucydides in the well-known passage on the evils of revolution (3.82–83) roundly condemns conspiracy and oath-breaking. In general, trickery and deceit were not approved (cf. Soph. *Oed. Col.* 228). It is only in Homer that we find the prevalent attitude that prevarication and skillful deceit are acceptable, and in some cases admirable.[27] We may reasonably suppose that the audience would regard the chorus' actions here as being in the old, Homeric style of cleverness but at the same time definitely unscrupulous by modern (i.e., fifth-century) standards. Neoptolemus has obeyed Odysseus well, and the chorus are indeed supporting him; yet they are also doing far more. Another aspect of their character is now emerging. They appear as willing and accomplished liars, they undertake on their own initiative to equal or even excel their chief in fraud—in short, they now clearly show themselves to be capable of independent action and dedicated to the task at hand, possessing the Homeric attributes of inventiveness and unscrupulousness which we associate so closely with Odysseus.[28]

Philoctetes' reply to the chorus shows that they have succeeded in firmly establishing both Neoptolemus and themselves (404) in his confidence. They remain silent while Philoctetes questions Neoptolemus about the fate of his noble friends among the Greeks, but when Philoctetes begs Neoptolemus to rescue him, the chorus promptly respond with another brief song (507–518) that is the antistrophe to their earlier song (391ff.).

26. Joseph Plescia (*Oath and Perjury in Ancient Greece*, 86–87), cites Eurip., *Hipp.* 612: ἡ γλῶσσ᾽ ὀμώμοχ᾽, ἡ δὲ φρὴν ἀνώμοτος, as evidence that forced oaths did not require observance and that "the poet separates the proposition of the oath-formula from the intention of the oath-taker." But Hippolytus did *not* break his oath since, as he says (1060ff.), he would not be believed anyway. In fact, we do not hear the actual oath-taking, nor even a description of the circumstances surrounding it; Euripides avoids the whole issue.

27. Stanford in his commentary on *Odyssey* 19.396, the description of Autolykos (Homer, *Odyssey*, ed. W. B. Stanford [London, 1948], II, 332), calls this "a form of trickery that many Greeks would commend" and cites the passages from Herodotus (4.201) and Thucydides (3.34). But this cannot be shown to be valid for fifth-century Athens; cf. Bowra (*Sophoclean Tragedy*, 270), who maintains with respect to Odysseus' conduct that the Greeks in general disapproved of lying.

28. Unlike their leader, they have received no specific instructions; the religious theme was only vaguely introduced by Neoptolemus; and even if one assumes a signal of some sort (above, note 8), their assertions are far beyond what is required for mere confirmation of Neoptolemus' statements. Cf. Schmidt, *Philoktet*, 89.

Separation of strophe and antistrophe by a length of dialogue is an uncommon phenomenon in Greek tragedy. The only other instance of such separated responsion in the extant plays of Sophocles occurs at *Oedipus Coloneus* 833–886. There the strophe is an excited exchange among Creon, Oedipus, and the chorus, with much iambic trimeter and antilabe. The argument continues during the following thirty-two lines (844–875) and right on through the antistrophe (876–886), in which the structure and order of speakers are identical to those of the strophe. Thus there is no discontinuity and scarcely even an impression of separation.[29]

Aeschylus uses a similar device in three of his dramas. In *Seven against Thebes* (375–630), three strophic pairs of choral lyric alternate with iambic trimeter dialogue that actually consists of only two balanced speeches—one by the messenger and one by Eteocles—in the order: dialogue/strophe/dialogue/antistrophe. But the lyric pieces each have only five lines, and the interposed dialogues average about thirty-five lines. The final antistrophe is followed by another pair of messenger-Eteocles speeches (631–675), and a few lines of choral iambic trimeter (677–682). Then comes another lyric-iambic system (683–708), shorter than the last. In this second system Eteocles' iambic trimeters—only three lines in each set—alternate with two pairs of very brief strophic lyrics (the first pair each have only three lines, the second only four) in the same order of iambics/strophe/iambics/antistrophe. A spate of stichomythia between Eteocles and the chorus (709–719) is then followed by a full choral ode (720ff.). The entire passage has the continuity and balance of a unified whole and is essentially a kommos.

The other Aeschylean examples involve a variation of this technique: the choral strophic pairs alternate with iambic trimeter speeches by a single character in the form strophe/speech/antistrophe/speech. This occurs at *Agamemnon* 1407–1447, where the speaker is Clytemnestra, and again at *Eumenides* 778–891, where the speaker is Athena. In each case, both lyrics and speeches are short and a kommos follows almost directly after them. As in *Seven against Thebes*, the effect is of a balanced, kommos-like unit, and bears little resemblance to the situation in *Philoctetes*.

Euripides makes greater and more varied use of separated strophic responsion. He employs the second Aeschylean type of strophe/speech/antistrophe/speech in *Electra* (859–885). There also the parts are very short

29. In three other places Sophocles uses brief passages of iambic trimeters (less than ten lines) within the body of a kommos: *Aj.* 866–973, *Ant.* 1261–1346, *Oed. Col.* 1447–1499. They do not separate the lyrics, but are an integral part of the kommos.

and close together, and the entire system, although not associated with any nearby ode or kommos, nevertheless functions as a balanced unit with the dramatic effect of a kommos. A more daring attempt is found in *Orestes* (1353–1549), where the strophe and antistrophe are separated by more than two hundred lines which contain the Phrygian's lyric tale and some trochaic tetrameter dialogue (1506–1536).[30] Clearly this is a substantial distance, but the chorus' participation in the intervening monody, the equally frenzied nature of both stanzas, and their verbal similarity all combine to bridge the gap with relative ease;[31] the passage still retains the effect of a dramatic unit. Only in *Hippolytus* do we find an example of strophic separation comparable to that of *Philoctetes;* here the strophe (362–372) and the antistrophe (669–679) are separated by a dialogue scene of nearly three hundred lines that also includes a choral ode of two strophic pairs (526–564). Moreover, the strophe is sung by the chorus, but the antistrophe by Phaidra, although the contents are almost identical: both songs express Phaidra's desperate circumstances, misery, and certain doom.

In all of this it is tempting to try to discern some chronological progression in the development of separated responsion: to say, for example, that Aeschylus first attempted the division of strophe from antistrophe, although he kept the distance short and maintained an essentially lyric unit; that Euripides, the daring innovator, boldly disconnected the parts entirely in *Hippolytus* (428 B.C.) but, perhaps unsatisfied with the results of this experiment, returned to the Aeschylean unity in *Electra* (*ca.* 413 B.C.), although he later lengthened the distance in *Orestes* (408 B.C.), and perhaps finally abandoned the whole idea; that meanwhile the more prudent and meticulous Sophocles tried out a separation of moderate length without unity in *Philoctetes* (409 B.C.), but then returned to the technique of brevity and continuity in *Oedipus Coloneus* (405 B.C.). But the paucity of the evidence allows us to say only that the disjunction of strophe and antistrophe was not a regular or conventional usage, and that during the latter part of the fifth century both Sophocles and Euripides were experimenting with variations on the Aeschylean technique.[32]

30. The authenticity of this passage has been questioned by B. Gredley ("Is *Orestes* 1503–36 an Interpolation?" *GRBS* 9 [1968], 409–419), who considers it a later interpolation. If this were true, it would reduce the gap to about 170 lines, still an unusually long separation.

31. Note the beginning of the strophe (1352–1353): ἰὼ ἰὼ φίλαι, / κτύπον ἐγείρετε, κτύπον καὶ βοάν; and of the antistrophe (1537–1538): ἰὼ ἰὼ τύχα, / ἕτερον εἰς ἀγῶν', ἕτερον αὖ δόμος.

32. Mention must be made here of *Rhesus*, since it contains the most radical example of strophic separation in all of the extant tragedies. In fact, it occurs twice in the play: in the first

The few instances of strophic separation in the extant tragedies do show that the audience was not entirely unfamiliar with the device, and therefore we may suppose that the poets had some purpose in using it. That purpose seems usually to have been the maintenance of a scene as a dramatic unit, as, for example, that of *Hippolytus*, where the strophe and antistrophe enclose the scene of the revelation of Phaidra's love to Hippolytus. But in *Philoctetes* the action is continuous and the scene does not separate itself from the occurrences on either side of it. Rather, the separated responsion serves to make it indisputably clear to the audience that the chorus are still lying. Philoctetes' request to be taken home is to be used to further the conspiracy against him, but this, of course, cannot be made explicit in his presence. If, at the end of Philoctetes' moving speech, the chorus were to suggest that Neoptolemus accede to his request out of pity and piety, it is not unlikely that the audience would take their words at face value, especially if they were spoken in iambic trimeter. The danger of such a misunderstanding is partially alleviated by the chorus' phrase, "If, my lord, you hate the horrid Atreidae"; but the poet has gone as far as he can verbally. Metrically, however, he has clinched the matter, for the audience is made to recall the rhythms of the earlier song, in which the chorus vividly displayed themselves as consummate liars. With this in mind, and aided by the obvious falsehood of line 510, it would be natural to conclude that here also their pious behavior is pure deceit.[33]

Besides maintaining the clever and unscrupulous behavior that they

---

instance a short strophe (131–136) is followed by fifty-eight lines of dialogue and then the antistrophe (195–200). The passage is obviously not a unit, nor is there any relationship between the two songs in content. In the second instance the strophe (454–466) and antistrophe (820–832) are divided by dialogue, lyrics, and even the departure and return of the chorus; it is difficult to discern any connection between the two parts. Insofar as it concerns *Rhesus*, the general phenomenon of separated responsion is discussed briefly by William Ritchie (*The Authenticity of the "Rhesus" of Euripides* [Cambridge, 1964], 328–333), who suggests rather halfheartedly that the function of the separation in the second instance is to reestablish the identity of the returning chorus. Despite the obvious association with *Hippolytus*, however, he seems to regard the strophic separation of *Rhesus* as possible evidence against Euripidean authorship.

Ritchie subsumes Eurip., *El.* 859–885, under the rubric "epirrhematic" rather than "separated responsion" (pp. 341–342). That term is so broad—and therefore unhelpful—that it usually includes separated responsion (cf. Popp, "Das Amoibaion," esp. 230–232). For the purpose of evaluating the dramatic effect of a passage on the audience, the distinction would better be made between inserted anapestic systems or iambic trimeter couplets on the one hand, and the longer and therefore more intrusive iambic speeches on the other. Thus Aesch. *Sept.* 683–708 could be called "epirrhematic," but not *Eum.* 778–891.

33. Cf. Reinhardt, *Sophokles*, 283n3; Parlavantza-Friedrich, *Täuschungsszenen*, 52.

manifested in the earlier strophe, the chorus are actually advancing the intrigue to its next stage. Philoctetes has just made perhaps the most moving speech in the play; his solemn supplication must surely evoke the spectator's pity. He has scarcely finished when the chorus thrust themselves forward to pull the audience, and Neoptolemus, back to the conspiracy. It is they as much as Neoptolemus who initiate the next phase of the plot by taking advantage of Philoctetes' words, leading him and Neoptolemus into the artful little scene in which the young man appears to accede, somewhat reluctantly, to Philoctetes' request. They are increasingly becoming more devious and forceful in guiding the plot toward its desired conclusion.

This forcefulness appears even in the announcement of the arriving characters (539–541). It is a common assertion that one of the chorus' chief functions is to announce new arrivals. Certainly such announcements are important to the drama, to call attention to the new characters and identify them for the audience. Nevertheless, the chorus are not the chief announcer in Sophocles' plays. Most new arrivals are announced by other actors, or by the characters themselves, who often simply walk in and state their identity.[34] Clearly this is not the task primarily of the chorus and so not something that we should automatically expect from them. Nor is it at all usual for a Sophoclean chorus to use imperatives in an arrival announcement as they do here (ἐπίσχετον, μάθωμεν [hortatory subj.]).[35] This gives the effect of urgency, to be sure, but also makes the chorus active participants rather than passive observers, for they might simply have described the newcomers without telling Neoptolemus and Philoctetes what to do. The chorus seem to be giving orders and directing the movements of the principals in an authoritative, perhaps military, manner.

The scene with the pseudo-merchant (542ff.), which among its other effects exhibits Philoctetes' strong antipathy to the idea of going to Troy, leads into the display of the great bow and the notion that Neoptolemus may actually get his hands on it. At this point the chorus perform their first and only stasimon of the play (676–729), which has become, not un-

---

34. Fewer than half of all the entries in Sophocles are announced by the chorus (excluding, of course, the entrances of the choruses themselves). The approximate figures for each play are as follows (the ratio is that of the number of chorus-announced entries to the total number of entries in the play): *Antigone* 8/12; *Ajax* 5/14; *Oed. Tyr.* 4/13; *Trachiniae* 4/10; *Electra* 3/9; *Philoctetes* 3/7; *Oed. Col.* 2/11.

35. There are only four examples apart from *Philoctetes: Oed. Tyr.* 631, *Ajax* 1040ff., *El.* 1428, and *Tr.* 178. The first three are entirely appropriate to the emotional intensity of the dramatic situation, and the fourth (*Tr.* 178: εὐφημίαν νῦν ἴσχ') has the connotation of a ritual phrase.

reasonably, an object of some bewilderment and contention. The chorus begin by expressing sympathy for Philoctetes and the sufferings he has endured; nothing here is strange, for they have expressed similar sentiments in the parodos. But in the second antistrophe they give voice to the joyous notion that Neoptolemus will convey Philoctetes to his home. They apparently ignore the mission they have undertaken, the deception they have promoted, and the fact that Odysseus is waiting at the ship. This is inconsistent with what has been said and done thus far; the reader must stop and seek some explanation. Yet because the audience could not stop long to deliberate, we must presume that in the original performance the ode was readily comprehensible; consequently, we must first consider whether the visual aspects of the production might have been part of the intended dramatic effect. At this point there are three possible movements which the actors could execute, each of which could lead the audience to a different interpretation of the chorus' words. We shall examine them in turn, to see whether one is more logical within the plot and therefore the one most likely intended by Sophocles.

1. *Neoptolemus and Philoctetes remain on the scene* throughout the entire ode. They do not exit into the cave but remain in front of it, and the chorus are, of course, completely aware of their presence. Under these circumstances one would naturally assume that the chorus are again furthering the deception with their lies. The entire song is directed at Philoctetes; they wish to make sure that he goes with Neoptolemus, so they sing to him of the evil that he has suffered and the good things to come, knowing full well that Neoptolemus has no intention of taking him home. This interpretation, in no way contradictory to the chorus' previous behavior, is confounded by Neoptolemus' invitation, "Do go in," and Philoctetes' reply, "And indeed, I will lead you in, for [my] illness desires your companionship" (674–675). These are patent exit cues; without some attempted motion toward the cave the lines would be entirely pointless. Then, as Neoptolemus and Philoctetes are about to go in, the chorus stop them and sing the stasimon, at the end of which Neoptolemus repeats the invitation to enter (730: ἕρπ', εἰ θέλεις).[36] But the chorus do not actually stop them from leaving. We can find examples of characters who declare their inten-

36. Errandonea (*Sófocles* [1958], 265 and 374–375; cf. *Sófocles* [1970], 189–190) believes that the attribution of lines 671–673 to Philoctetes instead of Neoptolemus somehow solves the problem, that Neoptolemus only says, casually, "you may go in if you like," and Philoctetes continues to linger onstage while the chorus sing.

tion of departing but then fail to carry it out, as earlier in *Philoctetes* itself, when Philoctetes and Neoptolemus were also preparing to enter the cave (533ff.), or later, when they are about to leave for the ship (1408). In every case, however, the departure is literally prevented by the command of another character, as the chorus earlier stopped Philoctetes and Neoptolemus (539: ἐπίσχετον) or Heracles later detains them (1409: μήπω γε). But here the chorus, far from telling them to wait, do not even address them. Finally, the elaborate description of the herbs and arrows that Philoctetes wants to fetch from the cave (645–653) loses its main function, to provide a pretext for entering the cave, if he and Neoptolemus remain onstage. The articles are never mentioned again; when Philoctetes wakes after his fit, he seems to have forgotten all about them. If the two men do not go into the cave, it would have been more logical, and would have made the choral ode more appropriate, for the poet to have them heading toward the ship when the chorus begin to sing. Taken together, all of these cues prove that both Neoptolemus and Philoctetes are supposed to exit to the cave, surely at line 675.

2. *Philoctetes and Neoptolemus leave the scene at line 675 and do not return until the end of the stasimon;* therefore, they hear nothing of the ode.[37] It is an entirely normal procedure in Greek drama for the chorus, left alone on the scene, to speak without the influence of other characters' presence; and it would be especially significant here, since only now for the first time can they speak their own thoughts unhindered by the necessity for ambiguity and deceit. The audience would probably accept their expression of sympathy as sincere and natural to their character, except for the perplexing contrast between the final antistrophe and the chorus' previously effected deceit. Critics have proposed three different reactions that the audience might have to this stanza. The simplest is to suppose that the chorus fully believe what they are saying—that Neoptolemus is about to take Philoctetes home, as he has promised. This means one must also assume that, when Neoptolemus earlier agreed to Philoctetes' request, he succeeded in deceiving not only the castaway but also his own men.[38] Such

37. Schmidt (*Philoktet*, 132–133) believes the chorus are wholly engaged in deceit, because they expect to be overheard by Philoctetes. His evidence is Odysseus' injunction to silence (22) and Neoptolemus' calling Philoctetes out of the cave (1261–1262). But the former is too vague (and early) to serve as a statement that everything outside the cave can be heard within, and the latter does not occur until after the present scene. There is no way the audience could know that the chorus can be overheard or that they want to be.

38. Thus Webster, *ad* 676ff. and 719ff.; and *Introduction,* 100.

an assumption, however, ignores the fact that it was not Neoptolemus but the chorus themselves who suggested that he take Philoctetes home (in the "antistrophe," 507ff.), and that it was made unmistakably clear at the time that they were lying, in full awareness of the deception. Hence one would have to suppose that a complete change in the chorus' understanding has taken place somewhere between that song and the present ode. It is inconceivable that the audience would believe in such a drastic change without any previous hint from the poet or the action.

The opposite view holds that, in an effort to evoke the audience's sympathy for Philoctetes and to produce a form of his famous joy-before-disaster effect, Sophocles has deliberately removed the chorus from their dramatic role. The audience does not hear the chorus speaking as a character in the play, but rather responds emotionally to the poetry of their song.[39] The main difficulty in this view lies in the fact that the poet has thus far stressed Philoctetes' hatred of Odysseus while simultaneously portraying Odysseus as the author of the whole deception. These two themes have run parallel through the play and have just been brought together by the scene of the pseudo-merchant. That Philoctetes abominates Odysseus has been testified to even by Odysseus, and Philoctetes himself, in response to the merchant's story, avows that he would sooner listen to the snake that bit him than to Odysseus (631–632). At the same time, the very presence of the merchant vividly announces that Odysseus himself lurks behind all the action, and at no great distance. Sophocles has deliberately led the spectators to the point of knowing that if Philoctetes goes to the ship with Neoptolemus, as he seems about to do, he will be confronted by the object of his hatred, Odysseus. It is not clear what precisely will happen, but if things go on as they are, something catastrophic must occur. Having raised the tension to such a pitch, the poet could hardly expect his audience to abandon, however temporarily, all apprehension and to share in the chorus' alleged mood of joy.

In the third view, intermediate between these two, the audience would presume that the chorus are mistaken, not about the plan of action but about the human relation between Neoptolemus and Philoctetes. The chorus think that the two characters have reached such a complete mutual

---

39. Wilamowitz, *Dramatische Technik*, 287; Kranz, *Stasimon*, 221; Burton, *The Chorus*, 238–239. Waldock (*Sophocles*, 210–211) believes that Sophocles was so carried away by the composition of the ode that he forgot about the continuity of the play as a whole; it has also been suggested by Seale (*BICS* 19 [1972], 98) that the poet deliberately keeps the audience in a state of confusion and uncertainty in order to sustain the element of surprise.

understanding that both desires can be fulfilled together—for Philoctetes, that he will eventually return home, for Neoptolemus, that Philoctetes will first help him at Troy. In this ode the chorus are expressing their belief that all of Philoctetes' past troubles are over at last, that his deliverance and eventual return home will be the ultimate result of Neoptolemus' successful mission. The truth is that their mutual situation is still ambiguous; Neoptolemus is still concerned more with the success of the deception than with Philoctetes' human situation.[40] The proposition cannot be dismissed as inherently unreasonable; still, it is none too obvious. Now that the chorus are at last alone, they are presumably free to speak their mind, yet they make no specific mention whatsoever of the visit Philoctetes must necessarily make to Troy before he can go home. The very notion that to be taken to Troy would be advantageous to Philoctetes is entirely new at this point, and difficult, if not impossible, to grasp without at least a slightly broader hint than the poet appears to have given.[41] No one has yet said anything about curing Philoctetes' foot; indeed, the divine origin of the wound probably implies that it cannot be cured by human means. Moreover, the upcoming kommos shows that the chorus are not the least bit interested in Philoctetes' future, since they are quite willing to abandon him. If the audience succeeded in perceiving the chorus' kindly motives, and their misunderstanding of the principals' relation, the later unexplained change in attitude would still result in confusion. On the whole, the obscurity of the references and the consequent demand upon the audience's imagination, together with the later inconsistency in the chorus' character, render this solution weak and generally unsatisfactory. If we can find another answer that requires less effort from the audience, we would do well to reject this one.

3. *Philoctetes and Neoptolemus exit, and then return before the final antistrophe.* The chorus, left alone during the first three stanzas, sing of Philoctetes' past sufferings with genuine sympathy. Then, as the two actors

---

40. Müller, "Chor und Handlung," 214–216; cf. Schlesinger (*RhM* 111 [1968], 137–138) and Kamerbeek, 104.

41. Some see 720ff. as a prediction of health and glory to be gained at Troy; cf. Webster, *Introduction*, 100. Schlesinger (*RhM* 111 [1968], 136–137) takes the phrase πλήθει πολλῶν μηνῶν as a reference to a visit to Troy and not to Philoctetes' past exile, since he has clearly spent years, not months, on Lemnos. This is a very oblique allusion indeed; it is possible that μηνῶν presented itself as an appropriate substitute for the metrically unsuitable ἐτῶν, to correspond with the strophe, 711: πτανοῖς ἰοῖς.

appear from the cave, the chorus revert to the deception.[42] The main objections are that such an action is unprecedented in Greek tragedy and that, if the actors were supposed to hear the antistrophe, the chorus would have addressed them directly.[43] Although the proposed action is indeed not precisely equaled in any extant tragedy, there are, nevertheless, parallel situations in which actors enter during an ode, just before the final antistrophe, as in *Trachiniae* (962) or Euripides' *Alcestis* (234). It is true that in these cases the arrival is actually described by the chorus. But there are several places where it is clear that an entrance occurred, yet the exact point of the entrance cannot be determined. In *Agamemnon*, for example, during the first lyric passage (40–257), the chorus address Clytemnestra (83–103) but then apparently ignore her until their final anapests (258–263), which are also addressed to her. It is impossible to tell from the text exactly when she arrives.[44] Likewise, Oedipus must overhear some of the parodos of *Oedipus Tyrannus;* and Creon, part of the kommos of *Antigone.* Many other characters of whose presence the reader is aware only when they "speak" may possibly have entered during a preceding ode; it is, after all, a long walk from the parodos to the center of the scene. The only reason for our uncertainty in these cases is the lack of specific stage directions. There seems to be no solid evidence for the "sanctity of the ode," for the convention that actors did not move during a choral performance unless addressed by the chorus. On the other hand, it is evident that those characters who are undeniably present during an ode hear (and are meant to hear) the chorus' words, even though they are never addressed directly— clearest proof of this is found in Antigone's comment (*Oed. Col.* 720–721) on the hymn to Colonus. There is no reason to believe that the proposed action—characters enter during a song by the chorus, who are aware of the entrance—would be shockingly contrary to the established practices of drama. |

42. This movement was assumed by Jebb (*ad* 718f.) and has been widely accepted since by, for example, Kitto (*Form and Meaning*, 118), Linforth ("Philoctetes," 122–123), and Knox (*Heroic Temper*, 130). Kamerbeek (*ad* 676 and 727) believes it does not matter whether they are overheard or not.

43. Kranz, *Stasimon*, 221; Webster, *ad* 719ff.

44. See the lengthy discussion of Clytemnestra's entrance by Oliver Taplin (*Stagecraft*, 280–288); he further believes that entries do not take place during what he terms an "act-dividing lyric," although they may be announced during the song (173–174). But this conclusion rests on the assumptions that odes perform a "dividing" function (51), and that the entrance of an actor during the song "would destroy the whole effect of the allusive imagery through which the transition is made" (173). These assumptions may perhaps be valid for Aeschylus, but not for Sophocles.

Nor is this suggestion incompatible with many elements of the ode it-self. The structure of the song is a type used elsewhere by Sophocles and Euripides: $\alpha\alpha'\beta: \beta'$, that is, the first three stanzas have a certain unity of content, and the final antistrophe is in contrast.[45] Here the structure is es-pecially tight. The first three stanzas are intimately connected both by grammar and by content; the fourth is so distinct from them that a physi-cal distraction such as an entrance would easily fit in. In this it greatly re-sembles the parados, for there, too, the chorus' expression of pity was in-terrupted by an action (Philoctetes' cry, or at least their perception of it) which caused them to drop all speculation and return to the immediate problem. We must also note with respect to the elaborated description of Philoctetes' home (725–729) in the second antistrophe that the only other time this usually plain-speaking chorus employed geographical references was in the blatantly deceitful strophe (394). There is, therefore, nothing in the ode itself which would contradict this proposed action—on the con-trary, every part of it has a precedent. In particular, the chorus' increased participation in the duplicity, each artifice more clever and unorthodox than the last, has prepared for this final display of cunning. If Philoctetes and Neoptolemus reappear before the last stanza, the audience would im-mediately understand what the chorus are up to.

With this stasimon the deception aspect of the plot reaches its climax. The chorus speak consistently within their character as it has developed through the play to this point; indeed, the song opens with an iambic trim-eter, suggesting the conversational tone of the parados. Their statements are matter-of-fact, with relatively little poetic elaboration. Again there is a tone of amazement at Philoctetes' powers of endurance (686). Now the em-phasis is more on his humanity than his beastliness, which was the theme in the parados; he is a child without his nurse, a man bereft of the benefits of civilization, and especially that most human benefit, wine. Still, there seems to be a certain reserve in their words. They make no personal state-ment of pity now, and though they declare his sufferings undeserved (683), they do not mention the relationship of their actions to those sufferings. Pitying, even sympathetic, though the chorus' words may be, the audi-ence's knowledge of the previous deceit surely prevents any relaxation of the dramatic tension during the first three stanzas. Then, as Philoctetes reappears, the chorus' instant relapse into the deceit increases the audi-ence's anticipation of the approaching inevitable confrontation.

45. Cf. Kranz, *Stasimon*, 178, 197–198.

For some time it has seemed to the spectator that the trick will not work out according to plan. Now, with Philoctetes' attack of illness, a certain doubt begins to affect Neoptolemus. This is no psychological inference; the text makes it quite apparent. Philoctetes' dreadful cries, the frantic antilabe, the stumbling meter, show that Neoptolemus is not standing calmly by, but is deeply involved in the scene. His rapid questions and horrified exclamations do not seem feigned (759: ἰὼ ἰὼ δύστηνε σύ), although upon receiving the bow he does appear to revert to the ambiguity of deceit in his brief prayer (779–781, cf. 527–529). But the pressure on Neoptolemus does not decrease; Philoctetes' words, uttered in agony, show that Neoptolemus' silence signifies a reaction to what is happening (805: τί σιγᾷς; etc.). With such an introduction, Neoptolemus' reply (806) that he has long been distressed by Philoctetes' troubles is surely to be heard as truth. Now his involvement increases to the point of physical contact as he actually touches Philoctetes for the first time (813–818). This is the climax of the scene, physically, metrically, and dramatically. When Philoctetes sinks to the ground (820), he leaves Neoptolemus standing with the great bow in his hand. With this powerful scene the poet has altered the audience's expectations, transferring them from the general to the particular, from the passive to the active; instead of expecting that something must happen, one now feels that Neoptolemus himself must do something.

The chorus, apparently responding to Neoptolemus' injunction to let Philoctetes sleep (824–825), begin to sing an invocation to Healing Sleep. When they are evidently satisfied that he is quite asleep, they turn to Neoptolemus in the middle of the first strophe and bid him take advantage of this new opportunity. There is nothing unusual in this change; we have seen before how impersonal their pity is, how they are alert to seize every chance to further their purpose. It is fully in character for these shrewd and practical men to brush aside Neoptolemus' higher speculation and return to the immediate problem (843), just as they did in the parodos (201, 210). The sequence of thought and the priority of action in the antistrophe are exactly parallel to those of the strophe: the chorus are concerned first to be sure the man is asleep, and then to deal with the immediate future. Their analysis of the situation (855–864) is militarily sound and their tactics practical. Using numerous imperatives, and addressing their chief four times as τέκνον (833, 843, 845, 855) and once as παῖ (863), they are displaying the full measure of their forcefulness, self-reliance, and capacity for independent action.

With this kommos the poet brings the relationship between the chorus and Neoptolemus to a turning point. Under circumstances which suggest that he is not speaking in deceit, Neoptolemus has just declared that it would not be right or proper for him to leave without the sufferer (812: οὐ θέμις). Now, urged on to take action appropriate to his mission, namely, to abscond with the bow, he declares that it would be useless to do so (839–842). Critics have questioned Neoptolemus' sudden possession of this knowledge; a widely accepted answer is that the use of hexameters, the meter of oracles, insinuates the idea that truth is being uttered.[46] This is a reasonable explanation, but not an entirely necessary one; it has been implied from the beginning that deceit is wrong, and surely stealing is much the same as lying. Nor is the notion that Philoctetes must be brought to Troy a new one (cf. 112); in fact, only the chorus have suggested taking the bow without Philoctetes, and that only just now. These four lines have another and perhaps more prominent effect: oracles may speak in hexameters, but so do heroes, the great epic heroes of Homer.[47] This is the son of Achilles, at last beginning to assert himself, to speak with the authority of a Homeric sceptered king. The young Neoptolemus and the veteran chorus are engaged in a contest for mastery, which he wins; for instead of taking their advice, he takes control of them in an authoritative and final manner: "I command you to be silent, and to give over this insanity of yours!" (865).

The change in Neoptolemus' attitude is neither instantaneous nor yet complete. He has asserted himself over his own men; now, prompted by his sense of honor (902–903, 906, 908–909), he rejects deceit and reveals at least some of the truth to Philoctetes. When at the end of Philoctetes' bitter invective (927–962) the chorus-leader turns and asks Neoptolemus what is to be done (963–964), it is clear from these words that they fully accept Neoptolemus' leadership and acknowledge his right to decide. They do not express approval or disapproval; they do not advise. In sharp contrast to their previous mode of address during the kommos, Neoptolemus is called not τέκνον, but ἄναξ (963). At the same time, it is evi-

46. Kitto, *Form and Meaning*, 119. Some even suggest that Neoptolemus is divinely inspired here and speaking as a prophet (e.g., Whitman, *Sophocles*, 183; Bowra, *Sophoclean Tragedy*, 280); but there is no indication of this in the text. Easterling (*ICS* 3 [1978], 34) offers a convincing picture of Neoptolemus coming to realize the true meaning of something he has always known but never understood.

47. See also Winnington-Ingram on the hexameter as the meter of "heroic action," contrasting with the nonheroic theft of the bow (*BICS* 16 [1969], 50–51), and on the dramatic effect of the "agonistic" imagery in the lines (*Sophocles*, 287–288).

dent that, although Neoptolemus has renounced the principle of fraud, he has not yet renounced the fruit of that principle since he refuses to return the bow (925–926, 950–951). Philoctetes appeals both to his honor (921–922) and to his pity (952ff.) to restore his ill-gotten gains. The chorus, by stating the alternative courses—either to sail away or to comply with Philoctetes' request—establish the possibility that Neoptolemus may change his mind on this matter also. The chorus-leader's words introduce a very brief scene, the dramatic effect of which is to show Neoptolemus' vacillation. The intensity of his indecision is especially portrayed by the fact that he does not reply to Philoctetes' impassioned speech but speaks only to the chorus or to himself (965–966, 969–970, 974). That this leader is not yet in full command of himself, and still depends upon the advice of his followers, is made manifest in his final question, "What shall we do?" (974: τί δρῶμεν, ἄνδρες).

The audience never learns what their reply would be, for Neoptolemus' indecision is resolved for him as Odysseus explodes onto the scene in the middle of a line (974) and takes command of the situation. During the verbal duel that follows, Philoctetes' situation rapidly worsens. A victim of base fraud, deprived of his only weapon, confronted by his archenemy, denied even the final recourse of suicide, he is reduced to total helplessness by Odysseus, yet still will not submit to him. At the end of Philoctetes' speech of defiance, the chorus-leader makes what is usually considered a platitudinous or "buffer" comment about Philoctetes' stubbornness (1045–1046). The final words (1046: κοὐχ ὑπείκουσαν κακοῖς) closely resemble the words of the chorus in *Antigone* (472: εἴκειν δ' οὐκ ἐπίσταται κακοῖς) in a dramatic situation nearly identical to that of *Philoctetes*. Antigone is completely helpless and under guard, yet she, too, gives voice to self-justification and defiance. When she has spoken, the chorus address Creon with a similar statement about her stubbornness in the face of misfortune. It is true that choruses often seem to summarize a character's speech as harsh words needing modification; it is also true that the "Sophoclean hero" is often urged to yield (εἴκειν), to give up obstinacy, to listen to reason.[48] But only in these two passages (*Ant.* 472 and *Phil.* 1046) does Sophocles use the particular phrase [ὑπ]είκειν κακοῖς, "yield to misfortunes, ills."

Aeschylus uses the phrase once, at *Prometheus* 320, where it also de-

48. Knox (*Heroic Temper,* 16) has found that the use of [ὑπ]είκειν "to characterize the demand made on the hero of the play is almost exclusively Sophoclean." He does not, however, examine the further implications of the phrase εἴκειν κακοῖς.

scribes the attitude of an overpowered but defiant man. We may compare these usages to *Odyssey* 14.157 and Thucydides 1.84 and 2.64, where it seems clear from the context that "giving in to one's misfortunes" implies a certain dishonorable compromise for the sake of material advantage, a cutting of one's losses. The principle that this kind of compromise is dishonorable may be found in Sophocles' *Electra* (330–398), where Electra condemns Chrysothemis for urging her to yield to those in power (396) so that she may live a comfortable and easy life, instead of enduring a prisoner's lot. These examples are, of course, too few to serve as incontrovertible proof, but they suggest that the phrase itself, [ὑπ]εἴκειν κακοῖς / συμφοραῖς, may have had a somewhat derogatory connotation, such as "surrender to, collaborate with, evils" in the way that the English words "expedient" and "politic" contrast with "reasonable" and "prudent." This is not to say that here the chorus praise Philoctetes—quite the contrary. They are just the sort to think that the wise course is the expedient one, as their past conduct only too clearly shows. So also the Theban Elders, who are the silent subjects of an absolute ruler (*Ant.* 211ff., 220, 504–509), and Oceanus, who fears Zeus' anger (*Prom.* 323–324, 330, 374), have managed to survive the dangers of a superior and arbitrary power by behavior that is more politic than honorable.[49] By putting the probably unpleasant phrase ὑπείκειν κακοῖς into the mouth of these men, Sophocles has not only added to the characterization of the chorus, but may also have intended the audience to perceive, and respond sympathetically to, the helpless and desperate man who clings to his principles in contrast to the prosperous compromiser.

The scene in *Philoctetes* also significantly corresponds to that of *Antigone* in the mood and order of the speakers. Contrary to the popular concept of the general, or platitudinous, choral remark, Sophocles' chorus-leaders almost always address their unsolicited remarks directly to a character.[50] More than half of these remarks are responded to by a character; the most common pattern of response is: *A* makes a speech to *B*, who is often a supe-

49. The only Euripidean usage, *Suppl.* 167 (ἀνάγκη συμφοραῖς εἴκειν ἐμαῖς) may seem at first glance to lack this pejorative connotation. In the context of Adrastus' speech, however, and of his own character, it is suitable. He has, after all, waged an unjust war (232ff.) against the advice of the gods (157ff., 230–231), and now he admits that his present action is shameful (164ff.), yet he must do it to gain his end (the burial).

50. Only three in Sophocles are clearly "general" in address: *Tr.* 1044–1045 (to themselves), 1112–1113; *El.* 763–764. A few others do not have a specific address in the text, but are directly responded to by a character (e.g., *El.* 610–611, 990–991; and *Ant.* 471–472), and so may have the effect of being specifically addressed. Kitto (*Greek Tragedy*, 163) wishes to note "the habit of Sophocles' characters of addressing their reply to the chorus when they

rior; the chorus address *B* about *A*, then *B* replies to the chorus about *A*.[51] We may reasonably deduce that the dramatic effect of this discussion, in the third person and while *A* stands listening, is to stress that *A* is isolated and is often subordinate to, or even dependent upon, the power and status of *B*. Even further, *Phil.* 1045–1046 belongs to a subgroup of this pattern, consisting of four scenes, in which *B*, after replying to the chorus about *A*, turns directly to *A* and issues angry and threatening orders to him or her. It is almost a trial in which the petitioner's case is pleaded and judged, and sentence is passed.[52] The defiant Philoctetes is held prisoner while Odysseus and the chorus talk about him. This and the arrogance and smugness of Odysseus emphasize Philoctetes' isolation and desperate circumstances. He is helpless in the power of his enemy, condemned to die alone and wretchedly.

The impression of Philoctetes' desolation deepens as, released by Odysseus' command, he addresses in turn each character on the scene. Odysseus spurns him utterly (1065). He makes a last appeal to the son of Achilles, whom Odysseus prevents from replying. Finally he turns to the chorus, but they refuse a direct answer and refer him back to Neoptolemus (1072–1073). Nor does Neoptolemus then speak directly to Philoctetes; instead, he, too, addresses the chorus about Philoctetes, in the third person (1075). In addition to the continued emphasis on the isolation of Philoctetes, this exchange has another, equally important function. Neoptolemus has been standing in silence throughout the entire confrontation between Philoctetes and Odysseus. Now the chorus, in drawing him into the scene, remind the

---

are too angry to answer directly." But of the four examples he cites, only one is actually not in direct answer to the chorus (*Oed. Tyr.* 429). Of the thirty-two unsolicited comments made by the chorus in Sophocles (unsolicited in that the chorus have not been directly addressed and are not responding to a physical occurrence, such as an entrance or exit), fully seventeen are immediately answered by a character, five are not answered directly but appear to affect the character's response, and the remaining ten are ignored.

51. Twelve certain cases: *Aj.* 525–526; *El.* 369–371, 464–465; *Oed. Tyr.* 616–617; *Ant.* 278–279, 471–472, 724–725; *Tr.* 291–292; *Phil.* 963–964, 1045–1046; *Oed. Col.* 629–630, 1346–1347. The chorus-leader's interference also functions to expand the dialogue temporarily from two participants to three and thus to create triangular patterns of speech; in some cases this seems to be used to achieve a dramatic effect of unity and harmony (see below on *Oed. Col.* and *El.*).

52. The other three are *Ant.* 278–279; *Oed. Col.* 1346–1347; and *Oed. Col.* 629–630. This last is an exception in that although Theseus (*B*) does first speak to the chorus about Oedipus (*A*) and then addresses him directly, his attitude is friendly rather than hostile and threatening. Still, the effect of judgment and sentencing, though favorable in this case, remains. We may consider *Ant.* 471–472 as similar to these three, despite the fact that Creon (*B*) does not speak to Antigone (*A*) directly, since he does issue angry orders (489–491).

audience that this παῖς is indeed their captain (1072: ναυκράτωρ), that he has asserted control over them. Their words create a vivid contrast between Odysseus' arrogant commands to Neoptolemus (1068–1069) and the chorus' own deference to him. Moreover, Neoptolemus does not obey Odysseus entirely, but, admitting the possibility of criticism, he bids the chorus remain a while; and he seems to have assumed a military manner, in that he issues a sequence of technical and efficient orders.

Philoctetes is left alone with the chorus, who are remaining not by their own request so much as by their chief's orders. Since the audience does not know exactly what will happen, except perhaps that Philoctetes will eventually get to Troy, it seems that he is going to be left behind. Neoptolemus and Odysseus have gone, the ship is being prepared to sail, and the chorus are just about to go (1076–1077, 1080).[53] The element of suspense here is strong, for Neoptolemus has suggested the possibility that Philoctetes might change his mind (1078–1079), and the audience must wonder whether the chorus will persuade him. The ensuing kommos (1081–1217) may be regarded as a genuine attempt on the part of the chorus to persuade Philoctetes, an attempt which Sophocles deliberately designed to fail, in order that we may see Philoctetes' refusal to go to Troy as a natural consequence of the brutal treatment he has received, rather than as merely petulant obstinacy. Therefore the poet has purposely given the chorus weak arguments and inadequate delivery.[54] This is undoubtedly an important part of the dramatic effect of the kommos; but it is by no means the whole, for the chorus seem to be engaged not so much in persuasion as in recrimination.

In the first strophe Philoctetes, rejected by men, addresses his grief to his wretched abode (1081–1094). We might expect the chorus to express some sympathy for his circumstances, as they have done before, but none is forthcoming here. "It is your own fault," they cry, "you had a choice"— but the choice was to defy his enemy or to surrender to evils (εἴκειν κακοῖς). Philoctetes ignores them entirely and sings of the loneliness to come, and of the treachery that leaves him helpless in his ills (1101–1115). Still the chorus offer no pity; before, they laid the blame on him (1095ff.), now they blame destiny (1116). The chorus are right about his illness; but

53. On the notion that the audience would believe that Odysseus is only bluffing, see, for example, Kitto (*Form and Meaning*, 124; *Greek Tragedy*, 306), Linforth ("Philoctetes," 136, 140), and, most fantastically, Calder (*GRBS* 12 [1971], 160–162). This is well refuted by Knox (*Heroic Temper*, 192); see also Winnington-Ingram, *Sophocles*, 293.

54. Cf. Kitto, *Form and Meaning*, 124–126, and *Greek Tragedy*, 306–307.

Philoctetes is talking about the plot, which Odysseus himself has admitted was his own doing (980). Thus they are wrong to deny their part in Philoctetes' troubles, when they have played a major role in the deception. Again Philoctetes ignores them; he speaks to the absent bow, now in the power of the enemy, and of the treachery of its new master (1123–1139). To this the chorus reply that Odysseus was only acting under orders.[55] At best, this is a poor justification for fraud, and hardly valid, seeing that the emphasis has been entirely on personal gain and glory (81, 112ff., 1052, 1061–1062). Still Philoctetes ignores them; and now he sings to his former victims about the terrible fate he is to suffer—death by starvation (1146–1162). It is a prospect which might draw pity from the coldest heart; but the chorus evade the issue of his abandonment and speak instead of escape from his disease (1163–1168). This is no specific offer of healing, merely another version of the idea that he has the choice of staying or accompanying them, and it pointedly ignores the fact that if he stays he will die not from the disease but because they have stolen his bow.

It is obvious that this kommos is unique in Sophoclean tragedy in the complete absence of communication between chorus and character. Philoctetes three times ignores the chorus, seeming not even to hear them. He addresses himself to the cave, the bow, the birds and beasts—to everything except the other human beings present on the scene. The chorus, on the other hand, do speak to Philoctetes, but they do not actually respond to what he says. Philoctetes has been deceived, defrauded, dishonored, and deserted. For this they have not one word of compassion or shame. They have not heard him. Philoctetes' lament is emotionally powerful and immediate, with its absence of mythological reference and the personification of the bow (1130–1131: φρένας εἴ τινας ἔχεις), culminating in the horrifying imagery of lines 1155–1157, in which he invites the birds and beasts to dine upon his flesh. Yet even this Neoptolemus' men ignore. They show not the slightest understanding of the injustice that has been done to Philoctetes.

At last Philoctetes speaks to the chorus, and at the same time the structure of the kommos moves from the formal balance of strophic responsion

55. Kitto (*Form and Meaning*, 125) assumes that the chorus are referring to Neoptolemus and not to Odysseus (1143: κεῖνος); but it is surely clear that Philoctetes has been speaking of Odysseus, since he has already placed the responsibility for the whole stratagem squarely on Odysseus (978–979, 1006–1015) and speaks of him as wielding the bow (1063–1064). It is perhaps possible that we are intended to perceive the chorus as having misunderstood Philoctetes' reference, but again the recollection of his recent words to Odysseus makes this unlikely: . . . τῶν Ἀτρέως / διπλῶν στρατηγῶν, οἷς σὺ ταῦθ' ὑπηρετεῖς (1023–1024).

to the irregularity of the astrophic epode (1169–1217). But the hope of communication offered by this more conversational mode quickly fades. The chorus do not understand that for Philoctetes the "cure" of going to Troy is worse than the disease itself, nor does he accept their attitude of compromise for the sake of gain. "I think it best," they say, and he rejects them (1177). The readiness to abandon him which they display (1178–1180) in response to his dismissal of them is in startling contrast to Neoptolemus' behavior during Philoctetes' illness. The young man did not release Philoctetes' hand, though bidden to do so, until the frenzy had passed (815–818); but here Philoctetes himself, in the frenzy of despair, must explain to these men that one ought not take offense at another's anguish. It is reasonable to suppose that the members of the audience would recall the earlier scene, especially the reversal of visual effect. There they saw Neoptolemus in close contact with Philoctetes, clasping his hand; but here the chorus and sufferer are probably far apart (1164). The spate of questions at the end of the epode also points the contrast with the scene between Neoptolemus and Philoctetes, for Neoptolemus, too, questioned, but he ended up understanding the answers (753–755, 814–818, and especially 839–842). The chorus, however, never do achieve comprehension of, or sympathy for, Philoctetes, as is emphasized by the petulant tone of their parting shot (1218–1219)—which is again ignored, or goes unheard, by Philoctetes.[56] This scene, this dialogue of the deaf, completes the isolation of Philoctetes—he is alone not only physically, but spiritually. In part, Sophocles is delineating the suffering of a great soul by comparing the reaction of the small soul, the "average man."[57] Yet these men are not average: they are a very specific type—the expedient, the timeservers, the followers. They have no sense of shame or honor, as Neoptolemus so clearly does (906, and especially 1011–1012); yet they are the survivors, while the hero will perish, and between the two lies an unbridgeable gulf of misunderstanding. They are Neoptolemus' men, but they behave like Odysseus.

With the return of Neoptolemus and Odysseus, the chorus fall silent; but their role is not over, for their physical presence and their silence itself

---

56. On the interpretation of the kommos in general, cf. Schmidt, *Philoktet*, 190–192; on the failure of communication within the play, see also the wider speculations of Podlecki (*GRBS* 7 [1966], 233–250), who does not, however, appreciate the function of the chorus (cf. 241). Taplin (*GRBS* 12 [1971], 42–43) argues convincingly that the style of lines 1218–1221 suggests they are a later interpolation ("doggerel"); but if a transition were suitable here, this would be a smooth one, since the first two lines round off the previous scene and the last two introduce a new one.

57. Müller, "Chor und Handlung," 217.

serve as a foil to the continuing action. It is curious how even those readers who admit the dramatic importance of the single actor—Neoptolemus, for example, holding the bow during the confrontation between Odysseus and Philoctetes—can lose all interest in fifteen men as soon as they cease to speak. Neoptolemus has only recently established his authority over the chorus, and the chorus reminded us of this just before the kommos; it is now in front of these same men that he finally asserts himself against Odysseus. They who have hitherto always been ready with a timely word now stand silent and motionless as the action is played out by greater men than they. While Odysseus flees and the other two principals each yield in turn, having achieved some measure of understanding—Neoptolemus to Philoctetes, and then Philoctetes, who can distinguish between the true messenger of Zeus and the false (899–902), to Heracles—the chorus' visible presence displays the contrast between the honorable and the politic, the leaders and the followers, the understanding and the uncomprehending.

Only at the very end of the play do the chorus speak again. These lines are seen, as are all the concluding choral statements in Sophocles, as the poet's way of setting the final tone for the play—here it is that of a joyous departure, a happy ending.[58] The final lines of *Philoctetes*, however, differ from the rest of Sophocles' endings in that they contain no comment whatsoever on the things which have occurred, no general statement such as "let us rejoice that all has ended well," or "behold how Zeus has accomplished his will." We cannot tell whether the words were recited by the chorus in unison or by the leader alone, nor whether the chorus were standing still or moving off. Nevertheless, Euripides' use of one closing for five different plays (and another one for two others) makes it not unreasonable for us to postulate an entirely conventional action or mode of delivery to indicate the end of the performance. All the extant tragedies end either with a lyric passage or with a meter other than iambic trimeter (trochaic tetrameter, dactylic hexameter, or, most commonly, anapests). In the latter case, there is usually no occurrence of a meter other than iambic trimeter after the last lyric and before the final passage of the play. This final passage may be long and complex, but there is no return to iambic trimeter. It is therefore possible that the final change of meter, especially when it was to anapests delivered by the chorus, could have functioned as a sort of ver-

---

58. Cf. Bowra, *Sophoclean Tragedy*, 9–10; Errandonea, *Sófocles* (1958), 382. In his brief study of the final lines of Sophocles' plays, Hester expresses the belief that the poet wanted the ends of his plays to have a "relaxing" effect on the audience; this one he sees as a clear case of "relaxed diminuendo finale" (*Antichthon* 8 [1973], 9).

bal curtain, without breaking the dramatic illusion as Aristophanes does.[59] That is not to say that the chorus' final utterance would not be heard within the context of their dramatic character. On the contrary, their exhortation to depart after suitable prayer is equally consistent with their previous behavior, for they are advising the proper military procedure. Their words are neither banal nor inappropriate to their character and at the same time convey a definite sense of finality.

Because of the extent to which the chorus participate in the plot and aid in the deception with outright lies, they are usually granted more character than other choruses in Sophocles. It is generally agreed that their chief characteristics are complete devotion to Neoptolemus' interests and at least some genuine sympathy for the unhappy Philoctetes; they are, however, relatively insignificant in their function as a minor character, an "assistant conspirator."[60] But the audience has seen them as the poet has presented them: veteran soldiers whose behavior is at all times sensible and practical. Their large share in the deception, for which they themselves devise some of the most convincing parts—the "false oath," the pleading for Philoctetes' return home—shows them as capable of independent thought and action, clever, unlikely to pass up a good opportunity. They were, after all, the first to think of stealing the bow. The early references in the parodos (135–143, 150–151) establish their relationship to Neoptolemus as his faithful subordinates, but thereafter greater emphasis is laid on their devotion to the stratagem than to Neoptolemus, until their final submission to his authority (1072–1073). They are loyal to the mission. The contrast between them and their chief presents some negative aspects of character: they are neither noble nor honorable, hence their vision and understanding are limited. But they are clearly not utter villains; the moderate amount of pity they display is indicative of their humanity.

This very pity, however, can lead critics to the opposite extreme of the "voice-of-the-poet" view—excessive psychologizing, a varietal strain of the "documentary fallacy." If the play is to succeed, the action of the drama must necessarily be both logical within the plot and readily comprehen-

59. The few exceptions would cause no confusion: Eurip., *Iph. Taur.* 1621ff., is a farewell speech, as is *Phoen.* 1758ff., and *Or.* 1549ff. is an arrival announcement; *Helen* 1621–1641 reaches an impasse which could not be heard as the end of the play and which is solved by the entrance of the Dioscuroi.

60. For example, Kirkwood (*Sophoclean Drama,* 187, 192), Linforth ("Philoctetes," 114), and, worst of all, Waldock (*Sophocles,* 209; they have only "faint glimmerings of personality").

sible to the audience; therefore, any action significant to the story which is not either physically performed or verbally described cannot be supposed to occur. Whereas the audience has been carefully prepared for the return of the guard in the character of the pseudo-merchant, one may readily eliminate the hypothetical early silent entrance of the chorus, or the suggestion that Odysseus keeps returning in disguise (as the merchant and as Heracles) in his attempts to get Philoctetes to Troy.[61] This principle may be applied also to the characters' "feelings." Neoptolemus is the clearest example, for his emotions at every stage of the plot are described explicitly—his initial distaste for fraud (79–80, 88) struggling with his desire to do his duty (93–95), his decision to go ahead with the deception (120), the fact that he is affected by Philoctetes' pain (804–806), his realization that the scheme will not work (939–941) and that it is shameful (902–903, 906), his confusion and indecision (908–909), his resistance to Philoctetes' entreaties (934–935, 951), and his sense of honor, which in the end compels him to make restitution (1011–1012, 1224ff., especially 1234). Nothing relevant to the plot is in any way left to the imagination. With this clear evidence of Sophocles' practice of openly presenting his characters' mental processes, it would be illogical to assume that he leaves others so hidden that the audience can only guess at them. These characters are the creation of the poet; they have no existence save what he imparts to them.

Thus to suggest that Neoptolemus in the parodos is suppressing his inner guilt or that Odysseus is only bluffing when he says that Philoctetes is unnecessary is to give these characters a level of existence which they do not possess. If the structure of the plot requires a character to say one thing and mean another, as is often the case in *Philoctetes,* or to undergo an emotional reaction while another is speaking, Sophocles utilizes his expert stagecraft to tell us exactly what is happening. The metrical responsion of the separate antistrophe (507–518) indicates that the chorus are lying; Philoctetes' questions to Neoptolemus—"Why are you silent? What are you thinking?" (805)—tell us that his silence is indeed significant. When, therefore, it is alleged that the chorus are actually pitying Philoctetes while they lie, that they are concerned throughout the play for his well-being, that they sincerely believe "they must be cruel to be kind," [62] we must reject this as unwarranted psychologizing. The poet has shown us the exact amount of sympathy the chorus have for Philoctetes—they pity his wretched circum-

61. Errandonea, *Sófocles* (1958), 246–255, 278–284, 291–292.
62. Linforth, "Philoctetes," 114, 123.

stances in a general way, but they are quite ready to abandon him even after his illness. They display, in short, no more sympathy for him than did his former visitors (cf. 307–309).

In this character, then, the chorus serve the poet as an extremely useful and versatile instrument; besides providing smooth transitions and continuity, they have a vital part in the plot as they nurse the deception toward maturity. In addition, their character functions in relation to the principals. With respect to Neoptolemus, they show up his kingly qualities, his youth and inexperience, his indecision, and his eventual move from reliance upon their advice to independence of judgment. With respect to Philoctetes, they display his pitiable circumstances, his physical and mental isolation, and the contrast between his great will and their lack of understanding. It is when we examine their relation to the character of Odysseus, however, that we see the chorus' wider function in the drama. He bears many characteristics of the Homeric Odysseus—he is clever, unscrupulous, adaptable to every situation. He is also the skillful speaker (98–99), the prudent counselor in the Homeric assembly which the false merchant so aptly describes (608–619). At the same time he seems to be representative of a familiar type of fifth-century B.C. political leader, the man who suits himself to the occasion and for whom virtuous conduct is subordinate to immediate self-interest (1049–1052). We may compare Thucydides' remarks on such men (3.82), Cleon's defense of the Mytilenean decree (3.39ff., especially 40), or the attitude of the Athenians in the Melian dialogue (5.89–90, 98, 105). This Odysseus stands as the representative both of the Atreidae, so often referred to throughout the play, and of all such cynical, expedient demagogues.

Besides these leaders there is another prominent political element in the play: the great host of the Greek army at Troy, the Achaeans-Argives-Danaoi, is referred to at least twenty-eight times, and Odysseus himself is described by the chorus as "one from many" (1143: εἷς ἀπὸ πολλῶν). Surely the fifteen members of the chorus are a group of these same fighting men who went to Troy with their chiefs, who formed the assembly of the army, who were the ἑταῖροι of the great heroes.[63] Thus they have a close relationship with Odysseus: they imitate his attitudes, his actions, even his

---

63. Beye (*TAPA* 101 [1970], 66) suggests that in respect of Philoctetes' solitude the chorus are by their numbers "symbolic of the *laoi*, of society." It is interesting to note that the play contains an unusually large number, for Sophocles, of Homeric words, most of which are uttered by the chorus; cf. Earp, *Style*, 52–55. Perhaps this might contribute toward the chorus' identification with the Homeric λαοί.

words; on the other hand, their personal sympathy for Philoctetes distinguishes them from Odysseus, who is completely blind to his sufferings. The political analogy is obvious: these particular men are typical followers of the demagogue, the sort of men who accept the principle of expediency which is offered them, who are concerned not with higher concepts of honor and justice but only with the immediate gains of their group's interests. Decent enough men in their way, they are able to be controlled by competent leaders, but are basically short-sighted. They make good soldiers, but poor generals. By introducing this group into the play, Sophocles has achieved a twofold broadening of the entire scope of the drama. A sordid incident on a desert island has been expanded to include the whole Greek expedition against Troy, and at the same time a power struggle between leaders has become a political dispute taking place before their people.

CHAPTER 3

Ajax

Of all the heroes of Attic tragedy, our age most admires the Sophoclean Ajax. The mighty Homeric warrior has captured the gaze of later readers, and in their sight looms far above the other, wiser giants of legend, eternally massive, stern, implacable. His great strength, which made him the bulwark of the Achaeans at Troy, is still much admired, but it is felt that this mighty physique must have been endowed with something more, some quality that made him both epic hero and religious hero. "Noble" he is called, and "splendid," and many would probably acknowledge, with Kitto, that Ajax, son of Telamon, is "incomparably the most magnificent figure of them all."[1] Despite his obvious faults, indeed his crimes, many find in him a noble spirit that through its own greatness came inevitably into conflict with the universe, an indomitable fighter who by yielding in the end not only preserved the honor that he so greatly feared to lose, but also became a worthy object of reverence for future generations. For them, Ajax's death is a religious sacrifice, an act of expiation and consecration.[2]

Those of a more humanistic view, who do not agree that the hero is "rehabilitated" within the play to the level of cult-hero, nevertheless admire his grim determination and find his suicide both poignant and noble. In general they agree that his is the tragedy of the passing away of the old order, the heroic ideal that can no longer be applied in a nonheroic age. In

---

1. Kitto, *Form and Meaning*, 183.

2. The view that the canonization of Ajax is the goal of the play and the belief that the poet succeeds in attaining this goal (inasmuch as he causes his audience to admire Ajax) were especially advocated by Jebb (introduction, xxviii–xxxii) as providing an answer to the problem of the unity of the drama; these views are still held by some, for example, M. Sicherl (*YCS* 25 [1977], 95–98), who maintains that the suicide is itself a ritual of atonement for the offenses against Athena.

their sight, his shaking his mighty fist at the universe as he defies by his suicide the inexorable powers of change is what makes him a tragic and at the same time admirable figure.[3] The members of a more civilized society still feel a wistful envy for the age of the mighty individual, when manliness and a man's place in the world were defined by a simpler set of rules.

This vision of Ajax's great and tragic stature tends to illumine and simultaneously to aggravate the most serious critical problem of the play— its unity. If Ajax is so prominent and imposing, the level of our interest can only decline when he dies. Our attention suddenly has no more focus than the hero's shrouded corpse, and thus the play becomes bipartite, a diptych. It cannot end, as modern taste would like, with the grand final gesture of the suicide. If Ajax is to be worthy of reverence, his character must be restored to full nobility. Or, from the humanistic viewpoint, we must be shown how such a man's inner greatness, as manifested by his determination, must be respected by lesser persons despite his transgressions against them. Even for those who do not question the essential unity of the drama, the interest lies mostly in the first part, the lessons in the second.

The dramatic portrayal of this hero's character appears to rely upon the chorus of the play for certain important effects. Consequently, they also become involved in the question of the structural unity of the play. Their role is usually seen as that of ordinary, lesser men, a standard against which the audience measures Ajax and finds him mightier, larger than life. They are relatively weak, timorous (perhaps cowardly), concerned chiefly for survival; in contrast to them Ajax appears strong, bold, unswervingly dedicated to maintaining his honor even at the expense of his life. If this is their function in the drama, to be a foil for Ajax, then they must naturally lose force when Ajax is present and eclipsing them with his greatness; and they must fade even more when he dies, for then they have no further dramatic reason for being. In the second part of the play all attention is concentrated on the burial of the body, and Teucer dominates the action; as a result, the chorus seem to recede far into the background.[4]

---

3. Among the many who esteem or at least condone the way Ajax stands up to the gods are Gellie (*Sophocles*, 20), Linforth ("Three Scenes," 26), and Whitman (*Sophocles*, 77); see the last for an example of the general approbation of Ajax's suicide as the best way for the hero to maintain his "honor": "His suicide is not weakness, or stubbornness; it is the supreme self-mastery." Stanford in his commentary (xxiv) calls it "the final splendor of self-fulfillment." Even Waldock agrees that at the moment of Ajax's death the audience perceives the hero as "noble" and possessing "intrinsic greatness of soul" (*Sophocles*, 61–62). In contrast stand the far more balanced views of Rosivach (*CJ* 72 [1976–1977], 47ff.) and Winnington-Ingram (*Sophocles*, 11ff.).

4. For a lengthy elaboration of this view, see Davidson (*BICS* 22 [1975], 164).

Even though the chorus are so intimately linked with Ajax, we should first examine them independently of the hero, because the audience actually sees considerably more of them than of Ajax himself during the course of the play. They are particularly remarkable for their extensive participation in the dialogue of the first part of the drama. The parodos, which technically consists only of the chorus' initial utterance, a long anapestic series (134–171), actually introduces a choral scene that lasts for nearly a hundred lines and involves, besides the anapestic introduction, an ode in the simple triadic form (strophe-antistrophe-epode: 172–200), an anapestic scene with Tecmessa (201–262) that includes another choral strophic pair (221–232, 245–256), a scene in iambic trimeters with Tecmessa, and a kommos with Ajax and Tecmessa (333–429). And they continue to be heard, speaking eight lines during the next iambic trimeter scene with Tecmessa and Ajax, then an ode of two strophic pairs. After Ajax's parting speech, they sing another ode of one strophic pair, and then they interview the Messenger, uttering thirteen more iambic lines during the scene. In effect, they function as a second actor until Ajax's appearance, and as a very much involved third actor when he is present.

As in the majority of Sophocles' plays, there has been no preparation during the prologue for the chorus' entrance, and we may therefore assume that their identity was readily apparent to the audience. The *hypothesis* calls them simply a "chorus of Salaminian sailors," and so they are commonly termed today. It is true that they are several times referred to as "shipmates" or "seafarers" (201, 349, 565, 872), but they are also "shield-bearing men" (565: ἄνδρες ἀσπιστῆρες); it is important to note that they are not specifically associated with the ships when they first appear. They are surely of the same class as Neoptolemus' companions in *Philoctetes*, the Viking-like warriors who both manned the ships and fought the battles.[5] This would be evident at once to the audience if they were costumed as soldiers. Their opening statements, that their fortunes rise and fall with Ajax's, at once identify them specifically as Ajax's soldiers. Since there is no indication of their age, aside from the fact that they came to Troy with Ajax and are therefore not raw recruits, we may presume that they are fighting men of otherwise indeterminate age.

Because anapests are traditionally considered a "marching meter," it

5. For the Homeric evidence that rowers and fighters were identical, see above, chapter 2, on the parodos of *Philoctetes*. Burton (*The Chorus*, 6–7) asserts that the chorus are not warriors, but ignores the testimony of both Homer and Thucydides—and also fails to consider whether, if the chorus are only sailors, the audience might wonder why Ajax's fighting troops are never summoned to protect his endangered family.

may be suggested that the poet deliberately brought the chorus on with an anapestic entrance to enhance or confirm the military aspect of their identity.[6] But the association of anapests with marching is merely a common assumption that rests on little or no evidence. Postclassical tradition seems to have inferred the notion of "march-anapests" from the fact that characters in Greek drama sometimes arrive or depart to the accompaniment of anapestic poetry.[7] Particularly noticeable is the tendency for the chorus to close the play, and presumably exit, with a few anapests. But we still know virtually nothing about the relationship among meter, musical rhythm, and movement. In fact, there is no proof that the Athenian soldiers of the fifth century ever marched in step, so the audience would not necessarily have associated the anapestic meter with marching or soldiery.[8]

Furthermore, there are numerous places in Sophocles where anapests cannot possibly connote any military aspect of the speaker, the most obvious of which is the heroine's entrance in *Electra* (86–120). It is usual to differentiate between the two passages by categorizing the anapests of *Electra* as "lyric" or "melic" and *Ajax*'s as "recitative." Yet there is actually no significant difference in the metrical quality of the passages,[9] and they

---

6. Burton, for example, although maintaining that the chorus are not fighting men, nevertheless asks "what is more natural than for a body of sailors, subordinate to the chief character, to march into the orchestra in formation?" (*The Chorus*, 8).

7. It is today almost universally assumed, with no more foundation than an occasional reference to the Spartan paroemiac ἐμβατήρια, that the anapestic dimeter was a marching meter. Cf. Webster, *Greek Chorus*, 62, 112, and passim; Dale, *Lyric Metres*, 47, 51; and Maas, *Greek Metre*, §51.

8. Thucydides' rather elaborate description (5.70) of the Spartans marching into battle to the accompaniment of flutes and his explanation that they did it not for religious reasons, but to maintain the battle line, suggests that the practice was not a familiar one. While noting that Thucydides attributes the "paian of attack" only to Dorians, W. Kendrick Pritchett (*Ancient Greek Military Practices* [Berkeley, 1971], 106–108) nevertheless seems to assume that there was among the Greeks an early and widespread need "for maintaining an unbroken phalanx in battle step." Yet there are no other fifth-century references to marching in step. Herodotus (1.17) says of Alyattes of Lydia that he made an expedition (ἐστρατεύετο) against Miletus with various musical instruments; but it was simply an invasion of the territory to destroy the harvest, and there is no clear sense of marching. Plutarch's admiring comments (*Lycurgus* 21–22) confirm the impression that the Spartan practice of marching into battle was unique among the Greeks. A volunteer citizen army, recruited *ad hoc* for battles, is perhaps less likely to practice such refinements as synchronized marching than a professional standing army, such as those of Hellenistic and Roman times, or the Spartan society, which was dedicated to continuous military training in a communal manner.

9. Jebb (*ad El.* 86) maintains the distinction; Kamerbeek (*ad El.* 86) calls Electra's anapests "intermediate" between lyric and recitative. But see Dale's remarks (*Lyric Metres*, 52) on *El.* 86: "the dialect is Attic, and most of the chant is of the ordinary recitative type, except for two consecutive spondaic paroemiacs 88–9 and again (with one resolution) 105–6."

resemble each other rather strikingly in their dramatic function. Both passages convey important factual information about the present situation and attitudes of the speakers who, as new arrivals on an empty scene, must deliver the necessary information in a monologue: Electra's is in the form of an apostrophic prayer, while Ajax's men address a summons to their unseen leader.

The first information delivered by the chorus of *Ajax* in their anapests is the identification of their person. This the poet has intertwined with the introduction of a new mood and theme, which immediately advances the dramatic situation beyond that of the preceding scene. The prologue was a scene of isolation and secrecy: the solitary tent of Ajax, described as a remote outpost (4), beside which the lone, stealthy tracker Odysseus converses with the invisible goddess (15),[10] and is then himself hidden from Ajax's sight (83–87); the hero gloating over his unseen prey (101ff.), isolating himself from his patron goddess by his bold individuality; and after Ajax leaves, the ominous conversation between his goddess and his enemy. In sudden contrast, the chorus enter calling aloud to Ajax and bringing with them the crowd, the consternation, and especially the noise of the Greek camp. First they mention slanderous verbal attacks by the Danaoi, with the associated fear and danger (134–140); then they elaborate with such detail upon the charges being noised about (142: $\mu\varepsilon\gamma\acute{\alpha}\lambda o\iota$ $\theta\acute{o}\rho\upsilon\beta o\iota$) that they almost seem to be quoting directly (143–147), ending with the picture of the gossip passing from man to man, growing louder and more slanderous, each hearer maliciously savoring it more than the last (151–153).

Although the chorus have not yet given their own opinion about the truth of the rumor, their use of such phrases as "fabricating [slanderous] whispers" (148: $\psi\iota\theta\acute{\upsilon}\rho o\upsilon\varsigma$ $\pi\lambda\acute{\alpha}\sigma\sigma\omega\nu$) suggests that they have already made up their mind. Now, still without a clear denial of the rumor, they condemn the proclivity of the small to malign the great, offering as their philosophy the proposition that common people cannot survive without the help of the great, and the best order of things is a respectful alliance between the two classes, each fulfilling its natural function (154–161). This rather feudal outlook defines the chorus as humble men and very dependent upon their leader, but it also establishes them as good soldiers in the Homeric sense. The sentiments that Ajax's men express here are essen-

10. Invisible, that is, to him. On Athena's physical location in the scene, see the arguments of Calder (*CP* 60 [1965], 114–116); Ziobro (*CF* 26 [1972], 122–128); and in reply, Calder (*CF* 28 [1974], 59–61).

tially the same that Homer expresses about ugly, vulgar Thersites in the *Iliad:* it is wrong, unseemly (2.214: οὐ κατὰ κόσμον) for the lowly to impugn the motives of kings, and to dare to insult them; all the Achaeans at the assembly strongly disapprove of his reproaching Agamemnon for the wealth of war-prizes he has gained (2.222–223).

So, like Homer's Achaeans, the lesser men who follow Ajax are unquestioningly loyal to their leader and abhor the envy "that creeps up on the man who has [much]" (157).[11] The chorus' exhortations lead logically back to the motivation for their arrival: they have come to ask their leader to quash these insubordinate and disorderly upstarts. The passage ends with another picture of the Greek camp, this time prefiguring the hubbub (164: θορυβῇ; 168: παταγοῦσιν) suddenly silenced by the hero's appearance, a reasonable consequence, in a Homeric context, for the chorus to expect, since the Trojans fled in terror when Achilles only showed himself, unarmed, and uttered his war-cry (*Il.* 18.222–231).

Now the chorus move into lyric meters and presumably begin to sing. We cannot be certain of the extent to which the audience would hear a contrast between the anapestic and lyric sections, because we cannot be certain about the mode of delivering the anapests. If they were accompanied by a flute, the music would ease the transition between chant and song, whereas if the anapests were recited a capella the change in modes would be distinct and perhaps even abrupt.[12] Certainly there is some contrast, but the meter of the song suggests that the chorus do not break into a spate of frantic, tumbling lyrics. The beginning of the ode is dactylic (172–173); since this is itself a stichic or recitative meter, the lines may have been performed here in less than lyric fashion. There soon follows an iambic trimeter

11. Kamerbeek, *ad* 160, supposes the chorus' attitude indicates "a political preference on the part of the poet, a leaning towards ὁμόνοια as against στάσις." But if a character's words suit the dramatic context, as these do if considered as the ethos of Homeric warriors, it is always safer to leave them in the context rather than pluck them out and hang them around the poet's neck. For the significance of the grammatical structure of this passage, which he terms "reflective," and speculations upon the relation of metrical effects and content, see Davidson (*BICS* 22 [1975], 168 and 172–173).

12. The conversational tone of the parodos of *Philoctetes* suggests that the poet did not intend a jarring contrast between the lyric and anapestic parts, and therefore that the anapests, which are "recitative," had some slight musical accompaniment. There also the anapests convey information. On the other hand, certain of Sophocles' anapestic systems are so closely connected with iambic trimeter scenes that the intrusion of a musical accompaniment might seem incongruous. Such are the announcement of Ismene's entrance by the chorus in *Antigone* (526–530) and their later anapestic dialogue with Creon (929ff.); see below, chapter 4, on these scenes.

(176), which also may have had a more recitative delivery than the dactylo-epitritic meter of the rest of the ode.[13] It is as if the chorus, having delivered their information in the anapests, now begin to speculate upon that information. Their reaction is not despair or lyric emotionalism, but an effort to figure out the cause of what has happened and to work out some way of dealing with the situation.[14]

The simple structure of the ode reflects the uncomplicated, linear progress of their reasoning. In the strophe, they speculate on the possibility that a slighted deity may somehow be responsible, because, as they go on to say in the antistrophe, Ajax would never have done any such thing in his right mind. Then the chorus express the hope that the rumors are false and that, if they are, Ajax will not continue his disgraceful silence and passivity.[15] The epode follows logically upon the last statement of the antistrophe; they exhort him to rise up and take suitable action. To support this plea, they close with strong words on the urgency of the situation and a reminder that they are themselves grievously affected by their leader's inaction.

Throughout the parodos, Sophocles portrays Ajax's followers as men of action concerned to find an immediate solution to their present problem. Because he is their leader, they are dependent upon him and loyal to him. In the Homeric fashion that they extol, they do not presume to criticize or question him about the charges of slaughtering the herds. Nor do they

13. Dale (*Metrical Analyses* 1, 14) analyzes 172–173 (= 182–183) as dactylic tetrameter followed by hemiepes and epitritic dimeter. The tetrameter, however, is followed by two dactyls with diaeresis after the last; this phrase (ὦ μεγάλα φάτις) could as well be heard with the preceding one, thus suggesting, though not duplicating, the epic dactylic hexameter line. The next eight syllables constitute an iambic dimeter, with diaeresis at the end; this, too, could be heard as a unit that presages the upcoming iambic trimeter.

14. There is little evidence to support Davidson's belief that the transition between anapests and lyrics is strikingly abrupt (*BICS* 22 [1975], 169–170, 173). He maintains that the chorus' underlying fear, that the rumors may be true, erupts in an emotional outpouring which begins with an echo of the cult-formulae used to invoke deities. Claiming that "the name Artemis Tauropolos immediately creates an atmosphere of wildness and madness which sweeps aside the chorus' theorizing" (170), he hears the opening dactyls as so rapid and free that "we seem to be transported suddenly into the open spaces across which Artemis is imagined to range" (173). But neither the metrics nor the diction give any solid support to this interpretation. The mention of Artemis is probably intended as an allusion to Agamemnon's incurrence of that goddess' wrath by his arrogance when he slew a stag (compare the suppositions of lines 176–178 to *El.* 566–569). With such a precedent, it becomes perfectly reasonable for the Homeric warriors to suspect divine interference; cf. also Jebb, *ad* 172.

15. Cf. *Trach.* 813–814: "Do you not realize that by keeping silent you accredit your accuser?"

praise him or make any mention of his good qualities. In fact, despite their
ignorance of his true murderous intent,[16] they seem to have no illusions
about his temper, since they are not surprised by the idea that he might
have insulted a god. In the structure and content of the chorus' initial utterances, the poet has characterized them as direct and uncomplicated,
and he seems to reinforce this characterization through the meter and the
diction. Within the ode, their first speculation that Ajax might have neglected to sacrifice properly (176) and the chief part of their precative
hope that the report may be false (186) are both couched in iambic trimeter, which may have had a relatively matter-of-fact delivery. The structure
of the ode is simple, and the language relatively plain. They use only two
similes, both occurring in the anapestic section and both using the same
object of comparison: birds. In the first, they briefly (in four words) compare their fearfulness to a dove's (140); at the end of the passage they remark (still only in four words) that the Greeks "chatter like a flock of
birds," and then expand the image somewhat by picturing the birds falling
silent if a great vulture (Ajax) were to appear. Except for calling the rumor
the "mother" of their disgrace (174), they use no poetic figures at all in the
lyrics until the epode, when they enhance their plea for action with two
brief metaphors.[17]

Now that the chorus have been introduced, the audience may naturally
expect that their invocation of Ajax will be answered by his appearance.
That confrontation promises to be a shocking experience for the chorus,
since, as far as the spectator knows, Ajax is still hallucinating and his men
have no idea of the enormity of the circumstances. Sophocles has, however, once again deliberately manipulated his audience into anticipating an
event so that he can increase the dramatic tension by introducing new characters or situations that postpone or, in this case, contrast flagrantly with
the anticipated event. Instead of a raging warrior, the chorus are confronted with a gentlewoman. We cannot be certain of the extent to which
Tecmessa was part of the traditional story, but she does not appear in the

16. If the chorus are supposed to have arrived *after* Odysseus reported to the Greeks, why
do they not mention Ajax's intent to murder the chiefs, which is part of the scene that Athena
shows to Odysseus (cf. 66–67)? If they have come *before* Odysseus' return, why do they name
him as the source of the accusations (148–150)?—another apparent Sophoclean "inconsistency," which is apparent only to a reader. The ambiguity is deliberate, so that the chorus may
condemn Odysseus as Ajax's foe, without having to consider the morality of the hero's
motives.

17. 195: ἄταν οὐρανίαν φλέγων, and 196–197: ἐχθρῶν δ' ὕβρις . . . ὁρμᾶτ'.

extant pre-Sophoclean literature, nor do we have any testimony that earlier poets used her as a character. The fact that she is not actually named until just before Ajax's appearance (331), although she is identified much earlier by lineage (210), may suggest that perhaps the audience was expected to recognize her by patronymic. But it may also be the case that she was unknown by name in the tradition, and therefore her identification simply as a foreign princess taken as a prize by Ajax would be entirely adequate until a situation arose that called for including her own name. It is thus possible that Sophocles may be introducing a hitherto undeveloped character; in that case, her appearance here would be intriguing as well as startling.

Besides the immediate effects he achieves by Tecmessa's entrance, Sophocles also uses her to implement a dramatic contrivance. The sequence of lyric and anapestic exchanges between Tecmessa and the chorus (201–261) creates an atmosphere of dreadful discovery, in which she and the chorus learn the truth from each other: the chorus, that Ajax did indeed slaughter the animals and the herdsmen (232); Tecmessa, that Ajax's victims came from the Greek herds.[18] The learning process is not, however, simply an equal exchange between two parties. The chorus receive a far greater blow than Tecmessa; at the same time, the audience receives further information that advances the plot. The scene seems to continue the technical pattern established in the parodos, a combination of informative anapests and speculative lyrics. The information that is, for the audience, necessary to the plot, such as Tecmessa's identification and the fact that Ajax has ceased to rage, is again delivered in anapests, while the lyrics contain the chorus' speculations, which contribute significantly to the mood without actually conveying factual information to the spectator. Again we can only guess at the contrasting effect of the meter, since we cannot be certain whether the anapests were meant to be sung or recited. It would be reasonable to propose that the first and last anapestic sections (201–220, 245–256), which convey facts, were meant to be recited, perhaps with an accompanying flute. Tecmessa might then have sung her passage, which is enclosed between the chorus' lyric stanzas, contains no news for the audience, and is filled with descriptive elaboration of horrors.[19]

18. The device was noted in the *hypothesis*, lines 22–25.

19. Opinion is divided about the nature of the anapests. Stanford (*ad* 208–209, and 251–252) insists that the anapests of lines 201–262 are melic, and therefore sung, because of the Doric forms at 202 (Ἐρεχθειδᾶν), 208 (ἀμερίας, but easily emended; cf. Pearson, *ad loc.*), 234 (ποίμναν, and the epic/lyric ἤλυθε), 257 (στεροπᾶς), and 262 (surely an error, since he rightly understands μεγάλας ὀδύνας as accusative). But he admits the Attic η in 218

The scene is designed to introduce Tecmessa and quickly establish her relation to Ajax: a woman devoted to her lord and loved in turn by him (211–212). It also presents a good relation between Tecmessa and the chorus: they are respectful toward each other and allies in devotion to Ajax. Her greeting to the chorus, "Helpers of the ship of Ajax, of the race descended from the earth-born sons of Erechtheus" (201–202), with its Homeric flavor, is probably as close as one who is addressing a group of soldiers could come to the respectful patronymic form that they use toward her (210). In addition, it identifies the soldiers more particularly as ones who came to Troy along with Ajax, who were brought in his own ship (a reasonable inference from the use of the singular "ship"), and who are in fact his own countrymen, of the lineage of the ancient hero Erechtheus.

This additional connection between the chorus and Ajax serves to enhance a new theme, the chorus' fear of the rest of the army (227). Hitherto they have only hinted at it, but now they state the danger openly: the Greeks will kill Ajax (228–229). The notion is further developed after Tecmessa describes the scene of slaughter, incontrovertible proof of Ajax's culpability, for now they talk of death by stoning (254). And because of their affinity, as it were, with Ajax, they, too, may be killed along with him (255). Indeed, so imminent is the danger and so great their fear of it that they actually suggest running away on foot or fleeing in the ship (245–250). It is difficult to imagine a statement that could more effectively portray the danger of the situation.

Tecmessa responds not to the chorus' expression of fear but to their allusion to Ajax's frenzy (256). Her concern for him (257–262) provides a suitable transition to the subsequent iambic trimeter scene, in which the poet shows Tecmessa as a loving woman, single-mindedly devoted to Ajax. At the same time he employs another dramatic device, the alternative point of view, to further advance Ajax's dramatic situation beyond what the audience has observed. Tecmessa narrates the action of the prologue, and some that occurred even before that, from her own point of view on the other side of the door. Then the poet has her continue to narrate further events that have occurred on her side of the door, to bring the audience up to date.

---

and 238. Jebb, in his critical note *ad* 208, insists on the "dialogue tone" of the anapests and therefore emends all Doric forms to Attic, so that the passages are entirely recitative. There are no significant metrical variations that would classify the anapests as melic (cf. Dale's criteria, *Lyric Metres*, 51 and 50n2). Accordingly, the proposed compromise, a mixed delivery, does not contradict what little evidence exists and appears to suit both structure and content.

Such extensive offstage action, so early in the play, by a character who has already made an appearance is unusual in Sophocles.[20]

The scene also further illuminates the character of the chorus. In the parodos they behaved as men of the moment, trying to deal with the immediate problem and its projected consequences. While they could, they hoped and acted, but because of Tecmessa's news they have reached such a point of apprehension that they can see only flight as a solution. Then, when Tecmessa tells them that Ajax is no longer frenzied, they seize upon the news as a source of hope. But they have misunderstood Tecmessa's meaning, for she must instruct them about the true extent of their troubles. Now the poet again puts them through the cycle of despair followed by renewed optimism. The report of Ajax's actions leaves them appalled (331–332), as does the hero's sudden offstage cry (336–338); but when they hear him utter only a few coherent words (342–343), their optimism is renewed (344–345). Their shifts of mood according to the changing circumstances reflect their characterization as plain men of action rather than of vision. They are the sort of men who, without being fools, make "honest mistakes," who assume that Odysseus is an enemy (190) or fail to recognize that Athena is the deity actually involved (cf. 172–181).[21] Surely the poet has thus fashioned them in order that the audience may accept as reasonable their later actions, as when they fail to understand Ajax's intentions in the "deception speech" (646–692) and their mood changes drastically from the despair of the first stasimon (596–645) to the rejoicing of the following song (693–718).

The characters of Tecmessa and of the chorus have by this point been fully developed, the description of past and present circumstances has

20. Orestes' sacrifice at Agamemnon's tomb, in *Electra*, is not comparable since it is not reported until much later in the play. The closest examples are Oedipus' sending for Teiresias (287–289) during the parodos of *Oedipus Tyrannus* and the burial of Polyneices sometime between lines 99 and 222 of *Antigone*. But the former is insignificant, and the latter was clearly foretold in the prologue and hence entirely expected, whereas the information in the *Ajax* is new and important.

21. Tyler (*AJP* 95 [1974], 30n18) sees the chorus' speculations on divine intervention as guesses that are "ironically near the mark" and thus part of an Aeschylean structural pattern (most noticeable in *Persae* and *Agamemnon*) in which "a gradual accumulation of guesses by the Chorus and other characters about the relation of supernatural forces to human events" is eventually confirmed by "an authoritative revelation," in this case one issued by Calchas. This does not, however, truly apply to *Ajax*, because a revelation by no less an authority than the goddess herself took place before anyone onstage started guessing, whereas Darius and Cassandra do not appear until two-thirds of the way through their plays. Hence the audience of *Ajax* would take notice of the chorus' guesses because they are wrong rather than because they are "near the mark."

been completed, and all is now ready for the long-postponed confrontation with Ajax, which takes place in a kommos involving all present (348ff.). The main dramatic revelation of the scene is Ajax's own view of what he has done. The hero's attitude toward his men, however, is no small part of the action. Tecmessa had sought the chorus' help, implying that Ajax might perhaps be expected to listen to them (328–330), and the chorus have suggested that Ajax might, on seeing them, recover some sense of proper and respectful behavior (345: τιν' αἰδῶ λάβοι). He does begin to speak with friendly words, stressing their loyalty and their bond with him as countrymen who came on his ship, who propelled it to Troy themselves (348–350, 356–358). He calls them his sole defense (359–360). But in the next breath he bids them kill him (361). The relation rapidly worsens, for after the beginning of the next strophe (364), he ignores their pleas and advice and except for a parenthetical φίλοι (405) he ceases all direct address to the chorus. He addresses himself, the absent Odysseus, Zeus, nether darkness, the Trojan landscape—anything but his devoted listeners. This lyric-iambic sequence, so entirely lacking in communication between hero and chorus, would seem to be a precursor of the similarly ineffectual pleas of the chorus in the kommos of *Philoctetes* (1081–1217).

In *Ajax* the poet demonstrates, or at least reinforces, the failure of communication by using blatantly contrasting forms of utterance. The passage is termed a kommos, but Ajax sings all of the lyrics and the chorus have only iambic trimeter lines. We may reasonably assume, although we have no absolute proof, that such iambic lines, always involving a change of speaker and not intermingled with lyric meters, were not sung at all but spoken in the same fashion that such lines would be in the episodes. If this was indeed the case, it is likely that the lines assigned to the chorus were delivered by the chorus-leader alone and not intoned by the full chorus. These assumptions are supported by the pattern of the alternation of speakers. Ajax appears and sings a stanza, whereupon the chorus, so lately optimistic, apparently turn away to tell Tecmessa that she was indeed right about the gravity of Ajax's condition (354–355).[22] At the end of Ajax's

22. This suggests they are appalled by the sight of Ajax, which further suggests that the *ekkyklema* was used here for a visual effect. Acceptance or rejection of the hypothesis that this device was used in the fifth century has become almost a matter of faith. Those who do not believe in it argue that here Ajax simply appeared in the doorway and that the chorus are imagined to be able to see into the tent behind him (cf. Stanford, *ad* 348ff.). It is true that the carnage has been vividly described recently, but it is not specifically mentioned at this crucial moment. Ajax refers to the slaughter entirely in metaphor (351–353), and the chorus speak only of "the fact" (355). Between lines 347 and 353 something terrible has dashed the chorus'

antistrophe, the chorus issue sharp imperatives (362–363). The stanzas of the second strophic pair are interrupted by three lines of trimeter and end with two more lines, in which the several changes of speakers give the impression of dialogue. In each of the final stanzas, Ajax's lengthy song is followed by an iambic trimeter couplet, the first being spoken by Tecmessa and the second by the chorus; the pattern is reminiscent of the couplets that so often follow lengthy speeches.

The chorus' reaction to Ajax is entirely consistent with their previous behavior. They do not presume to blame him or discuss the morality of his past actions, even when he proclaims his true, murderous intent (372–373, 387–389). They concentrate their efforts wholly on urging him to deal sensibly with the results of his actions; their attitude is the natural concomitant of the danger they have been reporting.[23] They obviously do not agree with his view of reality, that death is the only cure for his particular shame. Not honor but survival is the concern of these practical fighters. Thus they beg Ajax to forget the past, which cannot be altered or rectified, and face the facts of the present (377–378, 383–384). Likewise they urge him not to aggravate his present condition by ill-considered violence (362–363, 386). Even when Ajax fails to heed them, they do not condemn or berate, but find themselves at a loss. This frustration is expressed in simple but accurate language at the end of Ajax's clear threat of suicide: "Indeed I do not know how to prevent your speaking [such threats], nor how to let you continue, since you have fallen into such [terrible] troubles" (428–429).[24]

---

hopes that Ajax may be recovered. It cannot be Ajax's uninformative words, so it must be the sight of him; but since they do not say so (e.g., "What a horrible sight is now disclosed before me!"), it seems reasonable to suppose that the audience could also see what the chorus perceived (probably some tokens of dead animals and blood) and therefore the poet felt no need to make the chorus explain their reaction more fully.

23. Commentators tend to suppose that in saying μηδὲν μέγ᾽ εἴπῃς (386) the chorus are bidding Ajax not to offend the gods lest he incur divine wrath for ὕβρις. Ajax has just uttered threats against Odysseus: "would that I could see him" (i.e., "get my hands on him"). Why should this, in the chorus' mind, incur divine wrath? The same warning is given to the hero at Euripides, Heracles 1244, after he has apparently, though somewhat vaguely, threatened to set himself against the gods (1241–1243). The connection between the two passages is not that the heroes have spoken irreverent words, but that they have threatened violent actions that in their present situations they could not accomplish; to "talk big" here is "to bite off more than you can chew." The scholiast to Ajax is wrong (pace Kamerbeek, ad loc.; cf. also Stanford and Jebb) to compare these usages to Soph., El. 830: μηδὲν μέγ᾽ ἀΰσῃς; that phrase has a different verb and hence a very different meaning (see below, chapter 6, note 23).

24. The lexicographical distinction that Ellendt cites (Lexicon Sophocleum, s.v.; cf. LSJ) between ἀπείργω and ἀνείργω, a distinction between preventing someone from doing some-

The mood of foreboding and consternation continues to build in the subsequent dialogue, a scene chiefly between Ajax and Tecmessa in which the chorus are used to interrupt the pattern of the duologue and thus to maintain a fairly rapid pace. At the end of Ajax's speech setting forth his decision that one should live nobly or die nobly, the chorus appeal directly to him in a four-line speech, twice the usual length for such a position (481–484). With careful assurances that his honesty and sincerity would not be doubted, the chorus urge him to let his friends influence him to change his mind. Their appeal recalls Ajax's role in the embassy to Achilles, one of his few appearances in the *Iliad*. In his brief, blunt statement he asks the reluctant hero to put aside his pride for the sake of the friendship of these comrades, his dearest friends of all (*Il.* 9.630–631, 641–642). This deliberately ironical reversal of roles for Ajax fits into the pattern of adaptations of Homeric scenes that is clearly recognizable in this play.[25] Ajax does not reply, since Tecmessa leaps in at once; but after her speech a brief exchange between the chorus-leader and Ajax (525–528) about Tecmessa creates a more complex transition to the next section of stichomythia and speech. Finally, the chorus-leader's expression of fear and foreboding (583–584) leads directly to the frantic antilabe between Ajax and Tecmessa with which the scene closes as Ajax withdraws.

The hero leaves behind him the chorus, and probably also Tecmessa;[26] it is hardly unexpected that the chorus now sing the first stasimon of the play,

---

thing not yet begun and preventing the accomplishment of something that has already been started, seems oversubtle when applied to *Aj.* 428, especially since ἀνείργω does not occur in Sophocles. At *Aj.* 1280 the reference is to action already under way: the flames are already burning the ships, Hector is leaping over the trench on his way to the ships (1278: φλέγοντος; 1279: πηδῶντος). Then Teucer, referring to Ajax, asks τίς ταῦτ' ἀπείρξεν. Kamerbeek, *ad* 428, accepts the distinction and therefore assumes that the chorus are saying they do not know how to prevent Ajax's intended suicide. This interpretation makes the chorus' second clause rather a non sequitur and destroys the parallelism with Tecmessa's exclamation at the end of the strophe (410–411). The construction does not differ at all from *Ant.* 270; cf. Stanford, *ad Aj.* 428, who rightly cites Denniston, *Greek Particles* (Oxford, 1966), 509.

25. On the pattern in general, and particularly the relation between the Hector-Andromache and the Ajax-Tecmessa scenes, see Kirkwood, "Homer and Sophocles' *Ajax*," 56–59 and 63, although he does not think a reference to Ajax and Odysseus as colleagues would be suitable to this play.

26. Most critics follow either Wilamowitz (*Dramatische Technik*, 55) in withdrawing Tecmessa into the tent with Ajax, or Jebb (*ad* 595) in sending her off to the "women's quarters" (against which idea Wilamowitz argues persuasively, ibid., 56). But if she exits apart from Ajax, there is no motivation for her re-entry; if she goes off with him, the audience would probably be confused, presuming Ajax was about to kill himself and wondering whether he was going to do it right before her eyes (and the child's). The key to the answer is generally

nor that it is filled with sorrow and foreboding. What is not anticipated by the audience, however, is that fifty lines after the end of the ode it will be matched by another, diametrically opposite in mood and tone but reverberating with echoes of this first one. We are not supposed to leap ahead of the audience in this fashion; but if we bear in mind the completed effect that the poet has devised, it may give us a better understanding of an ode of which the poetic qualities are usually appreciated but the dramatic force sadly neglected.

In this chorus' by now characteristic fashion, their utterances proceed in a simple, step-by-step progression. Their opening words, "O famous Salamis" (596), again recall their connection with Ajax and introduce the expression of the chorus' sorrow that occupies the first strophe (596–608). It is not unknown for a chorus to wish themselves away from present horrors. Here, however, they do not merely wish for escape from their situation but for a return to their home. The strophe is filled with the eternal, universal homesickness of the war-weary soldier in a distant land who must wait and wait—to return home at the end of the war, perhaps, but just as likely to die alone in a strange land. For a Greek it was not a fear lightly to be borne, that one might suffer or die away from one's city and family. If Electra in Mycenae, believing Orestes killed in Olympia, can say that he died a stranger (865: ξένος) in a foreign country (1136: γῆς ἄλλης), how much more lamentable is the plight of the Salaminian soldiers across the sea on another continent. And to the soldier's ever-present unhappiness the gods have now added a new misery—their leader has been stricken with madness (611: θείᾳ μανίᾳ). The chorus' explicit statements in the antistrophe (609–634) show they believe Ajax is ill with madness, in that he is no longer the same man with whom they set forth from Salamis, the mighty warrior of Ares (612–613: θουρίῳ κρατοῦντ' ἐν Ἄρει). This is quite a different syndrome from the madness imposed by Athena, which took the form of hallucinations. The poet has made it clear that the latter

---

agreed to lie in lines 579–580, where Ajax orders Tecmessa to "close up the house, and do not weep and wail outdoors [μηδ' ἐπισκήνους γόους δάκρυε], for truly women are enamored of mourning [φιλοίκτιστον]!" The emphasis is on Tecmessa's imagined wailings; he does not command her to come inside. There seems little point to his prohibitions if she is to go inside with him; but if she remains outside, they serve the purpose of explaining her silence, since we might otherwise expect her to make moan as much as the chorus (evidently only the protagonist sang lyrics, and an anapestic kommos like the first one might be too formal—and perhaps static—here). The scene of silent woman and child with singing chorus would be recalled later by a similar song with silent woman and child at 1185ff. Cf. also Gellie, *Sophocles*, 281n9.

madness was temporary, imposed when Ajax was on the point of killing the Greek chiefs (48, 51ff.) and removed after he went indoors at the end of the prologue (245, 271, 305ff.). The chorus cannot be referring to that since they have been carefully informed that that stage is past. They are talking about his present state of mind, in which he is now "herding his thoughts in solitary pastures" (614: νῦν δ' αὖ φρενὸς οἰοβώτας). Indeed, they go on to point out the inconsistency between this state and his past deeds of hand, acts of greatest heroic valor; the very order of the words emphasizes the contrast (617: τὰ πρὶν δ' ἔργα χεροῖν). The audience must surely be expected to assume that they are commenting upon what they have just heard, Ajax's brooding on his "honor" and the fearsome eagerness (583: προθυμίαν) with which he has withdrawn from them.[27]

In the next strophe the chorus consider what will happen when Ajax's condition becomes known to the others who care for him. They describe his mother's reaction in unmistakable terms of a funeral: she will not merely cry out in sorrow, but will sing a dirge, beat her breast, and tear her hair. This unhappy picture leads them in the antistrophe to the conclusion that the insane man is indeed better off dead. As far as they, and his family, are concerned, he might as well be dead because he is already as good as dead. He is no longer behaving according to the natural inclinations that are a part of his noble heritage, his "breeding," but has moved very much outside the pale. He is no longer Ajax. Such is the terrible news his father will hear, a thing never before known in that glorious family.

It is often noted that the chorus do not actually state that they believe or suspect that Ajax will kill himself. Some say it is because these simple men are too dull to comprehend the hero's intent, others because it would be too unlucky or unspeakable for them to utter such a foreboding aloud.[28] But the question is not relevant to the dramatic situation. If at this point the chorus were to talk explicitly about Ajax's intended suicide, they would of necessity mention his physical death and the terrible conse-

27. See Winnington-Ingram (*Sophocles*, 34–36) on the chorus' perception of Ajax's madness. He seems to find that in 617–620 they are referring to the Judgment of Arms, in which the Atreidae rejected Ajax's former deeds; but the lines are as likely to be heard as a reference to the new and dangerous anger of the Atreidae at the attempted murder.

28. For these views see Kamerbeek, 127, and Stanford, *ad* 596ff. Kamerbeek feels that if the chorus realized Ajax was going to commit suicide, they would have to either try to dissuade him or do nothing, but "both these possibilities would be unsatisfactory." Yet the poet has already had them try vigorously to dissuade Ajax, and they have failed. They must "remain inactive as they do" because the hero (and, of course, the poet) has firmly shut them out; since they could hardly be expected to storm the doors, there is nothing left for them but "outdoor wailings."

quences it would have for them and others. Besides being foolishly ill-omened, since he is not yet actually dead, such a song here might relax the dramatic tension because it would be just what one would expect. Furthermore, many of its expressions would probably have to be repeated after Ajax killed himself, thus vitiating the effect of his death. The poet has avoided that repetition by making the chorus more concerned here with Ajax's immediate behavior than with the deeds that are obviously consequent upon that behavior, with his "death" from spiritual illness that has, for them, already occurred rather than with his physical death yet to come. Thus the poet can use the chorus reasonably to create a funereal mood before Ajax's death, a mood, however, that differs considerably from the actual mourning that will take place. This prelusive foreboding serves to extend greatly the effect of the subsequent ironical joy-before-disaster sequence.

Sophocles uses his device of the joy-before-disaster ode elsewhere, most notably in *Oedipus Tyrannus* (1086–1109) and *Trachiniae* (633–662), but only here is it so intensified by a preceding descent into despair. Like a ghost at a funeral, Ajax suddenly reappears and leads his men, always ready for hope, to believe that he has changed his behavior and intentions (646–692).[29] As the chorus sing an exuberant ode of rejoicing (693–718), the omniscient audience cannot help comparing it to the last song, and to the events that must inevitably occur.[30] There is no complexity in the structure. In the strophe they invoke the well-recognized gods of celebratory dancing, Pan and Delian Apollo, in joyful contrast to their earlier homesickness; in the antistrophe they give the reason. To these once war-weary soldiers, the war-god, the god by whom Ajax was once so favored, has come as savior. For the men who yearned to leave the dreary Trojan shore,

---

29. For summaries and analyses of the conflicting interpretations of this speech, see Stanford's commentary (281–288: appendix D), Sicherl (*YCS* 25 [1977], 70–78), and Moore (*YCS* 25 [1977], 47–54). Commentators generally ignore the fact that Ajax's observations on the unreliability of friendship are false with regard to the chorus, who are his φίλοι. The poet seems to highlight this paradox by using the word "comrade" both when Ajax remarks on "the untrustworthy harbor of comradeship" (683: ἄπιστος ἑταιρείας λιμήν) and four lines later when he turns to the chorus and calls them "comrades" (687: ἑταῖροι). Knox, however, sees political implications in the word (*HSCP* 65 [1961], 36n120), while Stanford (*ad* 687) seems to think it merely coincidental repetition.

30. Unless one agrees with Waldock's contention (*Sophocles*, 78) that Ajax inadvertently "hoodwinks" the audience as well as Tecmessa and the chorus, it is difficult and probably wrong to believe that the Athenian audience was so malleable that, even knowing that Ajax would eventually kill himself, it was still drawn into sharing the chorus' rejoicing—but so Kranz maintains about all such odes in Sophocles (*Stasimon*, 213–214).

Zeus has made it habitable again. Their statement that mighty Time extinguishes all things (714), with its echoes of Ajax's theme of the changes wrought by time (646–648), leads into the terrible irony of the song's ending: if Ajax could change so, nothing is impossible![31] But Ajax has not changed, and Pan will not come to them.

The ode is followed by a spate of physical activity that is largely contrary to the audience's expectations and that depends for its effect upon the movements and utterances of the chorus. First the Messenger arrives—not to announce Ajax's death, as one anticipates, but to introduce the entirely new theme of the danger that threatens Teucer. The chorus do not summon Tecmessa, for although she is Ajax's wife, she is not their mistress; in fact, the Messenger delivers a part of his message directly to the chorus as if reporting to his own fellow soldiers (719: ἄνδρες φίλοι) and does not ask for Ajax until he has given them fourteen lines of information. So the chorus interrogate him themselves, and their wild hopes are changed to fear.

Much has been written about this speech and the prophecy of Calchas, chiefly in order to identify a more significant function for Athena's wrath than the merely technical one of clearing the scene.[32] The fact remains, however, that this whole sequence of actions appears designed to create as much suspense as possible. The audience knows that Ajax will kill himself, but not exactly how or when, and Sophocles is obviously exploiting this knowledge. He has already twice cheated the audience's expectations, first with Ajax's reappearance and then with the Messenger who turns out to be from an entirely different quarter. Sophocles is building up to the boldest stroke of all, the wholly unexpected departure of the chorus, the change of scene, and the final appearance of the hero.

Calchas' warning seems to be the best possible instrument to accomplish this stroke. The characters onstage must leave in a hurry; mere anxiety or vague rumor would not move them quickly enough. The word of a

31. The irony in the second part of the antistrophe is heightened by the numerous verbal echoes of Ajax's speech: χρόνος (714, 646), σέβων (713, 667), ἀέλπτων (716, 648), and even Ἀτρείδαις (718, 667).

32. Wilamowitz insists this is its only function (*Dramatiche Technik*, 53n1). See, for examples of different interpretations, Wigodsky (*Hermes* 90 [1962], 149–155): Ajax will find "salvation" in death; Tyler (*AJP* 95 [1974], 25–42): Athena is a part of a separate conflict within a double plot; Gellie (*Sophocles*, 18–19): Athena's wrath is a "psychological" explanation of Ajax's "craving" for suicide; Errandonea (*Sófocles* [1970], 44–46): the Messenger, sent by Odysseus, is lying. In contrast, see Winnington-Ingram's lucid observations on the theme of time in the speech (*Sophocles*, 39–43).

respectable, Teiresias-like seer would be believed, but it must be backed up with some sort of "proof" to convince them to leave immediately and without delaying argument. Omens and bird-signs would hardly be suitable here, but the seer's perception and "revelation" that Ajax's patron goddess has finally turned against him for his long-standing arrogance accords entirely with the chorus' earlier assumption that Ajax was perfectly capable of offending a deity through negligence, and thus makes it perfectly reasonable for them to accept the Messenger's statements unquestioningly.

As for the audience, Athena's antipathy toward Ajax has already been introduced in the prologue, so the concept is also quite acceptable here. At the same time, however, the poet does not repeat the contents of the prologue by attributing her anger to the attempted murder, which would not advance the plot in any way, but maintains the pace with new information and also explains why the goddess did not or could not avert her protégé's violent anger in the first place, as she prevented Achilles from drawing his sword on Agamemnon in the *Iliad* (1.188–220).

The one-day limit on the danger allows the chorus and Tecmessa just enough hope so that their reaction is a sense of urgency rather than static despair. There is no pause for reflection or lamentation. The men of action at once call Tecmessa forth, and the gist of the message is repeated to her. We may well ask why, if Sophocles wanted to suggest that Athena's wrath symbolizes something important, he does not take this opportunity at least to mention it once again. The obvious answer is that it has served its immediate dramatic purpose as a motive for departure, and its repetition would be irrelevant; the function of the exchange between Tecmessa and the Messenger is to emphasize the sense of urgent danger, and so to have all the characters leave at once (rather than, say, sending servants to look for Ajax). The simultaneous exit of the chorus, Tecmessa, Eurysaces, the Messenger, and the other servants, together with Tecmessa's extensive preliminary talk of departing, clears the acting area and effectively changes the scene.[33]

After Ajax's death the re-entry of the divided chorus from opposite sides, and without Tecmessa, creates an impression of frantic activity that is sustained by the rhythmic variety of the utterances surrounding the discovery of Ajax's body. The introductory astrophic dialogue between the separated semichoruses consists entirely of exclamations and iambic trimeters (866–878); the lyric part that follows is brief, and seems to end in an

33. An explanation of the technical production of these scenes is proposed in *CJ* 75 (1979), 10–14.

iambic trimeter (879–890).[34] With Tecmessa's cries the chorus return to using an amalgamation of brief exclamations and iambic trimeters, with two separately inserted bits of chiefly exclamatory lyric (900–903, 910–914). Then, after Tecmessa delivers a short iambic trimeter speech (915–924), also heavily exclamatory, the whole choppy, quasi-lyrical sequence is repeated as an antistrophe (925–960). The combination of frequent movement—the divided entrance of the chorus, the separate entrance of Tecmessa, the motions of discovering the body—with a kommos that has far more dialogue than lyric results in a scene of commotion that one does not ordinarily associate with the death of an awe-inspiring figure.

Nor does the content of the kommos suggest the lull, or relaxing of tension, that one may expect to follow a climactic event. There is no pause for any mourning. The chorus have in a way already expressed their reactions, and the reactions of his family, to Ajax's death before it occurred (596–645); but now that it has finally come to pass, the dominant theme of their exclamations is not sorrow for what is past but fear of what is to come. In their re-entrance song (879–896) the chorus cry out in desperation for some news of Ajax's whereabouts. And when, with terrible irony, their wish is answered by Tecmessa's discovery of the body, their first thought is that they are now doomed: "Oh, [gone is] my homecoming! Oh, you have killed me, my lord!" (900–901). Briefly they regret the solitary circumstances of his death and berate themselves for not realizing his intent (909–912), but the poet quickly shifts to the action of Tecmessa's shrouding the corpse (913–919). As soon as she has covered Ajax's body with her cloak, Tecmessa asks agitated questions about the immediate future, looking forward to Teucer's arrival. Although expressions of grief begin the antistrophe (925–936), their tone is that of plain and practical men trying to make sense out of the facts ("now I see, too late, what was really happening"), as they tried in the parodos to figure out what was actually going on and why. Then their compassionate exchange with Tecmessa (891ff.) moves almost at once into the fear of what will happen to her, of how Ajax's enemies, Odysseus and the Atreidae, will behave.

All this anxiety and dread is surely intended to create tension for the audience, since the danger is part of the unknown plot rather than the known myth. The prologue has shown that Odysseus is not as bad as everyone thinks, but nothing good has yet been said about the Atreidae. It is possible that Tecmessa's part in the story is largely original with Sophocles,

---

34. If the alpha privative in ἀμενηνόν could be scanned as long, the line (890) would be a trimeter. The lacuna in the responding line of the antistrophe (935) prevents it from helping.

and therefore dramatically possible that the Atreidae could drag her off into slavery (944ff.) or at least attempt it. As for the rest of the Greek army, their violence is reaching the point of explosion: Teucer was almost killed, and there is no good reason for the audience to think that the chorus could not also at least come close to suffering the death by stoning that they have feared.

This spreading flame of fear is fueled by the arrival of Teucer, whom the audience knows to be newly escaped from the angry mob from which the chorus were hurrying away at the beginning of the play. Tecmessa fades into the background, or remains beside the covered corpse of Ajax, and the chorus are retained in the part of second actor, receiving Teucer as they did the Messenger. Sophocles continues to mix rapid speech patterns—in this case, antilabe between Teucer and the chorus (981–985)—with action and alarm, as Teucer hurriedly sends someone, presumably Tecmessa, to fetch Eurysaces lest an enemy seize the boy (985–989). The chorus in response (990–991) discharge the duty that Ajax laid on them, to commend his son to Teucer's care, and this remark leads Teucer into the first lengthy mourning of Ajax since the hero's death. At the end of such a speech the audience might well expect an ode of mourning from the chorus, perhaps a kommos. But Teucer's reflections are abruptly cut off by the chorus' sighting of another character heading toward the acting area. The poet gives an air of alarm to the chorus' announcement of the arrival of Menelaus by having them enjoin Teucer, in imperatives, to act at once for his brother's burial (1040–1041), and by completing the necessary identification in dialogue rather than a single utterance by the chorus (1042–1046: "I see an enemy!" "Who?" "Menelaus!" "I see him!"). All this tension is, of course, also enhanced for the audience by the absence of any anticipation of Menelaus' arrival; he is a new and relatively unknown factor.

Although the next scene is chiefly between the two actors, the chorus are neither inactive nor wholly subordinate during it. When Menelaus finishes speaking, the chorus-leader firmly reprimands him,[35] not for his arrogance or bad temper, but specifically for proposing to "outrage the dead" (1092–1093). This reprimand creates a disruptive speech pattern:

35. Stanford, in his commentary, remarks on the chorus-leader's brusqueness to Teucer at line 1040 that "he would hardly have spoken like this to Ajax." But here he dares to address Menelaus in the familiar form with a prohibition (Μενέλαε, μὴ . . . γένῃ) and he certainly used "brusque" imperatives and prohibitions to Ajax's face (362–363, 371, 386, 483–484). It is reasonable to suppose that this style of address is meant to be heard as part of the chorus' general character rather than as a distinction between their behavior toward Ajax and their behavior toward Teucer.

the chorus address Menelaus, but Teucer breaks in to address them about Menelaus before turning to speak to him directly (1094ff.). Further, when Teucer has finished, the chorus-leader again disrupts the pattern by repri-manding *him* (1118–1119), and then Menelaus makes a remark about Teucer which is probably addressed to the chorus, since it is in the third person. The choral rebuke, that Teucer should not speak "stinging" (1119: δάκνει) taunts in such perilous circumstances, renews the awareness of present danger which is then continued in the heated exchange between Teucer and Menelaus; indeed, Menelaus exits with a blunt threat to return with force (1160). There can be no doubt about the dramatic immediacy of the threat, since the chorus confirm it in a brief anapestic system (1163–1167). "There will be a struggle of great strife," they predict, and then they once again issue urgent imperatives to Teucer to move, act, hurry. The occurrence of anapests here, usually considered an "archaic" element, may actually indicate the voice of the full chorus rather than just the leader's; or at least the abrupt change of meter may serve to reinforce the mood of haste and anxiety.

With Teucer's departure (1184) the play seems to reach the limit of the tension that has been steadily increasing. A confrontation, some unspeci-fied form of physical attack, is expected at any moment, while Teucer has left the chorus to defend the body (1183: ἀρήγετ') and has rushed off to prepare a grave. Sophocles has arranged what must have been a striking tableau of Tecmessa and her son, silent and vulnerable, huddled in this deserted place beside the shrouded corpse of their protector.[36] In the pres-ence of this tableau, the chorus sing a poignant ode of sorrow (1185–1222) that vibrantly echoes their earlier song before the death of Ajax (596ff.). Fully three-quarters of this final stasimon is devoted to the miseries of men in war, particularly these soldiers who are dragging out their unhappy years in a foreign land. By itself, the song is a powerful condemnation of the Trojan war as a "wretched disgrace for the Greeks" (1191), and of war in general as destructive of humanity (1198). Within the plot, the remem-brance of the pleasures of home, the sorrows of their present condition, and their longing to sail back to "sacred Athens" all reinforce both their dependence upon Ajax and their political relation, indeed their common Athenian origin. In this way Sophocles displays the enormity of Ajax's abandonment of these worthy, suffering soldiers of Athens. The general

---

36. On the tableau as a symbolic enactment of Ajax's transformation into a sacred hero, see Burian (*GRBS* 13 [1972], 155), Segal (*Tragedy*, 143), and, *contra*, Winnington-Ingram (*Sophocles*, 58n2).

reflections and the tone of despair might be thought to slacken the tension momentarily. Yet the chorus are still not mourning Ajax, nor reflecting upon the past; rather, they are speaking of their very present troubles, thus maintaining the mood and perhaps even increasing the suspense of the moment.

Teucer returns, now closely followed by Agamemnon himself, another unexpected character, and the two engage in the final confrontation. At the end of Agamemnon's tirade, the chorus-leader admonishes both of them to think sensibly, to be rational (1264–1265). Since Teucer has not yet replied to Agamemnon, the remark anticipates for the audience the coming impasse. This is acceptable, since both chorus and audience have already heard Teucer's defiant attitude and have no reason to think that anything in Agamemnon's speech would change him. The dramatic reason for anticipating the impasse is clear: Sophocles is going to use the actual moment of the impasse to bring on a *deus ex machina* in the person of Odysseus, and he will use the chorus there to form the verbal eddy that breaks up the duologue. The chorus-leader introduces Odysseus by addressing him with the suggestion of mediation (1316–1317), and Odysseus responds directly to him before being drawn into a dialogue with Agamemnon. When he has accomplished his part as peacemaker, the chorus are once again involved in the scene, this time in a unifying triangular dialogue, as the leader bluntly expresses full approval of the hero's behavior: "Odysseus, anyone who says you are not innately wise is a stupid man" (1374–1375). He in turn seems to half-reply to them as he turns to speak with Teucer: "And now I shall tell Teucer. . . ." The choral statement is a remarkable one, coming from men who had assumed Odysseus was an enemy; it may be taken as an inconsistency in their character, but it is much more likely that the poet deliberately brings them forward to show that they can recognize true wisdom when they see it. Indeed, he has them close the play with a remark that echoes the joy-before-disaster ode but now is both apt and ironic: "Men may know many things, but not the future until they have seen it" (1418–1420).

Viewing the chorus by themselves, we can see that Sophocles has made them a group of direct, uncomplicated soldiers, men of deeds more than of words. Still, they have certain principles of duty, both military and moral, according to which they act themselves and admonish others. Thus they rebuke Menelaus for his hubristic behavior and Teucer for his arrogance in adversity; in so doing, they display independence, which is not, however,

of the mutinous sort that they so strongly condemn in the parodos. In this
they present a considerable contrast to the indiscriminately and unscrupu-
lously devoted soldiers of Neoptolemus, who have no notion of the principles of heroic behavior. The men of *Ajax* are loyal to their chief, but they
are not fanatically devoted to a cause; their realistic view of the miseries of
foreign war is the view of sensible people such as Herodotus. At the same
time, they are no cowards. Their desperate suggestion that the only hope
lies in escape (245ff.) is made when Ajax is still alive and Tecmessa is
present; since it is uttered in the third person, it has a general tone that
could include both Ajax and Tecmessa. But when Ajax is dead and the
chorus must defend him alone, although they may wish they were far away,
there is not the slightest hint that they will not stand by his wife and child
and corpse to the end.

The general lines of the chorus' character are underscored by the consistent simplicity and directness of their language. Their lyrics tend to be
brief, with a simple progressive structure and a noticeably plain style. It
would be fairly difficult, and wholly inaccurate, to label this chorus a
"lyric instrument." Sophocles has made them an instrument of a different
sort, the instrument by which he creates the play's dramatic unity. Their
physical presence, of course, provides technical unity. But the examination
of the chorus' successive utterances shows that they introduce and then
amplify the theme of concern over present circumstances and hope or fear
about the immediate future. In so doing, they are chiefly responsible for
developing the atmosphere of danger that sustains the tension of the drama.
Both Tecmessa and Teucer are also used for this purpose, but the haste and
anxiety of the chorus begin with the parodos, and, rising without pause,
sweep over the suicide and on to the final confrontation and resolution.[37]
Given the poet's unrelenting insistence on the growing danger, and the almost continuous physical activity—there are twenty-six entrances and
exits in *Ajax*, more than in any other Sophoclean or Aeschylean play[38]—it
seems unreasonable to suppose that the original spectator, who had no idea

37. Errandonea (*Sófocles* [1958], 327–340; cf. *Sófocles* [1970], 41–42) has also observed
the unifying function of the chorus' fear.

38. Counting only the simple fact of entrance or exit without regard to the number of
persons taking part in the action, there are 24 in *Antigone*, unless Creon is assumed to exit at
780 and re-enter before or at 883, in which case there are 26. The calculation does not include
the entrance of the characters who open the play, the parodos of the chorus, or the final exit of
all persons at the end of the play. For the rest of Sophocles the figures are considerably
smaller: *Oed. Tyr.*, 21; *Oed. Col.*, 20; *El.*, 18; *Tr.*, 16; *Phil.*, 15.

of exactly what was going to happen in the "second half" of the play, could possibly have been so blasé as to lose interest in the drama after the suicide of the hero.

If Sophocles was thus able to maintain and even increase the suspense of the play after the death of the most interesting character, we must ask just how interesting he really is, and why. Is he actually a fascinating embodiment of the standards of the "Old Homeric" individual? Certainly a major element of the "heroic code" as we know it from Homer is personal achievement, *aristeia*, and the concomitant personal glory. But the *Iliad* and the *Odyssey* both clearly set forth other important aspects of heroic behavior that involve certain duties. First of all, one does not attempt to murder one's sworn allies. Achilles may have been about to draw his sword on Agamemnon (*Il.* 1.188–194), but that was an open challenge to one man, who was presumably also armed and able to defend himself, before the entire assembly of the army. In the case of Ajax's attack, however, Sophocles insists that it was a treacherous stroke in the middle of the night, when the lamps had been extinguished, the Atreidae were in their tents, and the whole army was asleep (21, 47, 141, 217, 285–286, 291). Further, he makes the enormity of the slaughter and the details of the torture of captives into so grotesque a scene that no one who knew the *Iliad* could possibly believe that any other of the heroes—least of all Achilles— would behave in such a degradingly underhanded and unheroic manner.[39]

The Homeric hero honors and defends his family. In Tecmessa Sophocles has created the ideal wife, by both Homeric and fifth-century standards. She is so wholly loyal, devoted, and obedient that the audience could not perceive her as other than fully meriting her lord's protection, especially since she is presented as the mother of his acknowledged son and heir, Eurysaces (569ff.). Yet Sophocles shows Ajax not merely treating her with cold disdain, but abandoning her entirely to slavery. Ajax expresses a few short words of pity for her before he leaves, but directly after the suicide

39. Knox (*HSCP* 65 [1961], 22–23) sees Achilles and Ajax as "kindred spirits," but he does not look beyond the limited field of their common fighting ability, pride, and violence. Not even in his wildest frenzy of slaughter, when he actually kills an unarmed suppliant (*Il.* 21.55ff.), does Achilles ever stoop to Ajax's treachery and sadism. And, of course, he is attacking the enemy, not his fellow Greeks. We may also note that Sophocles twice informs us that Ajax killed herdsmen as well as animals (25–27, 230–232). For Ajax's arrogance toward the gods—which is entirely contrary to Achilles' behavior (*Il.* 1.216–218)—and his "self-deception," see Rosivach (*CJ* 72 [1976–1977], 49–53) and Winnington-Ingram (*Sophocles*, 18).

Sophocles gives further examples of Tecmessa's worthy behavior as a woman (915–919, 961–973) and at the same time repeats the idea that she will probably be cruelly mistreated by Ajax's enemies (945–949). This careful delineation of Tecmessa's character and circumstances is no mere appeal to softness and sentimentality. Whatever the audience, or Homer, may have understood Ajax's legal responsibilities to be toward a captive wife, Sophocles makes Tecmessa plead in the name of Zeus of the Hearth (492) and of their marriage bed (493); and her statement that the sneers of the Greeks if he abandons her will be a shame to him and his family (505) gives the dramatic impression of Ajax's moral responsibility for her, an impression that nothing subsequent contradicts.[40] In a similar manner, Sophocles insists upon the danger to Ajax's son (499). The hero makes some reference to providing for Eurysaces' safety—the audience could hardly be expected to believe that any man would not do something about his only son—by commending him to Teucer to bring to his parents. But then the poet has Teucer almost killed by the Greeks, and when Teucer does arrive after Ajax's death, almost his first words are to affirm the danger that hangs over Eurysaces (985–989).

The duty that a "gentleman" owes to his parents is patent in the epics: we have the implication in Phoenix's appeal to Achilles that it is the function of a son to protect his parents (*Il.* 9.494–495), a duty that Achilles fully acknowledges (9.616). We have the conspicuous example in the *Odyssey* of the good and dutiful son, Telemachus. In the matter of this duty also, Sophocles emphasizes Ajax's failure. First Tecmessa, then the chorus vividly describe the sorrow of Ajax's parents. Again Ajax does make some small acknowledgment of their claim on him, in that he commends Eurysaces to Telamon and Eriboea, and in his final speech he again makes mention of his "aged father" and the cries of his "unhappy mother" (849–851). But these references only serve to accentuate Ajax's rejection of duty; he is aware of the misery he will cause, but he quickly dismisses all thought of it. Finally, Sophocles brings in Teucer after the suicide to tell how Ajax has by his last act ensured that Teucer will be unjustly banished by Telamon, and how he has left him surrounded by enemies at Troy: "All these things I have obtained by your death" (1023). The dramatic effect of these numerous references to familial obligations, not balanced by any-

---

40. The use of συναλλάσσω in the passive may deliberately suggest the duty of a party to an oath or treaty of alliance. After all, the Greeks went to Troy to recover Menelaus' wife for him; cf. Whitman (*Homer*, 186–187) on Achilles' love for Briseis.

thing more than the most superficial concern on Ajax's part and all repeated at least once after his death, is to show that Ajax's suicide utterly
fails to accord with the traditional Homeric standards of noble behavior.[41]

These are, however, essentially personal matters, and we must consider
that it is remotely possible that the fifth century might have condoned or
explained them away as many do today. But a military leader in any age has
a duty to stand by his men, and the Homeric warrior had a special responsibility toward his companions, his ἑταῖροι, because, as Alcinous says to
Odysseus, a loyal comrade is worth no less than a brother (*Od.* 8.585–586).
So Ajax addresses the chorus as he lays his final commands on them (687:
ἑταῖροι), appearing almost formally to invoke the relationship as reason
for expecting them to fulfill his wishes. The poet may well have intended
the audience to remember the passage in the *Iliad* that tells how "with the
son of Telamon many people and brave ones followed as companions, and
took over the great shield from him whenever the sweat and the weariness
came over his body" (*Il.* 13.709–711).[42] Such are the men of the chorus,
the hero's compatriots, whom Ajax deserts in a foreign land. By displaying
before the death of Ajax (596ff.) the danger to which the hero is exposing
his men, and by elaborating the danger after his death (900–903, 1185),
Sophocles seems to be trying to give the audience the clear impression that
in committing suicide Ajax is abandoning his comrades and therewith a
most important part of the heroic pattern of behavior.

The chorus thus function as a passive instrument, as men who unde-
servedly suffer the consequences of Ajax's actions. But they also have an
active role in reinforcing the dramatic impressions that Ajax's actions have
created. First, Sophocles gives the chorus suitable credentials as arbiters of
the heroic standard of behavior, by having them set forth in the parodos
their own distinctly Homeric view of the proper order of society and, toward the end of the play, their approval of Menelaus' rather harsh precepts
of governance (1091–1092). Then the poet insists several times upon the
chorus' Salaminian/Athenian origins and upon their status as Ajax's shipmates, who sailed with him from Salamis. From this we understand that

41. The text will not support Gellie's excessively sentimental perception of Tecmessa's—
and Sophocles'—description of Ajax's family as "a woman's family, compounded of affection
and gratitude, mutual support and dependence—a group of give and take," nor his claim that
Tecmessa's plea is therefore rejected, because it is "just the wrong sort of family to throw at
Ajax" (*Sophocles*, 11).

42. Lattimore's translation (Chicago, 1951): πολλοί τε καὶ ἐσθλοὶ λαοὶ ἕπονθ' ἑταῖροι.
The only other occurrences of ἑταῖροι in Sophocles are at *Oed. Col.* 1400 and 1403, where
Polyneices is speaking of his allies in the coming expedition against Thebes.

they have been with him since the very beginning of the war. If there is anyone, therefore, who can speak with authority about Ajax's previous condition, who can testify to his behavior before the judgment of arms and the attack on the chiefs, it is surely this chorus. And Sophocles makes them say again and again that Ajax must be sick with some form of madness because he is no longer himself, his present manner is entirely inconsistent with his previous behavior. It is made apparent that they are not referring to his murderous rage and hallucinations but to his subsequent brooding about his ills (431: κακοῖς) and the intimations of suicide (278–280, 337–338, and especially 609–615, 625, 635–645).

Sophocles presents no reason why the audience should not believe them. On the contrary, Tecmessa also asserts twice that Ajax is quite unlike his former self; once, when she describes his groans as the sort that he used to say were uttered only by low-spirited cowards (317–320), and again when she says that he is talking as he never would have before (410–411). Both of these assertions are made after Ajax has come to realize what he has done, when he is no longer subject to Athena's illusions. When Ajax, in the "deception speech," talks of compromise, the chorus rejoice to think that he is his old untroubled self again (711: λαθίπονος πάλιν). And indeed, in that moment he is most like the old Ajax of the *Iliad*, who brusquely told Achilles to stop fussing about his pride and pay attention to the words of his friends (*Il.* 9.628–642). These warriors, men who know and respect recognized Homeric standards of behavior, express the otherwise uncontradicted opinion that Ajax is a changed man, that he is not acting in his former, heroic manner. There is not the slightest suggestion that his suicide is a splendid or even faintly admirable heroic act.[43]

The notion that Sophocles intended his audience to admire any aspect of Ajax's actions during the play must surely rest upon the assumption that the fifth century was subject to the same Miniver Cheevy syndrome that afflicts many critics today. It may perhaps be understandable that a society that has gone from an era of social constriction and romanticism into an age of regulation and impersonal technology would heave a nostalgic sigh for the rugged individualism of bygone—and largely imaginary—heroes.

---

43. Tecmessa's last speech (961–973) is not uttered in admiration of Ajax's act, as some would have it, but against the notion that Ajax's enemies have the right to triumph over him. Ajax did not die unwillingly—there was no struggle in which he was the loser and they the victors—therefore they cannot consider his death a victory for themselves and gloat over it. This is obviously true, as Odysseus points out to Agamemnon at 1349: "do not rejoice in dishonorable gains" (cf. Stanford, *ad loc.*).

But it is most unlikely that fifth-century Athens, the enemy of tyrants, the defeater of Persia, a society so committed to the struggle for its democracy's survival that it felt the need for the institution of ostracism, would have had the same psychological reaction to the concept of the romantic renegade. Could Sophocles really have been trying to elicit from such an audience a grudging admiration for a general who, for personal reasons, deserts his men in a foreign country and calls down the Furies upon the entire army (844)?

The poet does not even describe Ajax's heroic deeds until long after he is dead, when they are needed to provide proof that he was once a good man and as such is entitled to decent burial. This postponement must be deliberate, since Sophocles does not take the obvious opportunity to have Teucer use Ajax's heroism as an argument against Menelaus, but waits until nearly the final confrontation with Agamemnon. Until then, one sees only the bad side of Ajax. The result is the play's obvious moral lesson: a man should be judged by the sum of his life and not by the moment, "for a day can both lay low all mortal things and raise them up again" (131–132). If once he was great and did great things, he must be accorded some respect for them after his death, even though in the meantime he has behaved shamefully. Not to recognize this truth, sanctioned by divine law, is to invite disaster as recompense for one's arrogant folly (Sophocles gives us no reason to think that Ajax's invocation of the Furies on the Atreidae deserved fulfillment, but Teucer's curse has more merit). This truth is not a matter of hero-cults, but of human wisdom. It is not presented in this play as a new notion that supersedes Ajax and the "old heroic code," but as a fixed universal standard. And it is significant that Sophocles makes the chorus of Homeric warriors, who are of Athenian origin, the first to recognize Menelaus' failure to uphold this standard (1092), and the first to applaud Odysseus when he acts in true heroic fashion according to this standard (1374–1375).

PART II

Men at Home

CHAPTER 4

Antigone, Oedipus Tyrannus, Oedipus Coloneus

The soldiers of *Ajax* and *Philoctetes* are men displaced from their native cities, and their views are therefore necessarily limited to the immediate and personal situation in which they find themselves. They act according to certain moral principles, such as that people have the right of burial, or represent a certain point of view, such as that the end justifies the means. In both plays the chorus function to set the characters and actions of their leaders in a broader context of ethical standards. Nevertheless, they are isolated from others of their kind, even though it is clearly understood that they represent the totality of their own particular group—all the soldiers of Ajax, all the men who serve Neoptolemus. The hostility incurred by their leader sets Ajax's men apart from the other soldiers in the army, so much so that they fear for their own lives; Neoptolemus' men are physically separated from the rest of the Greek host. These isolated groups, dependent upon individual military leaders, represent ways of thinking and modes of behavior but not the entirety of society as the audience would have conceived it.

The three "Theban" plays, so obviously grouped together by the cycle of legend from which they draw the basic elements of their plots, are also associated by the generally similar personae and function of their choruses. Each play is endowed with a chorus of "elders," mature men of responsible position who are functioning as citizens in their native countries and are involved in events that affect not only their own lives but the welfare of their cities. They are not isolated, self-sufficient units. The mass of their fellow citizens—including women, children, and warriors—is generally evident in the background. Occasionally these other groups are even visible onstage (the suppliants in the prologue of *Oedipus Tyrannus*) or are presented by the chorus' song (the warriors of Athens in the second stasimon of *Oedipus Coloneus*). The chorus' attitudes may even be contrasted with those of other groups, as the Elders of *Antigone* differ from the average citizens. Consequently, these choruses bring to their plays a broad political significance that could not easily be presented by a single character.

It is the purpose of this chapter to determine more precisely the nature and function of the political element that the choruses introduce. To do so, we shall consider the three plays in their generally accepted chronological order and compare the characters of the choruses and the dramatic effects that they create. Since the plays contain Sophocles' most famous odes, it is appropriate to repeat here that in concentrating on character we are not necessarily diminishing the role of poetry, but complementing it.

Of the three, *Antigone*—presumably the earliest—is most patently concerned with the topic of political morality, with philosophies of governance and the conflict of religion and law. Yet despite the immensity of these abstractions, the immediate dramatic intent of the poet is not the subject of critical dispute, in that critics do not tend to hold violently contradictory opinions about the poet's own views. Nearly everyone agrees that Sophocles intended to portray Antigone's burial of Polyneices as "right"—sanctioned by the gods according to Teiresias' revelations—and Creon's opposition to the burial as "wrong," insofar as his opposition arises from tyrannical behavior. It then becomes merely a question of the degree to which one condemns Creon or approves Antigone; the latter course usually involves an appraisal of Antigone's motives and of her behavior as a woman.[1]

The lengthy and frequent lyrics have exerted considerable influence upon the interpretation of the play's symbolism and judgment. Some of the odes are apparently so loosely connected to the action that they can be readily lifted out of context to function as independent poems. Or, when left in the play, they seem sometimes so ambiguous that their relevance to the plot is perceptible only through the most detailed and subtle analysis. It is generally agreed nowadays that the most productive approach to interpreting the choral lyrics is to assume that they arise from a distinct and

---

1. The extremes of opinion are almost exclusively occupied by Müller (in his commentary, especially 11–14), who sees Antigone as pure heroine and Creon as pure villain, and by Calder (*GRBS* 9 [1968], 389–407), who suggests that the sympathies of a Periclean audience "would have been with the government, not the opposition" (406). Of those who lie in between, perhaps more incline in the general direction of Müller's view than of Calder's.

consistent persona.[2] This being accepted, it is again a question of the degree to which one believes that the chorus support either Creon or Antigone. Some say that the chorus are utterly devoted to Creon throughout the play, or right up to the last possible moment at line 1259; some, that they begin by supporting the king but change their minds at one earlier point or another during the action.[3] Others see the chorus as vacillating between viewpoints until a decision is forced upon them by Teiresias; still others see them as Antigone's partisans, though necessarily secret ones, from the very beginning.[4]

The term "Theban Elders" implies the two characteristics that are most commonly agreed to define the chorus' persona: age and devotion to Thebes. Certainly they are old men; the poet twice calls them "aged" (160, 281) and later makes the chorus-leader declare that he has known Teiresias for a true prophet "ever since my hair turned white" (1092–1093), implying that his hair has been white for some time. Since they are so obviously old, it is likely that their age would have been evident at once from their costume and bearing. Later they are called rich (843); this, too, would be reflected in their costume. They must also be members of the aristocracy, for they are called "Lords of Thebes" (940, 988), but the term is used much later in the play. Unless their costume included some special insignia of their rank (for which there is no evidence), the audience would at first know nothing about their position in respect of power and influence. There is no preparation for their entrance, and they do not identify themselves until the end of the song. Throughout the parodos the audience would remain uncertain about the chorus' political status and about how

2. There are few exceptions: Else (*Madness*, 76) at one point sees the chorus functioning as "the mouthpiece of the poet and the gods"; Alexanderson (*Eranos* 66 [1966], 86, 102–105) accounts for the chorus' apparently sudden about-face, after Teiresias' statements, by suggesting that they play two consecutive roles: first as a character in the drama, then subsequently as the "mouthpiece" of the poet. Easterling ("Second Stasimon," 156) sees these two roles as mingled.

3. Cf. Müller's commentary (16, 266). For those who see an earlier shift in the chorus' allegiance, the conflict between Creon and Haimon is usually the turning point; cf. Coleman (*PCPhS* 18 [1972], 14) and, in a way, Errandonea (*Sófocles* [1970], 97). Kamerbeek (in his commentary, 15 and 24) sees them as the "wise, moderate and loyal elders" who are overwhelmed by events and take a long time to make up their minds against Creon. Similar is Burton's view (*The Chorus*, 87–90) that they respect authority and established religion and their loyalty is to the city rather than to any individual.

4. Kirkwood (*Sophoclean Drama*, 205–209) stresses the dramatic significance of the numerous ambiguities in the choral utterances; cf. also Winnington-Ingram (*Sophocles*, 137–138). For the view of the chorus as entirely pro-Antigone, see Schwinge (*Gymnasium* 78 [1971], esp. 297, 300–301, 320–321).

supports suspenseful mood of prologue

this chorus will react to the edict, of which they are as yet presumably ignorant (33 ff.), and to Antigone's deed. This deliberate uncertainty about the chorus' position serves to continue the suspenseful mood of the prologue despite the visual contrast between the two scenes.[5]

As the chorus sing about the recent victory and the deliverance of Thebes, the tone of their rejoicing becomes more personal than civic. Their song contains no sweeping prayer for the safety of the state, nor is it a hymn of thanksgiving offered to the gods for the rescue of the city. There is no invocation or address to any divinity until the mention of Bacchus in the last line, and there the god's presence is invited by a wishful optative in the third person rather than by direct address (154: Βάκχιος ἄρχοι). The chorus observe a fact—the gods have rescued Thebes—and express their own personal relief and rejoicing at it. Since there is no one else present onstage for them to address, and since they do not address a god, we may suppose that the song was heard as a "group monologue," that is, a group of persons all exclaiming to each other in the same manner about the same subject.[6] This impression is confirmed by their exhortation to themselves at the end of the song, "let us forget the war and go to all the temples of the gods with night-long dances" (150–153). It would probably be assumed that this "us" includes the rest of the town, that they are not setting themselves apart from other Thebans. Nevertheless, they are addressing neither the gods nor other characters of the drama, but only themselves.[7]

Although not directly invoked, the gods do play a large part in the chorus' utterance; indeed, the old men attribute the entire victory to the gods. This identifies them at once as pious men; but it also shows a curious disregard for the human participants in the battle. As the chorus tell the

5. See Kitto (*Sophocles*, 3) for a vivid summary of the contrasting effects, although we may question whether the Elders were dancing.

6. The chorus' initial apostrophizing of the sun's light, the new and glorious day (100–104), can hardly be called a prayer, since nothing is requested, nor does it seem reasonable to suppose that the rest of the song is still addressed to the sunlight. The comparable address to the message from the Delphic Oracle, in the parodos of *Oed. Tyr.*, sounds as much like an address to Apollo himself and is quickly replaced by formal invocation of deities. The anapests of *Antigone*'s parodos, which elsewhere in Sophocles are used by choruses only when they are directly addressing characters who are onstage or nearby, may be intended to enhance the impression that the chorus are addressing themselves.

7. Cf. Kaimio (*Chorus of Greek Drama*, 52, 143–144), who claims the choral hortatory subjunctive always includes other persons, that is, the chorus here represent and address the whole people of Thebes. But the only other Sophoclean usage, and the three Euripidean ones that Kaimio cites, give the *primary* impression that "each member of the chorus is addressing the others," as Kaimio admits (147).

story, Zeus (128ff.) and Ares (138ff.) appear to have fought the battle and accomplished the victory. There is no celebration of valiant Theban warriors fighting in desperate defense of their city, homes, and gods. In fact, the only allusions to the human defenders of the city occur as part of a reference to the noise of battle,[8] and in the brief statement that the Seven against Thebes were ranged against equals (142: ἴσοι πρὸς ἴσους);[9] perhaps their use of the epithet "many-charioted Thebes" (149) should also be included. The description of the attackers as beasts of prey (112–122) and the sense of the imminent destruction of the defenders (132–133) suggest that the Thebans were quite helpless, saved only by Zeus' intervention. The chorus certainly make no statement about the virtue of civic obedience and order as safeguards against invasion and destruction, or indeed about any such matter. By the end of the song, it is as if the story of a mythical battle between gods and monsters were being told by noncombatant spectators who are immensely relieved to have survived and wish only to forget the war and celebrate their escape from disaster.

So far the audience has seen a chorus of pious, elderly men who are at the same time passive, fearful, and very much concerned with their own survival. The choral character now receives a more personal definition from Creon as he describes his reason for summoning them. It is significant that Creon begins by stating that he has chosen these particular men out of all the Thebans and summoned them apart from the others (164: ἐκ πάντων δίχα). These are not the designated representatives of all the Theban people. Creon's reason for summoning them is equally revealing—their known, continuing devotion to the royal house. The emphasis is on the fact that they "reverenced the powers of the throne of Laius" (165–166). Creon says nothing about any concern for service to the city on their part; it is only their personal loyalty that commends them to him. The extended references to the royal succession, by Oedipus and then by his sons, show that the chorus have been functioning in Thebes for a very long time; they are the sort of men who manage to survive, without undue privation, terrible battles and successive changes of monarchy.

In the ensuing dialogue between Creon and the chorus, the poet com-

8. Lines 125–126, somewhat obscured by textual difficulties; cf. Pozzi (*HSCP* 75 [1971], 63–67).

9. When in the next lines the chorus finally come to the fight between Eteocles and Polyneices, neither is mentioned by name; both are subsumed under the dual (144: τοῖν στυγεροῖν, etc.). No details of the battle are given; the chorus say only that the two engaged each other in a duel (146: δικρατεῖς λόγχας στήσαντ') and died.

pletes his delineation of the chorus' concern for personal survival rather than civic involvement. First, after Creon's introductory speech they formally and lengthily acknowledge his absolute power and his consequent ability to command (211–214), without offering either support for or criticism of the principles of governance that he has just enunciated.[10] Next, when Creon tries to enlist the chorus' active cooperation in maintaining the prohibition against the burial, Sophocles makes the chorus misunderstand Creon by inferring from his general request a more specific meaning, so that they beg off on the grounds of age instead of making a statement of principle (215–216). They have a very different attitude from that of the physically enthusiastic Elders of Colonus (*Oed. Col.* 856–857). Finally, when Creon enjoins them not to aid the opposition, thus forcing them to make some kind of statement of their position, they agree only by expressing the fear of punishment (218–220). To this point Creon has shown no obvious signs of tyrannical behavior—in fact, he seems almost to be inviting the chorus to speak out at will (180–181, 184ff.)—but they conspicuously avoid making any statement either for or against his policies. There is no reason yet to suppose the chorus are afraid of Creon and therefore secretly opposed. The poet has taken pains to give them the dramatic opportunity to state their opinion and then has made them utter only self-concerned remarks without any mention of duty, order, or civic welfare.

After the Guard's report on the finding of the burial, the chorus offer the tentative suggestion that there is some divine influence at work (278–279), a remark that suits the attitudes that the chorus have expressed thus far: in the parodos they showed a tendency to attribute human acts to the gods, and subsequently they have avoided any comment upon human acts in a civic context. Nor can it be considered foolish of them to have suspected from the beginning of the Guard's report (279: πάλαι) that a supernatural agency was involved. The Guard's speech is so constructed that the burial could seem mysterious to one who has not heard the prologue. There was no sign of tools, digging, or transport; only a light coating of dust lay on the body, yet there was no sign of molestation by scavengers.

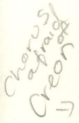

10. There is no compelling reason to remove Κρέον at line 211 and replace it with an infinitive, although it would be grammatically more convenient to do so (cf. Jebb, *ad loc.*, and Müller's commentary, 68). If the full patronymic form of address were retained here, it might serve to emphasize Creon's merely collateral relation to the royal line, as Coleman suggests (*PCPhS* 18 [1972], 6). But it would be even more emphatic of the formality and distance in the relation between Creon and the chorus; see below, chapter 5, on *Tr.* 665.

Indeed, it is such a reasonable suggestion from this chorus that it makes Creon's explosive reaction all the more unexpected and startling (280–281).

After Creon has begun to show temper by his rudeness to the chorus, overconfidence and poor judgment by his accusations of bribery and conspiracy, and tyrannical tendencies by his threats of torture (309), the chorus are left alone to sing an ode (332–375). Naturally the audience may expect to hear their real views on what has happened. Perhaps they will offer some comment on Creon's behavior, his hastiness and rudeness, or some speculations on who might have performed the burial and why. The style of this chorus' song is the same as that of their parodos, in that they engage in a discussion among themselves rather than a prayer or exhortation. The content of the ode, however, seems so unrelated to the immediately preceding action that it has generated seriously conflicting critical interpretations of the chorus' stance. Are they supporting Creon and condemning the person who buried Polyneices, or vice versa? But the very "detachment" of the song would have registered an effect on the audience. Since the chorus, being alone on the scene, can say what they please, it must seem to the audience that the chorus have chosen not to discuss the burial specifically; the logical assumption is therefore that they do not care who did it, or why. Nor do they comment on Creon's behavior, but they have already expressed their belief that he has the right to do anything he chooses in such matters. Instead, for three stanzas they proceed to enumerate Man's clever accomplishments and skills, and all the ones they mention are strictly limited to the context of the preservation of the self. They do not say that resourceful Man should use his talents in honoring law and justice in order to benefit the city. In their chronicle of civilization the only reference to the intellect and the state (355: ἀστυνόμους ὀργάς) comes after the development of hunting and the domestication of animals, and it is immediately followed by the invention of shelter against bad weather. In this context the phrase would probably suggest an early stage of human cooperation, of banding together to build houses and settlements for protection, rather than the establishment of law, government, and the arts.[11] In the end, the chorus' view is that Man should use his skill and cleverness to protect himself, to keep himself safe and secure in the protection of a strong city rather than endangered by the absence of that protection.[12]

11. The ἀστυνόμοι at Athens were apparently responsible only for the maintenance of the town (sanitation, streets, etc.); cf. also Benardete (*Interpretation* 5 [1975], 192).

12. 370: ὑψίπολις· ἄπολις. Against Jebb's translation of ὑψίπολις as "proud stands his city," see Ehrenberg (*Sophocles and Pericles*, 64*n*1), who argues for "stands high in the Polis."

Anyone who, using this innate cleverness, foolishly gets into trouble by breaking the laws—human or divine—is to be avoided as a danger to one's own security. Thus the audience hears the chorus removing themselves from the ethical problems that are being introduced. These Thebans ask no questions about right and wrong, offer no definitions of the good citizen. Their words contain no moral or political statement, but rather their own personal prescription for the survival of the individual.

Now, as the Guard leads in Antigone, the chorus, who have just been demonstrating the basic self-interest of their concern for expedience rather than general principles, are suddenly faced with the physical manifestation of the "lawbreaker" whom they have just been discussing in impersonal terms (370). The use of anapests instead of iambic trimeters may well reinforce the sense of shock and agitation contained in the chorus' initial exclamation that this sight is some stroke of the gods (376: ἐς δαιμόνιον τέρας). Their initial reaction is entirely consonant with their previous utterances: Antigone has been engaged in "folly" or "thoughtlessness" (383: ἀφροσύνη). When, however, they have had time to reconsider, when Antigone has defended her action by referring it to the gods' laws, the hitherto pious chorus notably fail to make any remark about the reasons she has given. Instead, the chorus-leader, apparently addressing Creon, says that she has clearly inherited her father's "crude" manner (471–472). Coming from this chorus, the statement is obviously a criticism, but it may also be heard as an attempt to excuse her behavior. When he goes on to say that she does not know how "to yield to misfortune," the audience would surely consider that unpleasant phrase, with its distinct connotation of expedience, quite suited to the sentiments that the chorus have so recently expressed.[13]

For double meanings, cf. Müller's commentary (85) and Bona (*RFIC* 99 [1971], 144n2). Certainly the adjective can be a possessive compound: "possessing a 'high' city," as in ὑψίπυργος (*Tr.* 354), "high-towered" (cf. Ronnet, *Sophocle*, 155n2). If it is thus construed, the question is whether the ὑψι- element signifies "lofty" in the metaphorical sense of "proud," or physically "high-built," that is, "strong, safe" (affording the protection of its walls and acropolis). There is no linguistic reason why the two words cannot mean "possessing a strong city" and "not possessing a city" (pure alpha privative), with the ὑψι- element functioning as the opposite of the alpha privative. The song's theme is not "the power of human wit to make or mar the polis" (Jebb, *ad* 37of.), but its power to preserve or destroy the individual, to lead one to good or ill, to the safety of a city or the danger of being an outcast.

13. For somewhat different views, cf. Linforth ("Antigone and Creon," 204), Bongie ("Daughter of Oedipus," 257–258), Schwinge (*Gymnasium* 78 [1971], 309). On the phrase [ὑπ]εἴκειν κακοῖς, see above, chapter 2, on *Phil.* 1046.

The chorus' failure to acknowledge Antigone's arguments sets them apart from her and contributes further to the isolation of Antigone that is created by the pattern of response between the chorus and Creon. Not only does Creon reply directly to the chorus' statement, but his entire speech (472ff.) seems to be addressed to them rather than to Antigone, to whom he refers only as "she" (480, 484, 488). The chorus remain silent and passive, but the poet makes their politic silence especially noticeable by having Antigone attribute it to fear (504–507). The following discussion between Creon and Antigone, about the fact that the Thebans dare not openly oppose Creon, is probably intended to include the chorus; the gestures would make it clear. Although the use of the deictic pronoun (τῶνδε: 508, 510) cannot be taken as proof that a particular character is physically present, we may assume that it does refer to persons already known to be present rather than to absent characters who are not specified.

The chorus' introduction of Ismene as weeping sisterly tears (526–530), like their shocked introduction of Antigone, portrays them as relatively compassionate in contrast to Creon, who sees Ismene only as a "viper" (531). Again, the metrical change to anapests may suggest agitation. But still the chorus remain entirely passive, making no attempt to defend either of the women until the very end of the scene (574–576). Even then, their mild inquiries about whether Creon has definitely decided to kill Antigone can hardly be heard as a serious protest against his decision.[14]

With the departure of the women, the chorus and Creon remain on the scene in what might have been a confrontation but is in fact another choral discussion, in which the Theban Elders fail to consider any of the issues that have arisen during the scene. Since it has already been suggested that the chorus would not speak out to Creon (509), it is not surprising that in the ode that they now sing (582–625) they do not criticize him in his presence. But neither do they seriously examine Antigone's actions. They have nothing to say about her motives for performing the burial or about the fundamental question of moral conduct and its relation to the safety of the state. Instead, they ascribe the whole problem to external causes. Their first two stanzas carefully set forth the belief that divine destruction once incurred may be handed down from generation to generation, spread-

14. The MSS give 574 to Ismene, and most also give her 576. There seems to be no reason why the lines would not suit the chorus, especially since the chorus later address a question to Creon that he clearly perceives as advisory (770–771); and he may also address the chorus at 561–563. Cf. Jebb (*ad loc.*) and Müller's commentary (111–112).

ing and increasing its destructive force like a coastal storm. Upon such an inherited fate they lay the blame for Antigone's ruin, upon some god (597), her thoughtless tongue, and a Fury of her mind (603: Ἐρινύς φρενῶν). The second strophic pair seems to begin as a prayer to Zeus, but it develops as a two-part statement of belief: Zeus' power is inescapable, and it is his law that "nothing that is great comes upon the life of mortals without bringing destruction"; Hope is the agent of this destruction. For the chorus, life is fraught with the danger of misfortune, whether inherited or incurred. This fearsome notion certainly accounts for their refusal to take up a moral position. For men so concerned with safety, the inevitable supernatural forces are of far more importance than questions of principle. For them, it is not a matter of right vs. wrong; Antigone is simply deluded. They say that bad seems good to one whom the god leads to destruction (622–624), but they never say whether the "bad" is the illegal burial of her brother or the folly of risking death by defying the king's power.

The chorus' ode is, like the previous one, ended by the arrival of a character; again, the chorus' use of anapests to introduce the arrival (626–630) may serve to intensify the emotional quality of, or add a sense of anxiety to, their speculations about what Haimon's attitude will be. After Creon's stern but restrained speech to his son, the chorus-leader expresses their agreement (681–682) with Creon's precept that obedience in all things, just or unjust (667), is necessary for safety and self-preservation (675–676). That is the position they have already taken, and it is not surprising that after Haimon's speech they mildly advise father and son to learn from each other, since Haimon's advice to bend with the wind (712–717) accords entirely with their own views and behavior. We may reasonably suppose that in making this conservative and obedient chorus approve Haimon's words, the poet is greatly enhancing the dramatic force of Creon's ensuing retreat into illogical stubbornness (745–746) and, eventually, viciousness (760–761).

The chorus maintain the same attitude after Haimon's departure that they displayed after Antigone's impassioned defense of her actions. They avoid any mention of the substance of the argument, just as they avoided comment on Antigone's motives, seeking instead external or emotional explanations of conduct. First, they attribute Haimon's anger to the impetuosity of youth (766–767). Then, after a brief exchange with Creon, which serves to present new information and to show that Creon is not entirely irrational (770ff.), the chorus sing an ode to Eros. The song is not a prayer, since the chorus address the god without ever invoking him. Love, they say, invincible and inescapable Love, is the cause of this family quarrel (793–794). Although they mention no names, they would surely seem to be saying that without the intervention of Eros there would have been no contention between Creon and Haimon. The chorus' words on the unopposable power of Love may sound ominous to the knowing audience, and the chorus may even seem to be hinting at Creon's stubbornness. Nevertheless, great human issues have been raised by Haimon—the responsibilities of kingship, the duties of son to father, the nature of true wisdom—but the chorus resolutely ignore every one of them and lay all the blame for Haimon's behavior on Love.[15]

The play thus far has consisted of a series of confrontations between Creon and other characters—the Guard, Antigone, and Haimon. Now, perhaps with Creon in the background, the poet confronts the Elders of Thebes with Antigone. The political significance of the chorus' role is plain: Antigone begins the first strophe by appealing to them as "citizens of our fatherland" (806: ὦ γᾶς πατρίας πολῖται). In her view, when they reject her, it is the city that rejects her: "Oh city, Oh richest men of the city" (841: ὦ πόλις, ὦ πόλεως πολυκτήμονες ἄνδρες), and so she appeals instead to the sacred places of the land itself to witness the injustice of her punishment (842ff.). The chorus pity her deeply, for they weep streams of tears at the sight of her being led forth to death (800–805). When she appeals to them, they offer praise—but only for the unique manner of her death, not for her actions (817–822). When she compares her fate to Niobe's eternal mourning, they claim it is a great thing for a mortal to share in divine misfortunes both in life and in death. For her, this is mockery (839ff.); for the audience, the chorus are once again ignoring the ethical problem and considering only the external, physical aspects of

15. Exactly as Creon does, insisting that Haimon is motivated solely by erotic desire for Antigone (e.g., 740). On the chorus' equating madness with love, see von Fritz (*Tragödie*, 235–237). It is a reasonable assumption that Creon remains onstage during the ode; certainly there is no evidence in the text to show he exits at 780, and at 883 he has clearly overheard Antigone's laments. *Oed. Tyr.* may, however, provide a parallel for the announced exit and the "eavesdropping" re-entry; see below, note 27. Cf. Kitto (*Form and Meaning*, 167–168), and especially Ziobro (*AJP* 92 [1971], 81–85), although the latter's proposal that Antigone is brought out between lines 765 and 766 is not convincing. It rests solely on the fact that she knows about the change in the method of execution, which could easily be another example of the deliberate Sophoclean inconsistency for dramatic purposes. Even more likely is the possibility that Creon exits at 780 and then re-enters with Antigone and her escort of guards at 806; he does seem to say that he will take her to the tomb himself (773–774: ἄγων . . . κρύψω), and this entry may be a form of sending her on her way to death. But whether he is present or not, the chorus' song is quite consistent with their previous utterances.

Antigone's doom. They are, nevertheless, still offering her sympathy and compassion, and speaking of "we" rather than of "you." Only after she has rejected their view (840), as vehemently as she rejected Ismene's, do they begin to rebuke her (853–856), and they still address her in kindly fashion, as τέκνον (855). Not until the very end of the second antistrophe do they set themselves apart from her with an accusatory "you" (875: σὲ δ').

Despite their compassion, however, the chorus are still the advocates of expedience, men who do not admit anything as the cause of Antigone's suffering except her boldness (853–855), the misfortunes of her parents (856), and her own self-willed passion (875). Their judgment is clear and uncomplicated: one is foolish to oppose power, whatever the reason, and bring on one's own destruction. So completely does Antigone reject their view that she calls herself "unwept of friends" (846, 876) despite the chorus' tears. The division between them is emphasized by the metrical contrast between Antigone's lyrics and the anapestic systems in which the chorus express their sympathy; and although the chorus' rebukes are expressed in fully lyric stanzas, the meter is so heavily iambic that the chorus' parts may have sounded wholly distinct from Antigone's lyrics.[16]

Creon's interruption does not end the encounter between Antigone and the Theban councillors. Sophocles makes Antigone place the responsibility for her death as much on the chorus as on Creon, for the plural forms in the challenge at the end of her final defense must include all present on the scene: "But if it is these [men, not I,] who act in error, may they suffer no greater evils than they have done to me" (927–928). Still the chorus remark only on her temper (929–930).[17] But in one last solemn utterance, Antigone invokes the city of Thebes and the ancestral gods and calls upon the lords of Thebes (940: Θήβης οἱ κοιρανίδαι) to witness this fate of the last member of the royal house, this punishment of piety. To this appeal the chorus respond with a rather impersonal ode on the legendary dooms of royalty. Twice they address her as "child" (949, 987), which gives some tone of sympathy to their words, but otherwise they say nothing about the

16. It is impossible to determine from the text whether the choral anapests are lyric or recitative; cf. Jebb's appendix (248) on 110ff. The choral lyrics can be analyzed as an uninterrupted sequence of iambs (with resolution at the beginning of 855/874; cf. Müller's commentary, 181), or as two groups of iambic dimeters separated by a tribrach.

17. If 933–934 are assigned to the chorus, the compassion implied in the exclamation would not conflict with the sympathy they have shown for Antigone's fate (though not for her cause). Nonetheless, the attribution rests largely on the desire for symmetry with 929–930, which in turn requires the excision of the words αὐταὶ ψυχῆς (cf. Müller, ad 930); and it does not seem to matter much to the characterization of either Antigone or the chorus.

present circumstances, so that critics often find the song irrelevant to the action and themes of the play.[18] Yet in the very first stanza the chorus plainly state the lesson that their mythical examples illustrate (951–954): nothing, not even noble birth and royal lineage, provides any protection against the suffering that Fate can inflict. As usual, the chorus respond not to the principal aspect of Antigone's complaint—the dishonoring of her piety—but to the side-issue of her royalty. They do not accept the civic responsibility she has laid on them, because, as they say, many royal persons have suffered terrible fates both justly and unjustly. Such sentiments as they express by these horror tales simply reinforce their fundamental fear, that "nothing that is great comes upon the life of mortals without bringing destruction" (613–614). The universe is filled with dread forces. These things can happen to anyone.

At this point the audience sees the king of Thebes and his courtiers alone for a moment on the scene. After all that has just been said, it must seem that the chorus have not much less part in Antigone's death than Creon does. The aged, wealthy nobles of Thebes, to whom Antigone appealed as to the city, have by their inaction condoned Creon's action. Haimon has clearly informed both the chorus and the audience that the common citizens (690: ἀνδρὶ δημότῃ) have only the highest praise for Antigone's act, yet the chorus made no attempt to intervene with the king on Antigone's behalf; despite their pity, they absolve themselves of responsibility by reproaching her headstrong opposition to power. Sophocles has not made Creon an unmitigated villain; the king is not holding a sword to the chorus-leader's throat. Tyrannies like his, which essentially operate on the principle that might makes right (666–667, 738), must rest upon the passive consent of timorously self-concerned and fatalistic men like these.

At the end of the song, Teiresias speaks (988–990). This is the only Sophoclean occurrence of a new character's entering from the parodos without being perceived and announced by those onstage.[19] The uniqueness of the situation suggests that it arises from the position of Creon and the chorus, that their attention is directed entirely toward the departing

---

18. As an extreme example, Else dismisses the ode as a meaningless breather (*Madness*, 68), and even Linforth ("Antigone and Creon," 233) explains its function only as something for Creon to be seen listening to. Cf. also Burton (*The Chorus*, 131–132). Most interesting, but least likely, is Errandonea's analysis: the chorus are knowingly, but allusively, predicting the deaths of Antigone, Haimon, and Eurydice (*Sófocles* [1958], 98–110; cf. *Sófocles* [1970], 95–102).

19. Except for the messengers in *Aj.* (719) and *Oed. Tyr.* (924). But they presumably come in at a rapid pace, and they are not individual characters with names, whereas the blind seer

Antigone and that Teiresias enters, unseen by them, from the opposite parodos. Only when he speaks do they turn and perceive him. His entering call, "Lords of Thebes," must have rung loud with irony in the audience's ears, an irony that would be heightened by the fact that the chorus do not participate at all in the ensuing scene between Teiresias and Creon. The confrontation between the power of the king and the knowledge of the seer builds steadily to a climax without any interruption from the chorus.[20] Because it is exceedingly unusual for a Sophoclean chorus to remain completely silent during a dialogue scene, from the very beginning through the exit of one participant, we may suppose that their silence was intended to have some dramatic effect, especially since the poet does not have Creon yield to Teiresias, but to the chorus. After Teiresias' exit, the chorus-leader breaks their noticeable silence with a four-line speech telling Creon that the seer has never been wrong (1091–1094). Creon's own indecision (1095–1097) may seem to encourage the chorus to act. Using a formal mode of address, the chorus-leader bids Creon take counsel (1098) and with two imperatives bids him take immediate action (1100–1101).[21]

The chorus' new stance is emphasized by two more imperatives with which they issue additional instructions to the king. This new behavior does not constitute an inconsistency in the chorus' character, since they have never supported Creon's policies, only his right to do as he pleases.

Teiresias must take a longer time to walk in. Both the Paedagogus and Orestes in *El.*, although supposedly disguised, must be immediately recognized by the audience. Cf. also Müller (commentary, 227), on the symbolism of the fact that the seer is unannounced.

20. The plural that Creon uses in his tirade against Teiresias need not include the chorus (as Jebb seems to imply it does, *ad* 1033ff.; cf. Müller, *ad* 1033–1036, who believes Creon is referring to Antigone and Haimon). The gestures would, of course, have defined the limits of the plurals for the audience. If Creon addresses only Teiresias and not the chorus, then he would be understood as accusing the seer of being the representative of a group (seers) that has been "trafficking" in Creon for a long time (1036: πάλαι). In the same vein he earlier accused the Guard of being the bribed tool of an established conspiracy (289ff.: πάλαι). There also he referred once to the Guard in the plural as the representative of the entire group (293: τούτους).

21. It is tempting to accept the emendation of λαβεῖν to Κρέον in 1098, thus making the chorus use the rare, fully formal mode of address; but cf. Jebb, *ad loc.*, against the change.

It is widely supposed that Creon disobeys the chorus' instructions by not performing the actions in the order that the chorus directed—free Antigone, then bury Polyneices. Even those who do not presume that Creon might have saved Antigone must nevertheless explain away the chorus' subsequent failure to comment on the reversal; Margon, for example, suggests that it simply "escapes their notice" (*CP* 65 [1970], 107). But it is likely that when Creon orders servants to fetch axes and go "yonder," adding that he himself will be present to free her (1108–1112), some members of his retinue are meant to exit at once. The audience

Nor is it surprising that Creon, formerly so rude, should now yield to them, for he earlier changed his mind about Ismene at the chorus' apparent instigation, even though there they only asked a question instead of giving advice (770–771). The dramatic effect of the sequence is to show that the chorus, under the influence of Teiresias' threats—which are directed not only against Creon but against the city itself (1080–1083, 1094)—are at last undertaking to perform their civic duty as Elders of Thebes and councillors to the king.

The change in the chorus' attitude is further manifested in the ode that follows Creon's hasty departure (1115–1152). For the first time in the play, the Theban Elders offer a prayer to the gods on behalf of the city. The god whom they mentioned so briefly in the parodos, the patron deity of Thebes, they now at last invoke with elaborate, ritual formality, naming all the aspects of his divinity and the places of his dominion, summoning him to come and heal the suffering city (1140–1145). The chief function of the ode is to create the joy-before-disaster effect. At this stage in the plot, time must pass before Creon's return, but the mere passing of time before an event which the audience fully expects—the report of disaster—would cause a relaxation of the dramatic tension that the poet has so carefully built up. It would be entirely possible, indeed likely, that the audience's attention might wander. Therefore he adds the twist of the chorus' dreadfully mistaken anticipation, so that the pungent irony of the song keeps the audience utterly engrossed in (and probably horrified by) the action of the moment. Thus the expected report will become a climax instead of a denouement.[22] Not the least of the ironies in this song is the fact that the chorus' first lyric utterance as truly responsible citizens, their first civic

---

would suppose that they are going on ahead to begin the task of opening the tomb with tools. As one listens to the Messenger's speech, one perceives that Creon assumed the tomb would be opened by the time he got there: someone heard a noise "from afar" (1206: ἄπωθεν) and went to tell Creon (1208); then, as Creon went along (1210: ἕρποντι), he also began to hear the still indistinct sounds (1209: ἄσημα), so he sent servants on ahead, telling them to pass through the opening that had been made into the tomb (1216). Creon's distance from the site is emphasized, and there is no hint that he is supposed to have caught sight of an unexpected opening. If the audience is not to make the natural assumption that the gap was made by the first contingent of servants, the poet must give some indication that it was made by someone else (e.g., Haimon, as Jebb maintains, *ad* 1216 and 1109); but he fails entirely to do that. Thus there is no "reversal" of actions, no "disobedience," and no race against time.

22. Many still believe that the chief function of such odes is to cause dramatic time to pass; Kamerbeek (commentary, 25) and Gellie (*Sophocles*, 226, 229) even revert to the impossible notion that these songs "raise our spirits against our better judgment" (cf. Kranz, *Stasimon*, 213–214).

prayer, comes too late, as their action came too late. The whole effect is climaxed by the juxtaposition of the chorus' invocation of the joyous god (1149–1154: προφάνηθ' . . . Ἴακχον) with the immediate arrival of the mortal messenger of disaster.

Having taken charge, the chorus remain in charge as the action proceeds to the moments of discovery with which the play ends. Henceforth they are no longer addressed as "lords" but as representatives of all the Thebans, both by the Messenger and by Eurydice (1183). They perform the tasks of responsible persons and are more involved in the activity than before: they receive the Messenger and question him at length before Eurydice comes out (1172–1179), they announce her arrival,[23] she addresses them in response rather than the Messenger alone (1183, 1190), and they then comment upon her silent withdrawal and rightly correct the Messenger's mistaken opinion (1251–1252), thus effectively causing him to go off to investigate. As Creon approaches, they finally offer their considered judgment of his actions (1259–1260).

The sense of activity that has surely been generated by the three entrances and two exits during these last hundred lines is sustained by the structure of the rest of the play. The exodos is a mixture of onstage action, reported action, and Creon's emotional reactions, all performed in a kommos-like utterance. Creon enters and straightway begins a lyric strophe (1261ff.) which the chorus-leader interrupts with an iambic trimeter line; Creon then utters a quasi-lyrical mixture of tribrachs and iambic trimeters to complete the strophe. Entrances occur both before and during the antistrophe, first as the Messenger appears from the house and converses with Creon in iambic trimeters (1277–1283), then as the corpse of Eurydice is disclosed in the very midst of Creon's antistrophe. When Creon finishes singing, the Messenger briefly describes Eurydice's death and Creon begins another strophe that is also interrupted by iambic trimeters, this time a five-line dialogue between Creon and the Messenger (1312–1316).[24] At

23. This is the first time they have used iambic trimeters for such an announcement, although eight of the twelve entrance-announcements in the play are made by the chorus. Sophocles may be deliberately contrasting their practical, responsible behavior here with their earlier anapestic announcements, which all consisted chiefly of agitated questions (159–162, 377–383, 628–630), except for their emotional description of the weeping Ismene (526–530) and their own weeping at Antigone's entrance. They return to anapests in their presumably agitated announcement of Creon's return (1257–1260), but announce the display of the corpse of Eurydice in a single iambic trimeter line.

24. Jebb and Pohlsander (*Metrical Studies*, 45) consider that 1306–1311 and 1317–1325 are two separate strophes. But there is no reason to suppose the dialogue divides them any more than in the epiparodos of *Aj.* (cf. 900–903, lyric; 904–907, trimeter dialogue; 908–

the end of the strophe, the chorus-leader speaks two trimeter lines to Creon, then takes the Messenger's place in the inserted dialogue of the antistrophe; and as soon as Creon finishes the song, the chorus close the play with the customary anapestic passage.

Thus the play ends with a complex and rapidly paced scene that is largely dialogue, and with an obvious contrast between Creon's mourning lyrics and the chorus-leader's calmer, conversational iambics. The chorus now clearly function as advisors without in any way contradicting their previous statements of principle. They now believe that Creon was wrong, but there is no indication that they always thought so. They blame him, but not to his face, and with some reserve (1259–1260). On the other hand, they do not commiserate with him, but advise caution, practical action, and the acceptance of fate (1326–1327, 1354–1355, 1357–1358). They do not repent of their former inaction or take any blame upon themselves, but neither do they reproach him with "I told you so," as if they had ever contradicted him. If Creon is meant to be led off into the house as the chorus pronounce the final lesson, then they may be heard as addressing themselves rather than Creon, just as they did in their first songs. Their brief statements of principle suggest that they, too, have learned a lesson. Where once they believed that power takes precedence over piety (872–874), now they admit that the laws of the gods must not be dishonored (1349–1350). Their comment that the proud words of boastful men are punished (1350–1351) would be heard as alluding to Creon's fate, but their final statement, that wisdom is taught in old age (1352), seems equally appropriate to themselves, since advanced age has been so prominent a part of their persona.

The chorus of *Oedipus Tyrannus* are prominent citizens of Thebes, but they bear no other resemblance to the Theban Elders of *Antigone*. In the first place, the audience is never uncertain about their status. At the end of the prologue, Oedipus orders someone to summon "the assembled people of Cadmus" (144: Κάδμου λαόν), so that the next group to enter will clearly be the representatives of all the Thebans. Thus from the beginning they are the opposite of Creon's hand-picked loyalists. They are not, however, common citizens. Iocasta calls them "lords of the land" (911: χώρας

914, more lyric); Müller (commentary, 263) evidently does not suppose so. Possibly some music might have been played during the inserted dialogue as a link; or Creon may not have actually sung to a musical accompaniment.

ἄνακτες), the same rank that the chorus assign to both Creon and Oedipus, and to the Messenger from the palace they are "always the most honored of this land." Although their rank would not be evident, their position as wealthy, and therefore prominent, men would be indicated by the richness of their costume. In addition, the poet does not insist upon their being old men as he does in *Antigone*. Oedipus once, late in the play, addresses them as "elders" (1111: πρέσβεις), and in their joyous speculation on his birth they once call him "son" (1098: τέκνον). But there are no other references to old age, nor any mention of infirmity, so we have no reason to suppose that it would have been a significant part of their initial appearance or bearing. They have been functioning in Thebes since Laius' day, so that they know the past, but otherwise their age is irrelevant.

The first impression the chorus give of themselves in the parodos is that they are filled with uncertainty and a consequent desire for fact. Their entire opening strophe questions the nature of the oracular response, expressing not merely curiosity but fearful anxiety (153). But they do not indulge in any speculation about the oracle; they make no assumptions, such as "perhaps the reply will be dire," and voice no hopes, such as "would that the reply might help us." Their apostrophe of the oracle contains only the desire for knowledge to relieve their own ignorance and apprehension.[25]

Unlike the parodos of *Antigone*, this first stanza already contains an address to a deity (154), and it leads into a formal prayer which lasts for the remaining stanzas of the ode. It is thus established at the outset that the chorus believe that the oracle is the voice of Apollo bringing the word of Zeus, and, further, that these men reverence and rely upon the power of the gods. Besides showing the importance of religion in their lives, this prayer for the safety of the city displays their deep concern for the welfare of the entire body of citizens. It is a solemn invocation especially of the gods of the city, Artemis γαιάοχος (160), whose seat is the agora, and

25. As he also does in the parodos of *Phil.*, Sophocles here avoids tedious repetition of background information by leading the audience to make a natural assumption, that the chorus have heard of Creon's return with an oracle but do not yet know the content. McDevitt's belief (*WS* 4 [1970], 29–30) that the chorus already know the details of the oracle rests entirely on the unfounded supposition that Oedipus subsequently speaks to the chorus "as if he expects them to know what he is talking about." But the reference to the oracle in lines 241ff. is perfectly adequate: first Oedipus makes the solemn proclamation, then he gives the reason for it: "I proclaim that we must discover and drive out the murderer of Laius, since the god says he is the cause of our ills." Since the chorus do not say in the parodos that they know this, why would the audience assume that they do? The assumption could hardly serve a dramatic purpose.

Bacchus, the eponymous god of the land (210). The devastation of the plague and the "numberless miseries" (168–169) that the chorus are suffering are not merely personal, but affect the whole city. They do not cry that their own wives and children are dying, but that the land bears no fruit, the women bear no children, and death is everywhere; the city itself is dying (179: πόλις . . . ὄλλυται) and it is for the city that they are praying. And, finally, the portrayal of the chorus as responsible leaders and representatives of the citizens, the λαός, is enhanced by the military metaphors of their song. They call the city their army (170) that has no weapon with which to defend itself (170–171) against the "bronzeless Ares" (190–191) of the plague.[26] In this legendary society that Sophocles is envisioning, the "lords" would be the king's generals, the men responsible for raising and marshaling the troops for battle and assisting at the preliminary prayers and sacrifices. This song gives the impression that the chorus are such men; functioning as if the leaders of a host, in the final strophic pair they marshal the gods themselves as allies in the battle against the plague (190–215). They are a far cry from the passive survivors of *Antigone*.

With the salient traits of the chorus' character now identified, the first episode establishes the relation between Oedipus and the chorus. Oedipus has come out of the palace at some point during the parodos, since he has overheard their prayer.[27] Thus the scene has a conversational beginning, since the king, instead of addressing the chorus without reference to their words (as Creon does in *Antigone*), responds to what they have been saying: "You pray; and concerning what you are praying for . . ." (216). This passage sets the tone for the rest of the scene. Oedipus speaks to the chorus not as a king to his subject, but as a "citizen among citizens" (222), and as if they are, or represent, "all Thebans" (223). In contrast to the edict of Creon, Oedipus does not threaten transgressors with the physical punishment that his royal power could inflict, but with his curse. His be-

26. As Kirkwood rightly observes (*Sophoclean Drama*, 204n31) against Knox (*AJP* 77 [1956], 137–138), Ares of line 190 is a metaphor, not the patron deity of Thebes, and the chorus are not being "un-Theban" in their hostility to him. But there is no need to distinguish this Ares from the war-god, since, as Kirkwood points out, "even the war god is only intermittently linked with Thebes." The martial metaphor is both obvious and apt, and, despite Kamerbeek's support (*ad* 190), the attempt to link it with some historical event simply misses the poetic point. See below, chapter 6, note 28.

27. Oedipus must be supposed to withdraw at the end of the prologue. He says that he has already sent for Teiresias "since Creon spoke" (287–289), and he must therefore have been offstage for part of the parodos. For obvious reasons of irony, it is tempting to speculate that he enters at the beginning of the final antistrophe, when the chorus invoke Lycean Apollo (203: Λύκει' ἄναξ).

havior toward the chorus is also quite unlike Creon's, for he charges them
with the civic duty of carrying out his edict (252–254), gently reprimands
them for their earlier lack of civic responsibility in not searching out the
murderer (256–258), and graciously praises them as just and righteous
(274–276).[28] In the exchange between the chorus and Oedipus, the chorus'
advice is earnestly solicited (283, 291), freely given (278–279, 290, 294–
295), and respectfully considered (280, 287). The spirit of the whole passage is that of a consultation between a concerned ruler and his councillors, a joint effort in the search for answers.

This cordial relation is not contravened by the next scene, in which the
chorus' attempt at intervention is ignored totally, because it is Teiresias,
not Oedipus, who ignores them. The chorus address their remarks to
Oedipus (404–405), but Teiresias then addresses Oedipus as if they did
not exist. His interruption underscores the intensity of his anger. Swept
aside during the principals' exchange of passionate and fearful accusations,
the chorus are left alone at the end of the scene to ponder and absorb these
new developments. They proceed to do so in a stasimon (463ff.) wholly
consistent with the character they have thus far displayed. Just as in their
reprimand to the quarreling principals they insisted that the welfare of the
city, and therefore the problem of the oracle, must take precedence over
personal matters, so now they commence with that same problem—the
identity and situation of the unknown murderer, revealed by the oracle,
who has done most unspeakable things.[29]

From this topic they move naturally to the accusation that Oedipus is
the killer. With intense expressions of anxiety and admissions of ignorance, they resolve the conflict between their respect for Oedipus and their
reverence for the seer not by any intuitive judgment but by very careful
and human common sense. They seek motive and proof, and find none; on
the contrary, Oedipus, they reason, has already proved himself wise and
useful to the city. To their cautious logic the poet adds an ironical twist,

28. The speech is, to be sure, an official proclamation to the entire city. But there seems to
be a subtle distinction in terms of address: whenever Oedipus speaks of the murderer or his
accessories, he uses impersonal terms. The only exceptions are the early references to one "of
you" who may know the identity of the guilty man (224, 233); otherwise the second person
plural is never used. But when he speaks of the other, dutiful Thebans, he emphatically uses
the second person pronoun (273: ὑμῖν δέ).

29. The audience may hear ἄρρητα (465) as a reference to the description of the murderer
just given by Teiresias (449–460; cf. 300–301: νωμῶν διδακτά τε ἄρρητά τ'), in which case
there is a close connection between the end of the scene and the beginning of the stasimon.

that in dismissing Oedipus' guilt for lack of motive they make the false assumption that the killer must have acted knowingly and deliberately.

It is reasonable to compare the subjects of the scene with the themes which the chorus treat in the first stasimon. Teiresias declared that Oedipus murdered Laius; Oedipus accused Teiresias of plotting with Creon to overthrow him; Teiresias stated that the day will reveal Oedipus' birth (438) and then described the murderer and his horrible fortune (449–460). Of these four statements, Oedipus' accusation of the usurpation plot is one of the most shocking, but it is an empty guess. No evidence of any sort is introduced in support of it, and the chorus ignore it totally. The remaining three, Teiresias' statements, may be considered to have some basis in fact, for the chorus' reverence for the seer borders on worship. To them, he is like Phoebus himself (284–285), godlike (298); in him alone of mortals is Truth (298–299).[30] His pronouncements would therefore merit serious consideration. They ignore the minor and personal question of Oedipus' birth and discuss only the civically important topics—the nature of the guilty man and the accusation against the king. Thus in their "selection" of subjects the chorus appear to abjure mere speculation in favor of evidence and individual personal matters in favor of those which concern the welfare of the whole state.

In the kommos (649–697) that follows the confrontation between Creon and Oedipus, the chorus continue to express their concern for the welfare of the city and to minimize less relevant, personal matters (665–668, 685–686). Of the two chief dramatic effects of the passage, one is to display to its fullest the chorus' reliance on reason, evidence, and common sense. They support their intercession on Creon's behalf with sound and sensible reasons: Creon has not previously behaved foolishly, and now has bound himself by a great oath (652–653). The stated principle on which their argument is based is consistent with both their piety and their practical logic: unproved rumor is insufficient ground for disregarding the evidence of an oath (656–657). The other effect is to demonstrate that Oedipus, despite his personal difficulties and errors, does not become the unjust and selfishly blind ruler that Creon does in *Antigone*. He continues

---

30. McDevitt's conclusion that the chorus are being impious in rejecting Teiresias (*C&M* 30 [1969], 87), despite their affirmation of the gods' true knowledge, is based on the untenable notion that "one cannot reject prophets without rejecting . . . religion." But that is precisely what Sophocles makes the chorus do, and he gives no reason for the audience to suppose that they are "impious" to do so.

to merit the respect of the citizens and to respect their advice. Although Iocasta also pleads for Creon (646–648), Oedipus does not yield Creon's life directly to her or even to Creon himself, but rather to the chorus of citizens (671–672: "for it is your words, not his, that move me"). But the poet does not end the matter there; Oedipus continues to insist that Creon and Teiresias are plotting against him (701, 705–706). It is not the act of a tyrant, but of a just and selfless ruler, to yield to the wishes of the citizens even though he believes that in so doing his own power, even his life (669), will continue to be in danger.[31]

The chorus' selection of subjects from the previous scene is of great im-

---

31. Oedipus does later say to Iocasta that he honors her more than "these men" (700), but this is only in answer to her request for information after the chorus have advised putting an end to further discussion. McDevitt (C&M 30 [1969], 81n7) supposes that at 689ff., "Oedipus is yielding to Iocasta, not the chorus." But it is the chorus who have just been pleading with him at length, not Iocasta.

Indeed, it is almost universally assumed that the chorus have gained such ascendancy in this scene that at lines 678–679 they are asking Iocasta to lead Oedipus into the house: γύναι, τί μέλλεις κομίζειν δόμων τόνδ' ἔσω. This interpretation supposes that the chorus believe Oedipus is exceedingly disturbed, even unstrung (cf. both Jebb and Kamerbeek, ad loc.). Yet there is no other possible indication in the text that Oedipus is perceptibly emotionally agitated or even incapacitated (hence Vellacott [G&R 14 (1967), 113–114] assumes that he is visibly "trembling and out of control"), nor that the chorus want him to leave. On the contrary, it is only the chorus who speak with the agitated tones of lyric meters, while Oedipus replies in iambic trimeters (except for one "iambic dimeter," 651); and it is likely that the chorus would prefer Oedipus to stay and work on the problems of state rather than withdraw for personal reasons. Without some further explanation, it would be difficult for the audience to understand why the chorus should for one moment suddenly become so dominant and patronizing that they want Iocasta to hustle Oedipus offstage for some unexplained cause. But it would be easy to suppose that they are asking the woman why she does not go back into the house now that she is no longer needed. If Creon were to exit to the palace, τόνδ' would certainly refer to him: "why do you not go inside with Creon?" But he has most probably exited down the parodos from which he entered, as he must have done earlier; cf. 515, 532–535, 672, 676, which strongly indicate that Creon is not a resident of the palace. (Thus 637 may refer to two different houses, as most assume; but at 288 Κρέοντος εἰπόντος cannot then mean "on Creon's advice," as Jebb, Kamerbeek, and Dawe interpret, ad loc. Oedipus and Creon have not conversed since Creon's departure, so that the phrase must be temporal: "after Creon spoke [i.e., delivered his message].") The easiest solution is to fully emend L's δόμον τόνδ' to δόμων τῶνδ' (cf. El. 39–40: μόλων . . . δόμων ἔσω τῶνδ'), and to interpret κομίζειν as intransitive, "go" or "betake oneself." Cf. Oed. Col. 589, where that meaning would (despite Jebb's disdain of it and Ellendt's denial) certainly suit the context. It may be regarded as equivalent to the usage at Ant. 444: κομίζοις ἄν σεαυτόν, with ellipsis of the reflexive pronoun. Thus the chorus of Oed. Tyr. are asking, "Madam, why do you not go [back] inside the house?" (The same interpretation suits the ἐσκομίζετε of Oed. Tyr. 1429 better than the notion that Creon spends eight lines admonishing silent extras; and the plurals addressed to Oedipus would echo the plurals that Oedipus has just used of himself at 1404ff.)

portance in considering the next stasimon (863ff.), a song which seemingly admits of so many interpretations that it has gained considerable critical notoriety. The many attempts to show that in their remarks on *hybris* the chorus (or Sophocles) are unequivocally (or allusively) condemning Oedipus (or Iocasta) have been ably and persistently refuted.[32] A more moderate view now generally prevails, that the chorus are expressing their fear for the future. Oedipus' behavior is not yet truly hubristic, but he seems to the chorus to be in danger of becoming so, either because of his inclination to disregard oracles or because of his recent arrogance toward Creon and Teiresias.[33] But the chorus are alone on the scene (861–862), with no suggestion that they can be overheard. Surely if they mean to refer to a specific person, there is no reason why they could not do so now. They have been quite outspoken thus far, with no sign of the fear of power that restrained the chorus of *Antigone*. Thus the poet gives the audience no reason to assume that the chorus are making furtive allusions to some particular character.

Nor has the poet given the audience any cause to expect the chorus to select and comment upon particular events in the preceding scene. The chorus have long since dismissed the quarrel between Creon and Oedipus as settled and irrelevant to the matters of state which require immediate attention (681–682, 685–686). Oedipus' past history is just the sort of personal matter that they have consistently eschewed. As to the possibility that Oedipus may have killed Laius, they warned against speculation without evidence when they told Oedipus to have hope until he should discover additional facts (834–835); directly after that, Oedipus presented the fact that he was alone, whereas the witness reported Laius was attacked by a group. Since Iocasta at once insists that everyone heard the witness say this, presumably including the chorus, who have also reported earlier that they heard the story of a group of killers (292), the scene ends with the case against Oedipus fairly well disproved as far as the characters onstage are

32. See Kitto's excellent arguments (*Poiesis*, 224–226) against such readings; cf. also Burton (*The Chorus*, 161–162).

33. Kamerbeek (commentary, 172–173) suggests that the chorus are afraid that if Oedipus should discover that he is himself the murderer, and if he should then follow Iocasta's lead in disregarding oracles, his *hybris* would become tyranny. In Winnington-Ingram's view (*JHS* 91 [1971], 133), the chorus see Oedipus heading in the direction of abuse of power. He (and somewhat similarly Müller, *Hermes* 95 [1967], 269–291) postulates an earlier Aeschylean version, in which Oedipus was guilty, which Sophocles introduces via the chorus in order to disprove it during the course of the play.

concerned. It would be strange if this chorus, always so careful and logical, should proceed to speculate anew on the question.

It is not at all surprising, on the other hand, that the chorus begin the song with a statement of faith, given their earlier prayers, their reliance upon the gods, and their statements of faith in the Delphic oracle. The audience may at once begin to suspect the chorus will discuss the new religious problem of the validity of oracles. The first strophe ends with a confirmation of the divine and eternal nature (872) of the High Laws of the universe; but the chorus do not define or specify these laws so as to lead the audience to think of any one (or more) of the actions that have been discussed or committed in the play so far. Then the antistrophe begins with *hybris*, which must surely have been understood as the breaking of the High Laws. This behavior, this vice, the chorus personify; they do not speak of the man who commits *hybris* but of the vice itself, the arrogant disregard of the High Laws that brings with it general destruction, although the struggle that benefits the general good is welcome (879–881).[34] They claim to rely upon divine leadership (882). In this context, their meaning would seem obvious: *hybris* is bad for the city, but certain rivalry is good; the god must distinguish between them, striking down the bad but letting the useful continue.

The chorus go on to explain this more fully in the second strophe (883–896). If someone commits hubristic deeds—again they do not specify the particular deeds, and again they assume such acts would be committed voluntarily—they pray that he may be punished. For if he is not, that is, if the gods allow the High Laws to be broken with impunity, then there is no safety anywhere and no reason for religious observation. The chorus fear it is possible that the gods might cease punishing wickedness. Step by step the chorus reach, in the final antistrophe (897–910), the reason for their fear: the process of the disintegration of religion, of the gods' shirking their responsibilities, has already begun. Iocasta has just shown that the oracle about Laius' death has not come true; with this evidence the chorus can only conclude that there is grave danger that oracular pro-

34. On the famous and still puzzling phrase ὕβρις φυτεύει τύραννον (873), Winnington-Ingram (*JHS* 91 [1971], 126) persuasively argues that it cannot rightly be understood as pejorative. Still, Blaydes' conjecture ὕβριν φυτεύει τυραννίς, which he and others accept, is not wholly satisfactory because the specific notion of kingship is never alluded to anywhere else in the general statements that constitute this ode. There has not yet been proposed a suitable emendation that could produce a more general, and negative, statement such as "*Hybris* destroys society," which would suit the tone of the ode and would not leave the audience wondering what the chorus were getting at.

nouncements in general have ceased to be reliable. These men, who have recently had to decide that seercraft is not as reliable as they thought it was, are now forced by circumstances to another decision: "No longer will I go with reverence [i.e., belief] to the great oracular seats—Delphi, Abae, Olympia—if they [902: τάδε] are not going to give accurate predictions that suit the facts in every case. Look to this, O Zeus, for already the oracles about Laius have been proved wrong and therefore set aside; hence the worship of Apollo and indeed all religion is beginning to wane."[35] These conclusions follow naturally from the chorus' previous attitudes about religion and the logical pattern of their reasoning as displayed in the previous scene. These practical men are not foolishly praying that Zeus will make the oracles of the past come true, but rather that he will restore the gods' credibility by preventing the utterance of false oracles in the future. Such is the sequence of ideas that the audience would most easily hear as this song proceeds.

At the same time, it has long been recognized that the listener could not possibly miss the tremendous ironies in the ode. At this point in the play, the audience has all the information needed to know that the chorus' wishes will be fulfilled, but in a way that they would never imagine or want. Somehow it will be shown that oracles will become reliable again because they never were false and that the gods will bring down *hybris*—not merely the voluntary kind that the chorus fear, but an involuntary kind that they have never imagined. The irony is particularly ingenious and terrible because it results from the general principles of religious belief, rather than mere personal joy, which the chorus espouse in all ignorance but which the audience then applies to the specific circumstances, so as to react with horror. The placing of the ode is crucial to the maintenance of the dramatic tension. The audience is surely expecting what will happen when the witness arrives. The poet must prevent the slackening of tension and the sense of anticlimax that would naturally accompany an action which the audience has been expecting; unless, of course, he deliberately

---

35. As this paraphrase indicates, there are problems of translation in the passage, but there are also reasonable solutions. It is far more likely that the deictic pronoun τάδε refers to the things that the chorus have just mentioned—oracular seats, χρηστήρια—than to the oracles about Laius or Oedipus (as is commonly supposed; cf., e.g., Jebb and Dawe, *ad loc.*), which have not yet been mentioned in the song. Χειρόδεικτα, since it is hapax here, is uncertain in any case; it could be predicate to τάδε, or be the object of ἁρμόσει. There is no reason for calling φθίνοντα "proleptic predicative adjunct ('so that they wane')" (Kamerbeek), rather than causal "because they waste away, [men] set them aside"; when an oracle goes unfulfilled because it is proved wrong, it can surely be said to "decay" or "pass away."

fosters the audience's expectations in order to cheat them, as in the post-
ponements of Ajax's expected suicide. It would be repetitious here for the
chorus to speculate on the facts: Did Oedipus kill Laius? Will he kill his
father and marry his mother? If they were, on the other hand, to condemn
him or Iocasta for foolishly scoffing at oracles, the audience would simply
nod in agreement and continue, perhaps with fading interest, to expect the
obvious. Sophocles has therefore given the chorus a song whose ironies
will generate such a feeling of horror, and pity for the chorus, that it must
engage the audience's full attention and participation.

The ode achieves a dramatic effect very similar to that produced by joy-
before-disaster odes, the most famous of which Sophocles now employs
before the final unraveling of the plot. In that third stasimon (1086–1109),
the purveyors of logic and common sense have been seduced by Oedipus'
confidence into an expression of wild and unsubstantiated speculation.
Even in their unusual indulgence in illusion, however, they retain their
basic characteristics of civic and religious concern. They rejoice at the idea
that Oedipus will prove to be a native Theban; and as the mountain is his
nurse and mother, so a god of the land may well be Oedipus' father. But
this foray into the realm of hope and speculation is a new venture for the
chorus and one that makes the coming descent into ruin all the more
precipitous.[36]

Disaster comes swiftly, for the chorus as well as for the principals. In
their ode following the terrible discovery of the truth (1186–1222), their
reaction is chiefly a horrified pity; they do not condemn Oedipus, but neither do they express loving compassion. They bewail his fate as it affects
them, the Thebans whose savior Oedipus once was and who now are also
cast down by his fall. In their anapests and kommos with Oedipus (1297ff.),
the chorus' sympathy seems rather impersonal, as their horror and curiosity vie with each other. But this kommos does not have nearly the metrical contrast of Creon's kommos in *Antigone*, where he utters a significant
amount of lyric while the chorus are given only iambic trimeters. Here the

36. Some find the ode too inconsistent with the chorus' previous behavior. Burton, for
example, notes that they do not take warning from what they have heard, especially from the
Corinthian Messenger, whose speech ought to have given them "at least an inkling of the
truth" (*The Chorus*, 169–170). He concludes that the poet has temporarily ignored their dramatic character. A change in behavior, however, is not necessarily an inconsistency in character. The chorus are here only following Oedipus' confident interpretation (1076–1083); they
know no more than he, so why should they be expected to be wiser than he? The fact that
here, at last, the civic-minded chorus have been led into speculation about personal matters
only heightens the dramatic irony.

first strophic pair consists largely of iambic trimeters distributed equally between Oedipus and the chorus (1317–1320, 1325–1328); in the second pair, Oedipus has much more lyric, but he does speak an iambic trimeter (1335, 1355) just before the chorus speak, and the chorus' utterances consist solely of an "iambic dimeter" but no trimeters (1336, 1356). The effect is of more controlled passion than in *Antigone,* and of agreement rather than of contrast. For Oedipus and the chorus do indeed agree: it were better he had never been born. The chorus continue to maintain their commonsense attitude, as they counsel Oedipus to wait for Creon's advice (1416–1418), but they are not in the same position as the chorus of *Antigone.* Their king has never acted against their better judgment, nor had to turn to them for help, and at the end of *Oedipus Tyrannus* it is not the chorus but Creon who admonishes and commands the chastened king (1515ff.).[37]

This chorus plainly have multiple functions in the structure of the drama. On the technical level they are exceedingly important, perhaps vital, to the poet's purpose. This is the most static of Sophocles' extant dramas. Almost no action occurs until the suicide and self-mutilation at the end of the play. There are considerably fewer entrances and exits than in *Antigone* or *Ajax,* and no offstage action of any kind—no homicides, burials, battles, poisoned robes, or kidnappings—and certainly no suspense about the outcome of the play. Yet *Oedipus Tyrannus* remains, in the opinion of many, the greatest of the surviving tragedies, because of Sophocles' consummate skill as a dramatist.

Part of his technique is the well-known *Dreigespräch,* the dialogue among three characters that is used here in successively more complex scenes: first Creon-Oedipus-Iocasta, then the more intricate patterns of Messenger-Iocasta-Oedipus, then finally the famous Oedipus-Messenger-Herdsman. The crowdlike effects of the *Dreigespräch* are supported and sustained by the constant participation of the chorus, not merely in their numerous odes but their involvement in every scene of this play, whether they introduce it, speak during it, or both. The chorus-leader never simply announces an arrival, but always engages in some dialogue with

37. Upon Creon's arrival they appear to cease speaking entirely. Even if the final disputed lines (1524–1530) are assigned to the chorus, they are not addressing Oedipus. Dawe's mordant evaluation of the passage (*Studies,* 266–273) provides evidence to support the widespread feeling—indeed, hope—that the lines are spurious (although his argument that this would be the only instance in tragedy of a break in the dramatic illusion ignores the possibility that the chorus [or chorus-leader] may address themselves; cf. Burton, *The Chorus,* 183–184).

one of the characters at the beginning of a scene. The chorus-leader is also given some interjection during every duologue, thus continuously generating triangular patterns of speech right up to the short, brutal exchange between Oedipus and the Herdsman. Even that scene begins with the chorus' identification of the Herdsman, although the poet quickly reduces the scene to a contest of two stubborn souls. Indeed, the chorus function largely as a third actor in duologue scenes, and as a fourth in the Creon-Oedipus-Iocasta scene, with its central kommos involving all three actors and the chorus, both leader and full lyric chorus, and serving as a transition that brilliantly unites two disparate episodes into a single scene.

It is of course the chorus' dramatic character as advisors to, almost colleagues of, the king that enables them to assist the progression of the drama in such fashion. But Sophocles further uses their character to establish, by contrast, aspects of Oedipus' character. He seems to have deliberately contrasted the chorus' plodding common sense with Oedipus' brilliant intuition, their caution with the king's bold passion, thus giving him a character appropriate to a man who would recklessly strive for knowledge and then blind himself rather than commit suicide. This is not to say that the chorus' behavior is in any way a moral judgment on Oedipus, for their approach to knowledge is in the end no more valid than his, and the outcome is perhaps more unexpected and shocking to them than it is to him. But neither do they seem to be merely the small men whose inadequacy points up the greatness of the hero. They draw the same conclusion that Oedipus does—that Teiresias should be consulted; and in the matter of Creon, their judgment is correct and Oedipus' wrong. The chorus are not so much inferior to Oedipus as different, and this difference is used to produce a definition of Oedipus' character vital to the plot of the drama: he is the sort of man who, without being a villain or a maniac, could single-handedly kill six men, solve the riddle of the Sphinx unaided, defy the prophet's dire threats and discover the secret of his own birth, and at last repeatedly stab his own eyes.

Equally significant to the drama is the chorus' function as representatives of the city and citizenry of Thebes, for they present the public aspect of the story of Oedipus the king. The prologue establishes the fact that Oedipus is the most honored man in Thebes, venerated by the suppliants—and priests—particularly for his ability to deal with matters involving the influence of the gods (34, 38–39, 42–43). But it is the chorus of Thebans who stress Oedipus' achievements as a man, who emphasize his actions as a benefactor of the city. Their attitude is not one of religious awe, but of respect for and trust in a great statesman. Nowhere do they give the slightest hint that their support of Oedipus is the result of fear or coercion; indeed, the presentation of Oedipus as a chosen king and the chorus' insistence on their own loyalty to him because of his past service to the state contain some implication that they could, if they wished, withdraw their support of him or even set him aside (689–696). Moreover, the relations between ruler and citizen in this play are reciprocal: Oedipus respects their advice, most notably in the matter of Creon's alleged treason. Through the chorus Sophocles presents the broader tragedy of the king of Thebes. The chorus' own loyalty is to Oedipus as the king, and it is their duty, when Oedipus' view begins to shift from his public responsibility to his private fate, to remind both him and the audience of the consequences for the state (406–407, 665–667, 685–686, 879–881, 1416–1418). It is truly as the representatives of the body politic that they say, at the end of their final ode (1220–1222), "from you I drew breath [of life] and through you I have closed my eyes [in death]."

In *Oedipus Coloneus* we seem to have another chorus of civic elders subordinate to a king and we may perhaps expect them to perform one or another of the political functions for which the Theban Elders were used. Certainly they are far more involved in the structure of the drama than the chorus of *Antigone;* and even the chorus of *Oedipus Tyrannus* do not have half the number of kommoi that the poet has given to the Elders of Colonus. The parodos itself is an elaborate kommos involving the chorus and two actors. The chorus have another kommos with Oedipus (510–548), two more that they share with two actors (833–886, 1670–1750), and a further series of stanzas, separated by brief passages of dialogue between two actors, that has much of the effect of a kommos (1447–1499). In addition, they sing no fewer than four odes (668–719, 1044–1095, 1211–1248, 1556–1578). They are also involved in dialogue scenes to a greater extent than any other chorus in Sophocles, whether they actually speak or are only addressed or mentioned by the principals. During the first confrontation between Creon and Oedipus (720–821), for example, although the chorus speak but once (726–727), they are addressed by Creon at some length (728–739) and are referred to by both Creon and Oedipus (783, 811–815). Indeed, there is only one episode of significant length in which they neither speak nor are spoken of, but that one is a *Dreigespräch* that is the most emotional scene of the play: Oedipus' reunion with his daughters and the announcement of Polyneices' presence (1096–1210).

The rich structural variety and the unusually large number, for Sophocles, of the chorus' utterances are concomitant with a character that is suitably complex and yet as transparent as any in the extant plays of this poet. The chorus' entrance is prepared by two items of information. First, the Stranger's explanations prepare the audience to assume that the members of the chorus, although governed by Athens (67), are not residents of the city of Athens (78), but are local inhabitants, the namesakes of the local divinity Colonus (58–65), who have at least some autonomy of decision (79–80). Then Antigone remarks when she sees them approaching that they are old men (111–112). Their advanced age is stressed again and again in the play and would therefore probably be evident in their appearance. The chorus' costume would also immediately identify for the audience another aspect of their persona that is later indicated by the text: they are not simple peasants but well-born locals (728); in fact, the "Lords of the land" (831). We may wonder whether, among other reasons, Sophocles chose to set the play in Colonus so that he might have such a chorus of elderly "gentry" without introducing the politically awkward concept of a feudal nobility in democratic Athens (and perhaps also because a kidnapping could not reasonably be supposed to occur within the city of Athens itself).[38]

These are the basic physical aspects of the chorus' role that are apparent even before they speak. Next, in the parodos (117ff.), the poet presents important aspects of their personality, the first of which is their piety. They enter with a strong tone of hostility, but their hostility is directed against Oedipus as the reputed desecrater of a holy place, so holy that they themselves customarily avert their eyes in silence as they pass it (125–133). The initial tension created by these jealous defenders of sanctity is, however, abated by their compassion, for as soon as they perceive Oedipus' blindness, they pity him (150–152) and offer to help him avoid religious pollution (153–154). This balance of piety and compassion in their character is carefully maintained; they are not religious bigots, but rather honest men

---

38. Contrary to the clear indications in the text (79–80, 728, 831), Burton calls the old men of Colonus "simple countrymen" (*The Chorus*, 295). He also interprets line 145, τῆσδ' ἔφοροι χώρας, as "guardians of this place," claiming that the chorus are in charge of the sacred grove (251). But χώρα most commonly means "land," "country," rather than "spot" (χῶρος). Ellendt, *s.vv.*, maintains the distinction throughout Sophocles. Although ἔφορος is hapax in Sophocles, its use at Aesch., *Pers.* 25 (referring to the kingly leaders of the Persian army), and its magisterial connotations (cf. LSJ, *s.v.*) strongly suggest that this chorus of ἄνακτες (831) are not simply the custodians of the grove but are meant to be perceived as the local nobility subordinate to the king in the city.

faced with a choice between holiness and kindness.[39] Although they firmly promise, out of compassion and a sense of justice, that no one will ever drive Oedipus away from the place (174–177), Sophocles places them in the moral dilemma of having to order him away at once when they learn his identity, lest he pollute the land (226–236). Then Antigone's passionate plea causes them to weaken in their resolve and to admit their perplexity honestly: they pity the wanderers' misfortunes, but fear τὰ δ' ἐκ θεῶν (254–257). They are reasonable men: when Oedipus argues that to turn him away would be in itself an impiety (276–277), they are content to resolve their conflict by referring it to higher authorities (292–295).

But the poet does not end here the chorus' involvement in this problem. They witness the meeting of Ismene and Oedipus, they hear Ismene's news of events in Thebes and the new oracles, they hear Oedipus' tale of suffering at the hands of his own sons. When he appeals to them at the end of this series of woes (457–460), they are again moved by compassion and offer him the help of religion, to appease the deities whose sanctuary he violated. The subsequent description of the ritual that must be performed, which has often been called irrelevant, is most impressive when viewed in proper dramatic context. The chorus' piety and reverent conduct have been heavily stressed in the play thus far; now they behave as knowledgeable priests, directing each detail of the sacrifice with solemn imperatives and framing the great prayer to the Eumenides for safety (486–487). It is as if the ritual were being performed before us, as if the chorus themselves have the authority to purify Oedipus. The audience would feel that the chorus make a right and reverent decision when they say that, if Oedipus will do this, they can and will stand by him (490–491).

Still, we may ask what the dramatic function of this elaborate ritual is, since it is never mentioned again. Surely it is not just to get Ismene offstage so that she can be captured by Creon. The instructions are given to Oedipus in the second person singular imperative; the substitution of Ismene is only made at the end of the scene. During the description of the ritual, the audience would suppose that Oedipus was about to do all these

---

39. Errandonea (*Sófocles* [1958], 61–83, esp. 82–83) sees their piety as superstition, which he considers part of their characterization as a historically genuine type, the well-known canny old Colonean sons of the soil with whose tricks Sophocles was only too familiar. They are determined, in his view, to keep Oedipus' promised benefits in their own land by every means at their disposal. To this end even the ode on old age is directed: the chorus are trying to prevent Oedipus from yielding to "the seductive temptation of going to reign in Thebes with Polyneices" (82)!

things and make this prayer. When Ismene leaves, it is not necessary to the plot that a lyric occur to pass the dramatic time while the ritual is being performed, since the performance will not be reported or even mentioned again. A messenger or another character could therefore enter at once and continue the story, yet Sophocles pauses to insert a lyric passage, a kommos (510–550). We may reasonably conjecture that the audience, being used to the fact that dramatic time passes with lyrics, would assume that the ritual was being performed during the kommos, and that there might even be some reference to it at the end of the lyric "interlude." The content of the kommos which the audience hears should therefore be considered in light of the assumption the audience is intended to make about the action, since it is likely that the kommos would function more than merely to characterize the chorus as rudely inquisitive.[40] While the audience supposes that a propitiatory, expiatory sacrifice to the Eumenides is being conducted nearby in Oedipus' name, to cleanse him from the guilt of his recent action, it hears the chorus catechize Oedipus about his earlier, graver sins, exactly the sort of sins for which the Furies pursue a man, even as they pursued Orestes, whom Apollo also sent to Athens to be saved from them. Oedipus defends his actions on the grounds of ignorance (the same cause of his trespassing on the sacred grove) and declares himself νόμῳ καθαρός (548). The chorus do not deny this defense, and soon they support his plea to Theseus (629–630). It sounds, indeed, as if they now believe that he is no longer a dangerous pollution that will bring ill to the land, as he clearly was before (235–236). In fact, the whole matter of ritual purification is never mentioned again. Thus by inference the question of Oedipus' original guilt, and hence his possible religious pollution of the

40. To some, the chorus' questioning seems impolite, even offensive; in this view, the function of the kommos is to point a contrast between the attitudes of the lowly chorus and of noble Theseus, between the hero's "unquestioning acceptance" of Oedipus and the chorus' "timid prurience" (cf. Knox, *Heroic Temper*, 152, and Burian, *Phoenix* 28 [1974], 414–415). Of course, there is some sense of a contrast in behavior, but it is hardly so detrimental to the chorus as is claimed. At this point in the drama, some explanation of Oedipus' past "crimes" should be given to the audience and to the other characters who have not known Oedipus before. Thus far the chorus have only implied that they recognize Oedipus' name by its terrible repute, and Oedipus has spoken to them of his past acts in only the most general terms (266–274). The information must be elicited, and questions are livelier than speeches, but only if they are asked once and not repeated. It would be a marked failure of dramatic economy for Theseus to question Oedipus all over again when the chorus have already done so. But if it were Theseus, rather than the chorus, who questioned Oedipus first, should we then call the chorus "heroic" for not questioning him later?

land, is resolved not by the authority of Theseus, who never mentions it, but by the old men of Colonus themselves.[41]

The poet now endows these pious and compassionate men with other admirable characteristics. When it has been decided that Oedipus must stay in Colonus, the chorus most generously welcome him to their land with a song setting forth all the beauties of the place. They sing of an abundantly fruitful land, blessed by the gifts of the gods and graced with their very presence (678–680, 691–693). It must have been a particularly impressive scene for the audience to behold: these well-dressed and prosperous Elders are offering an earthly paradise to the dirty, blind, ragged wanderer. From this point forward, the chorus are firmly loyal in their commitment to Oedipus (726–727) and valiant in defending him against those who would remove him. Indeed, there is a suggestion in the rapid antilabe of the kidnapping scene that the chorus make at least a token attempt at physically restraining Creon (836–837, 856–857). It is especially to be noticed that the chorus never criticize Oedipus' actions or his temper. The closest that they ever come to urging moderation is to ask only that Oedipus reply to Polyneices, for Theseus' sake (1346–1347); and when Oedipus then curses his son passionately, the chorus, far from disapproving, back him up by ordering Polyneices away at once with distinctly unfriendly words (1397–1398). All in all, the Elders of Colonus seem to possess all the civic and human virtues that one could ask for in a fellow countryman. Certainly the poet has taken pains to display such traits in this chorus as he never added to the otherwise politically respectable chorus of *Oedipus Tyrannus*.

These virtues are all presented in terms of the chorus' relation to Oedipus. They cleanse him with their piety, aid him with their compassion and generosity, and protect him with their loyalty and valor. The intimate

---

41. At the end of the "courtroom scene" between Oedipus and Creon (939–1043), Oedipus feels himself pure enough to call upon "these goddesses" (1010) to be his allies. Then the chorus, not Theseus, render the judgment that he is "worthy" (1014: χρηστός). There is no hint of any need for ritual absolution. When at 1132 Oedipus refuses to touch Theseus, it is not because he carries a μίασμα, which brings real disaster with it (cf. *Oed. Tyr.* 241, 353), but because of his κηλίς. The word seems to have the simple sense of "dirty," "blemished," "stained," commonly used metaphorically of one's appearance as seen by the world. Cf. *Oed. Tyr.* 833: "rather than see such a stain upon myself"; 1138: "after revealing such a stain on myself, how could I look these people in the eye?" For the basic physical usage, cf. *El.* 446 and LSJ, *s.v.* Because of the enormity of his misfortunes, Oedipus, though blameless, continues to appear "dirty" in human society, but without religious pollution (cf. 287).

relation between the hero and the chorus is further defined and sustained
by their old age, which the poet emphasizes throughout the play and
which he uses to achieve a stunning dramatic effect, the alliance of the old.
For Oedipus is also an old man, and much is made of his consequent
feebleness. Creon, upon his arrival, at once stresses the fact that he, too, is
an old man (733, 735). Then ensues the most physically violent conflict in
all of Sophocles' extant plays. Yet despite the participation of Creon's servants, the conflict is waged essentially by the aged: the sly, old Creon is
attacking the old and helpless Oedipus, who is defended by his aged allies
(815). Theseus comes to the rescue in the end, but the actual battle of
young men takes place entirely offstage. That battle, however, is presented
dramatically by the old men of the chorus, in an ode that suggests the chorus
regret they cannot join in the fray themselves (1044, 1081–1084). The visual effect of these combinations of old age and violence, both actual and
anticipated, must have been singularly impressive. Moreover, this display
does not culminate the poet's exploitation of the alliance of age with age:
when Oedipus reacts harshly to the announcement of Polyneices' supplication, the chorus sing their famous ode on the relentless sorrows of old age
(1211–1248). So great is the strength of the alliance of old men, so deep is
the chorus' understanding of Oedipus' suffering (1239), that they persuade
the audience that Oedipus is not simply being stubborn and querulous in
refusing to see his son, but has truly been dealt another blow by the storm
of troubles that beats down old age and ends at last in death. If such words
were sung by young men, they would be far less convincing; only those
who have endured long life can say with authority that not to be born is
best (1224).[42]

The poet has closely associated the chorus with Oedipus through their
age and behavior; and through their behavior he has also associated them
with reality and truth. After the chorus' initial, and very brief, misconcep-

---

42. Linforth ("Religion and Drama") rightly observes that the ode serves to elicit
sympathy for Oedipus. The extent of this sympathy is, however, somewhat disputed; see
Winnington-Ingram (*Sophocles*, 256ff.) on Oedipus' wrath and the theme of retaliation. On
his cursing his son, see Easterling (*PCPhS* 13 [1967], 1–13). Although modern readers may
feel that the scene between Antigone and her doomed brother must arouse our pity for Polyneices, it is hard to believe that Sophocles was trying to elicit the sympathy of a late-fifth-
century Athenian audience when he created a man who, for the sake of his pride (because his
brother laughs at him, 1422–1423), is going not only to invade his homeland with a foreign
army but to deceive his men and knowingly send them to certain death (1427–1430). If anything, Sophocles has contrasted the sister's filial affection and patriotism with the brother's
stubborn vanity and selfishness.

tion of Oedipus' position, they never make another mistake in their perception of the dramatic situation. There are no unfounded predictions here, no terrible ironies of well-reasoned misjudgment, such as in the second stasimon of *Oedipus Tyrannus,* no joy-before-disaster odes. Nor do the chorus have any bad characteristics or engage in deception even for self-preservation; these men are unreservedly honest and forthright. Thus their support of Oedipus has obvious political implications: the apparently unclean wanderer is accepted not just by the king, Theseus, but by a faultless group of "good citizens."

The chorus' role has a still more noticeable function in the drama; they are not only deeply involved in the action, but actually perform most of it. It is they who direct the sacrifice that will purify Oedipus; Theseus makes him a citizen after they testify to his intentions, indeed acting almost as his sponsor (629–630, 637); and then they are put in charge of him (638–639, 653). It is they, not the king, who formally welcome Oedipus to the land (668–719); they defend him against his enemies; they summon Theseus to help against Creon (884–886) and again when the thunder signals that Oedipus' time has come (1491–1499). They present, through their vivid description, the battle scene (1044–1095), and it is possible that they serve to simulate the theatrical effects of the thunder and lightning. Although a thunder machine of some sort—a sheet of metal struck with a padded stick, or a revolving drum containing stones—could have been used, such devices would tend to rumble on for a few moments after the loudest peal, so that the chorus would have to pause before continuing the song. The lightning flashes that are clearly supposed to accompany the numerous peals of thunder (1467, 1514–1515) would have been quite impossible to reproduce. But the desired effect could have been conveyed by the chorus' sudden cries (cf. 1456), and by their apparently frantic lyric interruptions (note the extended sequence of short syllables at 1462ff.), describing the noise and flash and loudly invoking Zeus, that are interspersed with the iambic trimeter dialogue between Oedipus and Antigone. It is as if during the thunder-stanzas (1461–1471, 1477–1485) the chorus are speaking entirely apart from, almost unaware of, the actors; this situation could create the effect of a natural phenomenon contrasting with the conversation of mortals. The same technical device—the sound of fifteen voices describing a terrifying event as it happens, together with appropriate cries and music—could easily serve to achieve the effect of the earthquake in Euripides' *Bacchae,* or the hero's offstage cries that, like the thunder at Colonus, are first perceived by the chorus in *Philoctetes.*

Finally, Theseus goes off with Oedipus to the place of his death, but when the principals have departed, the audience hears the chorus solemnly commending Oedipus to the gods of the Underworld (1556–1578). In everything they do and say, they act as representatives of the land and all its people. They are carefully distinguished from the city-dwellers in Athens (78). They are not the king's councillors, as are the Elders of Thebes, yet at the same time they are not common folk or simple peasants (728). Rather, they are the inhabitants and guardians of the land itself (145, 728, 831, 871), a land that is holy and blessed by the gods, the home of the Eumenides, the very root and strength of holy Athens. Theseus the king is the political authority, but he comes and goes; the men of Colonus remain, and summon him at their need as they summon the people and armed might of the land (841–843, 884–886), for the true authority is theirs. Theseus and Oedipus act and converse as heroic individuals, but the chorus embody the land that defends the suppliant Oedipus and that will ultimately benefit from him.

PART III

Women

CHAPTER 5

Trachiniae

Since the extant corpus of Greek tragedy represents only a small fraction of the total that was produced by the three great tragedians, it is impossible to draw statistically significant comparisons between authors. Nevertheless, it is worth noting that the surviving tragedies of both Aeschylus and Euripides nearly all have a female chorus (five of Aeschylus' seven, and fourteen of Euripides' seventeen), whereas the chorus is made up of women in only two of Sophocles' seven, *Trachiniae* and *Electra*. If we were to succumb to the temptation to speculate on the significance of these figures, we might imagine that a chorus of high-range voices would have been musically more useful to the poet, as a lyrical instrument, than the limited range of "mature male" voices.[1] Or, perhaps, because Sophocles was so greatly concerned with the conflicts between the individual and society, a chorus of men would have provided a more political setting and scope than could a group of women, who would best perform a limited, lyrical function in association with a female principal.

The latter explanation could readily fit *Trachiniae,* in many ways the most puzzling of Sophocles' plays. It is named for a chorus who speak only four lines during the last quarter of the play. Deianeira, on whose action the plot depends, also seems to vanish from consideration after her death. She and her husband Heracles never even meet during the course of the drama, a circumstance which has given rise to a brisk controversy over which is the hero of the play, or whether indeed there is a hero at all. And although the action, filled with monsters, oracles, and magic, is deeply concerned with the cause of Heracles' destruction, there is hardly the

---

1. It seems reasonable to assume that women's voices would have been represented in the chorus either by boys or by adult tenors.

slightest hint of the deification which, according to tradition, immediately followed. Such perplexing problems have naturally generated a wide variety of critical opinion that includes the notions that Deianeira is guilty of premeditated murder, that the play has no theme or essential point but is merely "high melodrama," and that it was not even written by Sophocles.[2] In view of all these problems and seeming anomalies, perhaps it is not surprising that no attempt has been made to focus attention on the eponymous chorus.

The Trachinian women are clearly defined for the audience as young and unmarried, especially by Deianeira's first address to them at lines 141–152. She calls them ignorant of her troubles (143) and contrasts the carefree existence of maidenhood with the fearful responsibilities of marriage. One who had been through that change, she says, could understand her sufferings, clearly implying that these women have not yet achieved that unenviable state. The chorus later address themselves with the words ὦ παῖδες (821), and the Nurse uses the same phrase to them (871). It is true that they are never directly called παρθένοι, only γυναῖκες;[3] but the latter word with its iambic beginning may be metrically more suited to the iambic trimeter. Certainly the chorus of Euripides' *Electra* are called γυναῖκες far more often than παρθένοι, even though they are clearly maidens and are once, but only once, addressed as παρθένοι (761).

That the text indicates that the women of the chorus are unmarried is not in dispute; the question is whether the distinction between women and maidens was immediately and continually evident to the audience, and therefore presumably a significant factor in the drama. The answer lies, as it often does, in the lost treasure-house of visual evidence, in this case, the costumes of the chorus members. There does not seem to have been the clear distinction in Greece that there was in Rome between the dress of married and unmarried women, but there were some differences. In Athens the peplos was worn ungirded only by young (i.e., unmarried) women, but they did not always wear it thus. Long hair unbound and hanging down was worn exclusively by girls, but again was not their only style.[4] Hence it cannot be said with absolute certainty that this chorus

2. Errandonea (*Sófocles* [1958], 165ff., esp. 191; cf. *Sófocles* [1970], 221–224) propounds the first view, that Deianeira is a murderer; Waldock (*Sophocles*, 103), of course, the second; and Adams (*Sophocles*, 124–126), the last.

3. Except, perhaps, at line 1275 (see below, note 25). It is unlikely that they are addressing themselves at line 211, despite Jebb's contention (*ad* 205).

4. Cf. Margarete Bieber, *Griechische Kleidung* (Berlin, 1928), esp. 18 and 24; M. M. Evans, *Chapters on Greek Dress* (London, 1893), 65.

must have been particularly costumed as maidens, but the evidence on Greek dress indicates that they could have been so identified by their costume if the poet desired. In view of the dramatists' practice of immediately identifying the basic persona of each character, including the chorus, it is unusual that these maidens are not readily identifiable as such when they first speak. Their arrival has not in any way been prepared, nor do they describe themselves in the parodos, as do the chorus of *Philoctetes*. Yet Deianeira recognizes them at once as maidens (143ff.). It may be argued that they are not strangers, that she has seen them before and therefore already knows their status; but that is outside the play. The audience would be in ignorance and hence surprised at Deianeira's knowledge. We may therefore reasonably suppose that the chorus' costumes enabled the audience to perceive at once, before Deianeira's speech, that these are young, unmarried women, rather than merely women of indeterminate age and marital status.

The costumes would also contribute to a further aspect of the chorus' dramatic role that is prominent from the very beginning: their independent social position. They are not slaves or servants, or dependents of the household. Almost their first action is to reprove Deianeira strongly and without apology, in sharp contrast to the deferential humility of the Nurse (52–53). They respectfully call her ἄνασσα, but never use the more servile term δέσποινα, as both the Nurse and Lichas, the servant of Heracles, do (49, 409, 430, 434, 472). Deianeira has already defined her family's own status—exiles in a foreign land, guests of a stranger (39–40)—and the chorus women, natives of that land, are clearly of an independent if not equal station. This social autonomy manifests itself, as a natural consequence, in their independence of action. They have not been summoned but have come of their own accord in response to news of Deianeira's sorrow (103, 141); they burst out unasked with a condemnation of Lichas' apparent perfidy (383–384); and at the end of Deianeira's plea to Lichas they intrude into the conversation and bid Lichas obey her, presuming to assure him, with great solemnity, of both Deianeira's thanks and their own (470–471).

The chorus are, then, young and single, possessing a frankness born of their independent social position. In their parodos they also display the joyful exuberance and confident piety which are natural characteristics, as Deianeira points out, of the young. These traits with which the poet has endowed the chorus may be expected to have a direct bearing on their relations with the other characters of the drama, especially with Deianeira.

That relation in particular is invariably seen by critics as a close one. The chorus are said to be affectionately devoted to her and deeply sympathetic to her problems and worries. Their function is to act as her confidante, to reflect and illuminate her gentle, passive character.[5] They have even been alleged to represent an extension of her emotions and a link with her past, to stand for "the Deianeira that used to be, echoing her longings, her enthusiasms, and trepidations."[6] Much of this is seemingly confirmed by superficial observation. The chorus are women and thus have a natural affinity with Deianeira; they do receive her confidence; indeed, she is the only person in the whole play with whom they speak at length. But closer inspection of the chorus' words and actions may require an extensive modification of the customary view of their attitude toward Deianeira.

The prologue has already established the background of the story and the character of Deianeira. It is especially clear that she is a loving and anxious wife, yet dependent upon the advice and actions of others—of her husband, of her son, even of her servants. It has also established the fact that Deianeira has a valid reason for her anxiety: Heracles' fate will be determined in Euboea (76–77, 79–81). Even the casual Hyllus is stirred to action by this revelation (86–91). Then the chorus arrive; there has been no preparation for their arrival, nor do they begin their parodos by addressing anyone on the scene, particularly Deianeira. This situation is unusual, for in every other extant Sophoclean play, if someone is on the scene when the chorus arrive, they speak at once to that person. Only in *Oedipus Tyrannus* and *Antigone*, where the scenes are empty, do they fail to do so.[7] In the first antistrophe the Trachinians turn to Deianeira's own situation and describe, in the third person, her unhappiness, a description which

---

5. This view is almost universal; see, for examples, Dale (*Collected Papers*, 216), Reinhardt (*Sophokles*, 56), and Burton (*The Chorus*, 41–42, 84).

6. Musurillo (*TAPA* 92 [1961], 377).

7. In *Ajax* the chorus immediately address Ajax, although he is not even on the scene. It is possible that Deianeira exits at the end of the prologue and returns during or after the parodos. But there is no motivation in the text for these movements, nor would they appear to serve any particular dramatic purpose here (especially the unusual movement of an entrance during an ode). Burton (*The Chorus*, 44) suggests that Deianeira is absent until the end of the second strophe: had she been present during the first part of the ode, she ought to have answered the chorus' question about Heracles (94–102) in her speech; also, her first line (141) "would not be very natural" in view of the chorus' statements at 103. But in her speech she is responding to the larger part of the parodos, which follows the question and concerns Deianeira herself. Further, the echo of the chorus' πυνθάνομαι (103) in Deianeira's opening lines is not at all awkward; rather, it points a sharp contrast between the chorus' merely *hearing* of her trouble (141: πεπυσμένη μέν) and the *reality* of her suffering (142: ὡς δ' ἐγὼ θυμοφθορῶ), of which they are ignorant.

would surely move the hearer but which contains no personal expression of sympathy by the chorus. Not until the second antistrophe do they speak directly to Deianeira, and then not to sympathize but to advise, instruct, and reprove. Their admonitions are gentle but firm and devoid of any words of familiarity or terms of endearment.[8]

The parodos is followed by Deianeira's long speech to the chorus (141ff.), the first one-third of which stresses the difference between them and her, implying that since they are young and unmarried they could not possibly understand what she is going through. Then she explains and justifies her fears, which, as was made apparent in the prologue, are not unreasonable under the circumstances. As she finishes, the Messenger is seen approaching, and the chorus enjoin her to be quiet and, in effect, not to utter such ill-omened words (178–179: εὐφημίαν ἴσχε). The use of a direct imperative by the chorus in an arrival announcement is uncommon in Sophocles, and this ritualistic phrase may have had an additionally striking effect. The impression received from this scene between the chorus and Deianeira is that the women are indeed concerned for Deianeira, but without deep sympathy or affection. They are different, they do not understand her position, and the poet has in the structure of the scene deliberately prevented any discussion between them. The whole scene differs sharply from the parodos of *Electra*, with its conversational kommos and warmly affectionate words. That warmth is distinctly lacking here.

This impression of an absence of intimacy between Deianeira and the chorus does not diminish as the action continues. The song of rejoicing into which they burst at Deianeira's command does not mention her, nor the specific reason for their joy (205–224). In their excitement at the approach of Lichas and the captive women, the chorus do call Deianeira φίλα γύναι (222), to which she responds φίλαι γυναῖκες (225). Nevertheless, the apparent warmth of this phrase, which they use only here, is probably mitigated by its context. In their announcement the chorus use several words that connote visual evidence (ἴδε ἴδ᾽ . . . ἀντίπρωρα . . . βλέπειν . . . ἐναργῆ). They seem to allude directly to proof of the Messenger's tidings and indirectly to proof of their own insistence that all will turn out well, that Deianeira should not have worried. In short, they seem to be saying to her, "there, look, I told you so," as they seem to do again at the end of Lichas' speech (291–292). Indeed, this scene with the captive

8. The kindly tone of the opening words of the antistrophe (122–123) remains evident despite the disagreement over their grammatical relation; cf. Lloyd-Jones (*YCS* 22 [1972], 263–264), Stinton (*JHS* 96 [1976], 130–132), and Easterling (commentary, *ad loc.*).

women is an outstanding example of Sophocles' ability to portray visual and verbal contrast simultaneously. The audience has before its eyes, on the one hand, the destitute, wretched captives, sent as slaves to a foreign land, and, on the other, the prosperous, carefree Trachinian girls, rejoicing in triumph. At the same time the contrast between Deianeira and the chorus is manifested in their respective attitudes toward the captives. Deianeira expresses profound pity at the sight (243, 298ff.); but at the end of Lichas' tale of vengeance, slaughter, and enslavement (281ff.), the chorus blithely call the sight an assurance of joy (291–292)![9]

The ensuing scene of the revelation of Iole's identity and the confrontation with Lichas enlarges upon a theme that was introduced in the prologue: Deianeira's inability to decide on a course of action. When the chorus remind her of their presence by their outburst against Lichas (383–384, surely without reference to Heracles), Deianeira in her confusion and extreme uncertainty turns to them for advice (385–386: τί χρὴ ποεῖν, γυναῖκες). They respond immediately and forcefully with advice that Deianeira gratefully accepts (387–388). Then the Messenger reminds her that she has not given him any orders (390). This little exchange is the introduction to one of Sophocles' most artful scenes. As Deianeira's hesitant and incompetent questioning yields no results, the Messenger, without asking permission, interrupts and assumes command of the situation.[10]

9. The dramatic impact of this scene is too often overlooked. That the Athenians did not always condone the complete sack and enslavement of a Greek city is attested by the rescinding of the Mytilenean decree in 427 B.C. (Thuc. 3.36.4: ὠμὸν τὸ βούλευμα καὶ μέγα). Whether this should be given any significance for the dating of the play is moot, for other such incidents occurred, and conscience did not prevail, for example, Scione: Thuc. 5.32; Melos: Thuc. 5.116.

10. The scene has been criticized, especially by Reinhardt (Sophokles, 50), for not being as cleverly managed a Dreigespräch as Oed. Tyr. 1123ff.; hence it is adduced as supporting an early date for the play (Schwinge, Die Stellung der Trachinierinnen, 73–75; cf. Seidensticker, "Die Stichomythie," 203–204). This presumes that both scenes attempt to achieve the same dramatic effect and that one may therefore seem more artful than the other. But, in fact, their structures and functions are quite different. The characters in Trachiniae are almost inversions of those of the Oed. Tyr. scene: the Corinthian Messenger is friendly and respectful, the Trachinian, sly and rude; Laius' Herdsman is sullen, and Lichas, haughtily formal; Oedipus is forceful and threatening, Deianeira, meek and imploring.

Although the Oed. Tyr. scene has an additional triangular pattern of speech at the beginning (1119–1123) as well as the main Dreigespräch, the entire scene is a steady progress toward a single climactic moment of understanding. But the Tr. scene is crowded with other persons and movements—the chorus, interrupting as if a fourth actor, the group of captives to which Deianeira draws attention by speaking to Iole, the exits of Lichas with the captives and his subsequent re-entrance after the Messenger's revelations—all creating a mood of confusion, deception, and uncertainty about the action still to come.

Only when Lichas finally appeals directly to her (434–435) does she speak, and as soon as she finishes the chorus again intrude into the conversation, giving assurances to Lichas on her behalf.

Because the scene dealt with Iole, and with Deianeira's compassionate behavior toward her, we might expect the chorus' ensuing stasimon (497–530) to enlarge upon the consequences of Heracles' passion for Iole, and indeed they seem to be starting with that theme as they sing of the power of love (497–502). But soon after they begin the tale of a contest for a bride (503–506), the hearer realizes that the prize is not Iole but Deianeira (507ff.). Moreover, the story is of her past; they do not mention the recent startling events. The song itself intimately links Deianeira and Iole, for the audience would at once perceive the similarity of their circumstances, and it ends on a note of pity with the image of the helpless bride snatched away from her mother. Yet one also perceives that the chorus' personal involvement here is minimal. They do not name Deianeira, they tell the story in a completely impersonal manner, they add no opinion or sympathetic expression of their own.[11]

When Deianeira returns, she again asks their advice, and they again give it instantly and firmly (588–589, 592–593); but as before (178–179), any extended discussion between them is prevented by the arrival of another character, this time Lichas. The next stasimon, which follows the dispatch of the robe to Heracles, is far less concerned with Deianeira than was the first. She is not mentioned until the middle of the second strophe, and then only briefly (650–652). The last two lines of the strophe are ambiguous; the "toilsome day" ($\dot{\epsilon}\pi\dot{\iota}\pi o\nu o\nu$ $\dot{\alpha}\mu\dot{\epsilon}\rho\alpha\nu$) which Ares has ended could as well refer to the end of Heracles' labors as to the end of Deianeira's (or the chorus') anxiety.[12] The chorus allude to Deianeira once more at the end of the ode; the text is uncertain, but the reference must surely be to the charm and to its desired effect on Heracles.[13]

---

11. Except perhaps at line 526. The critical dissatisfaction with this line rests chiefly on the inappropriateness of $\mu\dot{\alpha}\tau\eta\rho$ as applied to a chorus of maidens. For the many conjectures, see Jebb and Kamerbeek, *ad loc.*; cf. also van der Valk (*REG* 80 [1967], 124–125), who would retain the traditional reading, and Longo, *ad* 523–526, who would excise the lines as marginalia.

12. Ἐπίπονος in the sense of "toilsome" rather than "sorrowful" is used later specifically of Heracles' labors (829–830: $\dot{\epsilon}\pi\dot{\iota}\pi o\nu o\nu$ . . . $\lambda\alpha\tau\rho\epsilon\dot{\iota}\alpha\nu$), and perhaps also at *Oed. Col.* 1560. The word does not otherwise occur in Sophocles.

13. For the numerous readings of 660–662, see Jebb, *ad loc.* (and the appendix, 195–196), and Kamerbeek, *ad* 660, 661, 662, who ably seeks to retain the reading of the MSS; cf. also Easterling, *ad loc.*

In the next episode the chorus have their lengthiest conversation yet
with Deianeira; it is also their last scene with her. She comes out to them in
a state of new anxiety to which they respond with their by now characteristically detached interest. The contrast between her uncertainty and their
apparent clearheadedness is especially strong here. Her initial statements
are vague and distracted: "I may have gone too far, I may seem to have
done wrong, one should look before one leaps" (663–664, 666–667,
669–670). The chorus-leader, however, leads her into the story with brevity and precision: "What is it? Is it to do with your gift to Heracles? Tell
us if you can" (665, 668, 679), and at last she does begin, in a somewhat
muddled fashion, to bring out the whole story (672ff.). The formality of
the chorus' first response, "Deianeira, child of Oineus" (665), is entirely
consistent with the emotional distance between them and her. The use in
direct address of the full patronymic form of the name, that is, "*X*, son of
Y," is extremely rare in Sophocles, and used toward gods as well as mortals. There are only five other instances: twice the formula seems to under-
score the shift from ordinary speech to solemn invocation of a god (*Oed.
Tyr.* 158–159; *Oed. Col.* 712); once it is used for a very significant initial
identification (*Phil.* 4), once to summon a character forth onto the scene
(*Phil.* 1261), and once to convey a sense of being awestruck by horror (*Aj.*
331).[14] The use of the formula in description rather than direct address
is more common, but no less formal, as Lichas' haughty "identification"
of Deianeira to the Messenger demonstrates (405–406). By making the
chorus-leader use the rare formal mode of address here, the poet has emphasized still more the formality of the relation between the woman and
the girls.[15]

When Deianeira has told her tale, the chorus-leader replies not with
sympathy but with their customarily ready advice, not to give up hope be-

14. Kamerbeek (*ad Tr.* 665) cites this last as support of his assertion that "the formality of
address is in keeping with D.'s grave words." But Tecmessa has described the horrors fully;
Deianeira, however, has as yet said nothing substantial. Jebb (*ad* 665) says that the formula in
Tr. "implies earnest sympathy with the terror which they perceive in her" (with which Easterling, *ad loc.*, agrees), and to support this he compares *Ant.* 1098; but there the chorus are at
last assuming authority and giving orders to Creon, which is surely the effect of the formal
address.

15. The rarity of the full form of direct address—and hence the likelihood that its use is
intended to have a specific dramatic effect—becomes more readily apparent if one observes
that the common form of address, the vocative of a single name ("*X!*"), occurs 115 times in
the extant plays of Sophocles. And the simple patronymic form, "child [voc.] of *Y*," is still
used 35 times, as compared with the 6 uses of the full form, "*X* [voc.], child of *Y*." Even in
descriptions the full form occurs only 11 times in addition to Lichas' use of it at 405–406.

fore learning the actual outcome. This time she refuses their advice and sharply rejects the apparently sensible observation that she should not be blamed for acting unwittingly (729–730). She stresses the fact that they cannot comprehend her situation because they have not themselves experienced it, echoing her earlier statement to the same effect (151–152). Again the dialogue is abruptly terminated, this time by the entrance of Hyllus. The chorus say nothing throughout the confrontation between mother and son, and at the end their interference is limited, despite the fact that they know the true story, to protesting Deianeira's silent withdrawal. Such action, or rather inaction, would hardly be logical were it not for the way that this chorus have hitherto been portrayed. They have never understood Deianeira's feelings, hence they have no suspicion of her intentions; they regularly give her advice, but nothing more. In view of this, their failure to intervene on her behalf (they would have to interrupt Hyllus, or call him back after his hasty exit) would surely seem to the audience entirely natural and consistent with their character. The poet has thus avoided a snag in the plot without resorting to lame excuses or oaths of secrecy.

The pace of the action quickens, and the chorus are swept along with it. The stasimon (821ff.) is concerned with Heracles' fate; they speak of Deianeira only in the second strophe, and then return to Heracles: their "stream of tears" (851) is not for her. Their attention, however, is forcibly returned to Deianeira by the cries from within and the arrival of the Nurse with her dreadful news. The brief dialogue and astrophic kommos (871–879, 880–895) between servant and chorus unequivocally display the chorus' shallow understanding of Deianeira. The tone is more one of surprise and shock than of sympathy. The antilabe creates a mood of agitated bewilderment, but the kommos is largely iambic; the few lyric parts are all rapid-fire questions and responses, without any expression of sorrow or mourning.[16] The chorus cannot believe that she is dead (876–877), that she actually killed herself (882, 890): "Could a woman dare to do such a thing?" (898). The deliberate emphasis on the chorus' inability to comprehend the deed and the doer becomes even clearer when the scene is compared with the report of Iocasta's suicide in *Oedipus Tyrannus*. There the

---

16. Henderson (*Maia* 28 [1976], 21–24) so emends the kommos that the Nurse speaks only iambic trimeters, in accordance with the principle that minor characters do not sing. This proposal receives some support from Sophocles' observed tendency not to convey in lyrics factual information that the audience needs to have about the action of the plot. If only the chorus have lyrics in this passage, the lyrics are so brief, interrogatory, and iambic that we may suspect the passage may not have been accompanied by music.

chorus have already had misgivings about her intentions (1074–1075); when they hear the news of her death, they have but a single question, brief and to the point: "How?" (1236). The Trachinians, on the other hand, had no suspicions and take a long time to be convinced. When they do at last understand the whole story, they have only brief words of sorrow for Deianeira. They cannot decide which trouble is worse; and then their thoughts turn from her to the coming horror (947–952). Her passing is mourned no more than Iocasta's. As a final note, Deianeira's supposedly intimate friends make only two more comments (1044–1045 and 1112–1113), both expressions of sympathy for Heracles and dismay at his loss, and both uttered directly after Heracles has damned Deianeira and cried for vengeance on her.

This brief survey of the relation between Deianeira and the chorus reveals, first of all, that although both she and the Trachinians are women, the poet has given them two quite different characters. Their common sex is a useful aid to the plot, making it logical for the chorus to serve as Deianeira's confidantes and advisors, but there all similarity between them ends. The chorus are young, Deianeira is not; they are natives, she is a foreigner; they are maidens, she is married and the mother of a grown son; they are confident, she is pessimistic and fearful. It is a natural result of these differences that the chorus cannot and do not understand Deianeira, a fact to which Deianeira herself testifies and which is also closely allied to another, perhaps even more obvious, aspect of their relation: the chorus are interested in Deianeira and concerned for her welfare, but they are not on an intimate footing with her. This is consistently emphasized throughout the action of the drama. What little communication they do have with her is interrupted, with amazing regularity, by the arrival of another character. Their songs are at most only partially concerned with Deianeira, and the tone is distant and impersonal. Finally, and most noticeably, the poet has allowed no kommos between them and Deianeira. In their behavior and utterances, the women of this chorus contrast vividly with the intensely sympathetic choruses of *Electra* and *Oedipus Coloneus*.

On the technical level, we have already noted how the distance between the chorus and Deianeira renders credible their failure to interfere on her behalf in the face of the unjust accusations made first by Hyllus and then by Heracles. In addition, it intensifies the already noticeable contrast between their confidence and readiness to advise and her insecurity and vacillation. This facet of Deianeira's character is also displayed in her relations to both the Nurse and the Messenger, but it is made most conspicuous by the chorus. The dramatic function of the contrast is to show, beyond all possible doubt, that Deianeira is innocent.[17] She is incapable of independent action. Her every deed is performed at the instigation of someone else—the sending off of Hyllus, the questioning of Lichas, the dispatch of the robe.[18] Even her resolution of death (720) is finally accomplished chiefly by Hyllus' angry recriminations (932–933).[19] All these incidents combine to show that her use of the magic blood is to be regarded by the audience as natural and, considering her character, inculpable: she acted at the suggestion of Nessus, and the horrible consequences of her action are, as the chorus declare, "the results of a stranger's advice at a deadly meeting" (844–845). Once again, she is only doing as others bid her.[20]

Of the chorus' lyrics, perhaps only a third are concerned with Deianeira; most are about Heracles. The parodos begins with Heracles the son of Alcmena and ends with Heracles the son of Zeus. We have noted the unusual circumstance that the chorus do not address their first words to Deianeira; rather, they invoke the all-seeing Sun to give them news of wandering Heracles. The implication is strong that this man is of such importance that the very Sun keeps a watchful eye upon him. The chorus continue in this vein, singing of the Heracles who is subject to the mighty forces of the universe, whom some god always saves from Death (119–

17. Cf. McCall (*AJP* 93 [1972], 142ff.). The evidence is too meager to allow us to determine whether tradition perhaps regarded Deianeira as another Medea or Clytemnestra; see, for example, Errandonea (*Sófocles* [1958], 175ff.), who favors her guilt, and more reasonably, Kamerbeek (1–7). The perseverance with which Sophocles insists upon her innocence might suggest that a different version was current.

18. Adams (*Sophocles*, 110–111) suggests the play is named for the chorus because it is they who make the "fatal decision" (588–589, 592–593) and thus exonerate Deianeira. See also Winnington-Ingram (*Sophocles*, 79).

19. Because Deianeira has stated that if the stratagem fails, she will die (719–722), it is possible to argue that her death is her one independent action. But she has never acted independently before, and the text gives us no statement that she is doing so now. On the contrary, the poet has just made her own son emphatically blame her, curse her, and wish her dead (e.g., 735, 807–812), and continue in that vein when she has left (815–820); then the Nurse reports that Hyllus *knew* he had caused her death (932: ἔγνω, rather than some less positive word for "think, believe, suppose"). Deianeira's first statement (719–722) prepares us to assume, when she leaves silently, that she will die; Hyllus' rantings give the dramatic impression of her being driven to it, an impression which is then confirmed by the Nurse (932–933).

20. Errandonea (*Sófocles* [1958], 191–194) has also observed the chorus' detachment from the action and their noncomprehension of Deianeira. He believes, however, that Deianeira is a murderer and that therefore the chorus must be on the periphery of things, since they cannot be allowed either to help in the murder or to interfere with it.

121), reminding us that Zeus is mindful of his children (139–140) and that Heracles is the son of Zeus. They give the firm impression that they are familiar with the exploits of Heracles; they have followed his career and know, or at least believe, that he is a care to the gods.

Their song of triumph and exultation (205–224), on the other hand, does not even allude to Heracles, much less make actual mention of him. It is true that Deianeira's name and circumstances are also noticeably lacking. But the chorus here are rejoicing in response to the news of Heracles' homecoming, and they are extremely joyful, even frenzied. Despite the loss of the music and dance, the words and astrophic meter leave no room for doubt that the women are wildly enthusiastic about Heracles' return. In thanksgiving for it they call again upon gods—Artemis, Apollo, and the Nymphs—implying that these deities, too, watch over Heracles and are in some way responsible for his safety; and their words suggest that they break into a Bacchic dance (216–221). The gods reappear in the chorus' first stasimon (497–530): Aphrodite is introduced in the first line, with a description of her influence over the greatest gods: Zeus, Hades, Poseidon. Soon the chorus tell of her presiding alone in solemn official judgment (516: ῥαβδονόμει) at Heracles' battle for Deianeira. They are thus presenting Heracles as an exceedingly important man when they say that such a powerful personage deigned to be physically present (515: ἐν μέσῳ) at his nuptials. At the same time the chorus give us a new view of Heracles, as the heroic fighter. Deianeira made only slight reference to the battle with Achelous (20) without describing it at all, and the only allusions to Heracles' famous labors have been her complaints that he is always away from home on a journey for someone (34–35, 159, 170). Lichas and the Messenger have told, briefly, only of his slaying of mortals and his enslavement to a woman. Now the chorus give us a vivid description, with epic clashing and groaning, of Heracles locked in combat with a legendary monster, the very strength of a river in the shape of a bull (506–509). This is the audience's first glimpse of Heracles in his traditional role.

Following the scene of the dispatch of the magic robe by Deianeira, the chorus sing another song of joy for the return of Heracles (633–662), more formal but no less enthusiastic than the first. They continue to stress the gods' association with Heracles, proclaiming that the coming of the son of Zeus and Alcmena will be celebrated with sacred music (642–643); they now add Ares to the list of gods involved in Heracles' fortunes. Deianeira receives little mention in this ode; indeed, the chorus speak first at some length of their own sense of loss: "*we* have missed him from our city," "for twelve months *we* waited for him," "*we* knew nothing" (647–649).[21] Only then do they go on to Deianeira's anxiety. The song is, of course, a joy-before-disaster ode, since the audience must know that the robe will kill Heracles. In fact, it has a double effect of irony, since the chorus express two expectations that will be reversed by coming events. The hope that Heracles will return filled with renewed love for his wife—the purpose for which the robe was sent—is contained only in the last stanza of the ode; the larger part of the song expresses the chorus' own anticipation of Heracles' triumphant return as the victorious son of Zeus.

In the next song, the mood of joy has turned to one of horror and grief, but the chorus still remind us of the connection between the hero and the gods. Heracles is called "Zeus' own son" (826), and they say that the goddess Cypris is the author of these things (962). There is also a strong contrast between Hyllus' straightforward description of Heracles' affliction and the chorus' colorful imaginings. Hyllus gave the account of a human eyewitness to a human's sufferings, using only a simile and that only once (771). The chorus, however, present through metaphor a fearful picture of Heracles enveloped in a deadly cloud of poison by the Centaur's treachery, a poison born of Death and nursed by a serpent; he is gripped by the Hydra, and flayed by the Centaur (831–840).[22] The chorus are not showing us Heracles brought low by a magical garment, but rather struggling in mortal combat with the hideous and terrifying creatures of legend. It is this spectacle and its fatal results that move them to tears. The μεγάλαν ἄταν (850) that they foresee is the death of Heracles, for they have no suspicion of Deianeira's death. Their concern here is for Heracles' fate.

The chorus' anxiety for Heracles becomes greater, even after they learn of Deianeira's death. They do say that it is difficult for them to judge which trouble is the worse (947–949), but they seem to make that decision when they cease entirely to speak of Deianeira—"the troubles in the house" (950) is their last reference to that unfortunate woman. The spectacle of

---

21. The use of the first person plural, εἴχομεν, seems to emphasize the personal tone more than Jebb's inversion, "he was lost utterly to our land" (647). The difference between the chorus' twelve months (648) and Deianeira's fifteen months (44–45, 164–165) has been viewed as a mistake (e.g., Bowra, *Sophoclean Tragedy*, 121n2; cf. Burton, *The Chorus*, 58) or as an indication that the chorus refer only to Heracles' enslavement to Omphale (Kamerbeek, *ad* 648, and Easterling, *ad* 647–650). The discrepancy could also be intended to emphasize the difference in nature between the chorus' longing for Heracles, and Deianeira's; cf. below, on the oracle in the third stasimon.

22. Surely the general sense of the passage, despite the textual difficulties. On the Hydra, see Lloyd-Jones (*YCS* 22 [1972], 265–266), against Long (*GRBS* 8 [1967], 275–278).

the dying Heracles is the subject of their remaining utterances, and they seem to magnify his image. He is the great son of Zeus, and they fear that the mere sight of him would kill them (955–958). The ability to inspire such a fear is hardly the attribute of an ordinary mortal, but of a fabulous being, an "unspeakably great wonder" (961: ἄσπετόν τι θαῦμα). This attitude of awe is reflected in the chorus-leader's last remarks (1044, 1112), when she shudders at his sufferings and cries out in final despair that Greece herself will be plunged into mourning by the loss of this man.[23]

By spending most of their lyric time on Heracles, the chorus create and sustain one of the most important dramatic effects in the play. It is these fifteen persons who, by constantly singing about him, introduce in word the physically absent Heracles. They deflect attention from Deianeira and keep the audience ever aware of him; and therein lies the unity of the play. Through the chorus the spectator regularly hears about Heracles, and eagerly awaits his appearance; then at last he is seen in dismal reality. It is true that the chorus are not the sole instrument by which the poet maintains the dramatic awareness of Heracles. The audience learns about Heracles, but only about the man, from other characters. Deianeira presents Heracles the husband, desired but a source of anxiety; Hyllus, Heracles the father, desired but stern and commanding (797–802); Lichas and the Messenger, Heracles the lover, the avenger, the sacker of cities, brutal and ruthless. But it is the chorus who continually give us the mighty hero of legend, Heracles the battler of monsters, Heracles the care of the gods, Heracles the beloved protector of Hellas. Through the chorus Sophocles creates the final irony of the confrontation between this ideal image of Heracles and the terrible reality of the broken and helpless mortal who actually appears in the end.[24]

The relation between the chorus and Heracles appears to be entirely one-sided. Heracles is always in their thoughts and words, yet when he is at last physically present they do not speak to him, nor he to them. He

23. Kaimio (*Chorus of Greek Drama*, 171) believes that the chorus-leader's vocative address to the rest of the chorus (1044: φίλαι) "shows that the leader means only herself with the first person singular expressing her perceptions and emotions." But this vocative plural may as likely serve to include the rest of the chorus, so that the audience may not think that she speaks apart from them. Cf. below on *Electra*. The leader's movements and the chorus' responsive gestures, if any, could easily have eliminated any ambiguity or doubt for the audience.

24. On the portrayal of Heracles as "present while absent," see Musurillo (*Light and Darkness*, 62–64), who maintains (76–77), however, that the chorus serve in the final scene as a link with Deianeira rather than with the previously anticipated (i.e., legendary) Heracles.

never even acknowledges their existence. Throughout the play they refer to him with awe and reverence, and, finally, such fear that they seek escape lest the sight of him should kill them (953ff.). Despite their expressed desire for his return, their utterances manifest no intimacy between themselves and Heracles, but rather a remoteness, a distance which cannot be traversed by either party. We have already observed a similar distance between the chorus and Deianeira, exemplified especially in their failure to understand her, and in such details as the difference in their ages and the fact that Deianeira is not a native of Trachis. The latter difference also obtains with respect to Heracles. Lichas says that Heracles attacked Euboea with a "foreign army" (259: στρατὸν ἐπακτόν); when Heracles himself is brought in, the chorus describe a procession of foreigners (964). Nor is the chorus' relation to Heracles' son any more intimate; indeed, it is virtually nonexistent. They never address Hyllus, and he speaks to them only once, in a general way, after Deianeira has left (815ff.). If the closing lines of the play belong to Hyllus, then he does address the chorus personally (1275–1276); but, because these lines stand at the end of the play, they cannot of themselves serve to establish an earlier relation.[25] In these various ways the poet has created and sustained an obvious distance between the chorus and each of the principals.

If, then, the chorus of Trachinians are not linked in close relationship to any one character, we may legitimately wonder what they are doing in the play, what significant function they have. It would, however, have been easy for the audience to perceive the chorus as representative of a group of persons who are outside the scene of the action, but mentioned early in the play, especially in connection with Heracles. The newly arrived Messenger describes in some detail the scene of Lichas' announcement of Heracles'

25. The ascription of these lines to Hyllus seems most reasonable; otherwise we must take παρθέν' as being spoken by the chorus-leader to the rest of the chorus. Kaimio (*Chorus of Greek Drama*, 191) points out that such a singular vocative address by the chorus-leader would be unique in extant tragedy. But the objection to having Hyllus address the chorus-leader is considerably weaker, especially the supposition that "there is no reason for Hyllos to take notice of the chorus-leader." Principals often address the chorus in the singular (the fact that they do not often use the *vocative* singular is of no consequence here), and the poet makes Hyllus "take note" of the chorus in order to provide a cue for removing them from the scene. The view that Iole has returned and is being addressed here, either by Hyllus or by the chorus-leader, ignores the fact that an unannounced entrance with no subsequent identification of the character is utterly contrary to the needs and practices of the Greek theatre. Kamerbeek's desire (*ad* 1275) to retain ἀπ' οἴκων implies that the chorus, being young women, properly belong at home, or are playing truant; but such a notion is entirely new at this point and not at all relevant.

victory and imminent return. Lichas is speaking to a large crowd (188); indeed, says the Messenger, he is surrounded by all the Malian people, who are so insistent in their eagerness for news of Heracles that he cannot get away (193–199). Later, when Lichas has left, the Messenger again mentions the "public crowd of Trachinians" listening to the news of Heracles (371–373).[26] The chorus themselves twice invoke a general rejoicing by the people, once after the Messenger's announcement (205ff.) and again after the dispatch of the robe (633ff.). In the first instance, the chorus may be addressing only the members of the household, although the phrase ἐν δέ (207),[27] and the inclusion of men (Deianeira only mentioned women), may well suggest a wider audience. The opening strophe of the second song, however, is addressed to all the inhabitants of the land from the mountains to the Malian gulf. There will be joy for all these, and the impression of large numbers of people is even further extended by the reference to Ἑλλάνων ἀγοραί (638). In the second strophe, too, the chorus stress Heracles' absence as *their* loss, before they touch upon Deianeira's sense of loss. And we must note again the chorus' last declaration, that all Greece will mourn the loss of Heracles (1112–1113).

Surely the dramatic effect of this chorus, distant from the principals yet so deeply concerned by the fate of Heracles, is to show that the action is not private, but rather totally public. Deianeira's act and its consequence, the destruction of Heracles, affect not merely his own household but all the inhabitants of the land, indeed all Greece. The action and circumstances of this play turn on phenomena which could not exist in fifth-century Athens, upon monsters and magic and the improbable occurrences of legend. Sophocles has created a world in which such things would not be anomalous and incredible, a world alien to the reality of the fifth century. The chief characteristic of this world is the complete absence of any civil authority—there is no law, no assembly, no army of citizens, no council of elders, and, most noticeably, no king.[28] There is only the strength

26. For examples of ἀγορά as "a gathering" rather than a "marketplace" see Jebb, *ad loc.*, and often in Homer (e.g., *Od.* 2.69), although it can also mean "gathering place" (which Kamerbeek, *ad loc.*, prefers).

27. Kamerbeek, *ad* 207, renders it "and besides."

28. Sophocles appears to have deliberately avoided all reference to the mythical king of Trachis, Ceyx. Deianeira says only that they are now living ξένῳ παρ' ἀνδρί (40). She is called δέσποινα (and δεσπότις) by Lichas and the Messenger, but not by the Trachinian chorus. She is called ἄνασσα, and Heracles ἄναξ, once by the chorus, but the real terms of political authority, τύραννος and βασιλεύς, are never used of mortals in this play. For a somewhat different view of the contrasts between the world of *Trachiniae* and fifth-century Athens, see Segal (*YCS* 25 [1977], 119–122).

of Heracles, on which all depend. It is the chorus of Trachinian women who set the scene of the play in this strange world; by using a chorus of women rather than men, the poet has made them effective representatives of the Trachinians who people Heracles' world—independent of his authority yet utterly dependent on his strength, concerned yet distant, awe-filled, passive. We are led to compare the silent, mournful captives, brought low by Heracles' strength and will, with the silent and weeping chorus women at the end of the play, watching the final defeat of their champion. Further, as the crowd at Euboea watched the destruction of Heracles' strength (783–785, 795), so now this crowd of Trachinians watches the loss of the power of his will. The man who destroyed a city merely to achieve an amorous whim can no longer take personal vengeance, summon his family to his deathbed, or even command the obedience of his son.[29] This is the tragedy of *Trachiniae*, and it is not a private one. It is the chorus, purveyors of the heroic Heracles, who also give us the public aspect of that Panhellenic hero.

The chorus of *Trachiniae* have another function in respect of the wider themes of this play. It has been a regular complaint of critics that the religious aspect of Heracles is missing—specifically, that the poet neglects to include the all-important deification of Heracles which is the "divine reward" for his sufferings. It is indeed true that the plot itself contains no specifically religious actions, other than reported sacrifices; but, through the utterances of the chorus, the poet conveys from the beginning of the play the unmistakable impression of Heracles' association with the gods. We have several times noted that the chorus speak with great confidence of Heracles as the son of Zeus and a care to the gods. Nor are these merely general statements, for in their songs they refer, in connection with Heracles, to Zeus, Apollo, Artemis, Aphrodite, Poseidon, Hades, and Ares.

This religious content of the choral odes is strongly reinforced by their style and structure. The entire first strophe of the parodos is a prayer, in which the god is three times addressed and importuned (96, 99, 102). The chorus' subsequent assertions about the ways of the gods are spoken with an air of firm conviction, unqualified by any such phrases as "it is said

29. For Deianeira is already dead; Alcmena and the children have gone (1147–1154); Hyllus refuses his father's last commands and, at first, the marriage he arranges for him. Surely the dramatic point of introducing the "betrothal" to Iole as Heracles' dying wish is so that Hyllus may stubbornly resist (cf. Kitto, *Poiesis*, 170–172). Whether Heracles is only telling Hyllus to receive her as a concubine, as MacKinnon maintains (*CQ* 21 [1971], 33–41), or not, Hyllus utterly opposes the request (1233–1237).

that" or "we have heard that." They are clearly to be understood as believing that they are stating known truths. Their next song (205ff.) begins with an invitation to prayer and then moves into an apparently Bacchic strain. We cannot, of course, determine the nature of the accompanying dance, but the words, especially the references to ivy and "bacchic contest" (219–220) and the cry ἰὼ Παιάν, permit the speculation that it might have borne some resemblance to the dance of a religious celebration. The stasimon which follows the scene between Lichas and Deianeira is particularly interesting in this respect, for it appears to have the characteristics of a dithyramb, in so far as the genre is represented by the "dithyrambs" (*Odes* 14–19) of Bacchylides.[30] The stasimon is a lyric narrative of a heroic legendary event, traditionally an essential attribute of the dithyramb, and the sequence of questioning strophe followed by answering antistrophe may be compared with that of Bacchylides 17. If, then, we may recognize in this ode a deliberate resemblance to a dithyramb, the question remains of whether the religious aspect of the dithyramb was still significant in the late fifth century. Although the later dithyramb appears to have become almost wholly secular, there is little evidence on how it was regarded in the fifth century.[31] Nevertheless, the dithyrambic contest, like the tragic, was a part of religious festivals, and it seems reasonable to assume that the audience would, in recognizing the dithyrambic nature of this stasimon, associate it with those performances at the sacred contests.

The chorus sing two more odes which appear to be in a religious style. Their second stasimon (633ff.) is an invitation to sacred rejoicing which is issued to all the people of the land, especially of the "shore of the golden-distaffed goddess" (637). Although it lacks an injunction of sacred silence, this summons to the inhabitants may be compared to the opening lines of the parodos of the "Temple Maidens" in Euripides' *Iphigenia in Tauris* (123–125), which are a summons to worship. The Trachinian women then promise the people "sacred music" (642–643), and begin the final antistrophe with words which, although not addressed to a specific god, are nevertheless in the optative mood of prayer (655–656). We cannot, of course, state that this ode is in the exact style of priestly calls to worship,

30. So Kranz (*Stasimon*, 254), who relates this one to other "dithyrambic" stasima in Euripides, and Reinhardt (*Sophokles*, 253 [note to p. 46]). Others find an "epinicean" tone in the ode (cf. Easterling's commentary, *ad loc.*, and Burton, *The Chorus*, 58). On the likelihood that the six poems of Bacchylides are true dithyrambs, see Pickard-Cambridge, *Dithyramb, Tragedy, and Comedy*, 25–27.

31. Cf. Pickard-Cambridge, *Dithyramb*, 58–59.

but there is considerable likelihood that the audience would receive at least an impression of a resemblance to such ritual. In their next ode (821ff.) the chorus solemnly expound the "god-given word of the ancient prophecy" (822–823). This oracle has occasioned some concern because the time span of twelve years is mentioned here, whereas Deianeira said that Heracles spoke of fifteen months after his departure (164–165). There seems no reason to believe that the poet is presenting two entirely different oracles;[32] it is clear that he has given the chorus another statement of the same oracle. Moreover, the content of the oracle is differently presented. Deianeira spoke of Heracles' death (166–168); the chorus speak only of the end of Heracles' labors (825–826). The dramatic effect of these variations may well be that the chorus are presenting and interpreting the oracle independently, perhaps of their own separate knowledge. Their interpretation is logical and accurate (828–840) and contained in the metaphorical description of a sight they have never seen. In addition, they make an authoritative statement about Deianeira's motives (841–848), make a prediction of things to come (849–850), and fix the blame on a goddess (860–861). Much of this, especially prophecy, is the province of seers, or great mortals who are associated with the gods. This is not to say that the chorus are here portrayed as if they were such persons, but rather that their song has been deliberately invested with a mood of solemn and religious proceedings.

The chorus' odes, then, combine a theological content with a style which is suited to, or at least reminiscent of, the songs of religious festival and of worship. The only possible dramatic purpose of this combination is to maintain a strongly and consistently religious mood throughout the play. The chorus are not establishing a point of doctrine, or functioning as priestesses of a cult of Heracles; but the audience receives the continuous impression that the chorus believe that Heracles in a certain way belongs to the gods. Heracles is certainly human and mortal; yet at the same time the chorus portray him as a great hero, a legendary figure. Especially they suggest that Heracles has, and has always had, in his closeness to the gods a divine nature which the Trachinians recognize. Through the chorus' belief the poet can make the audience accept this dual nature of Heracles in this play—actively human and passively divine—an acceptance which is of the utmost importance for the understanding of the play.

For the central theme is not the notion that Heracles the superman is

---

32. Cf. Kamerbeek, *ad* 824–825, and above, on the second stasimon.

above the standards of human judgment and will be recompensed for his sufferings by the coming apotheosis.[33] Rather, Sophocles shows us that even in this lawless world, devoid of any human authority, there is still the natural authority of *Dikê*, the order of the universe, and that it is above even Heracles himself. The poet portrays some of Heracles' human actions as spectacularly contrary to the laws of Zeus' justice: he killed Iphitus by stealth, which Zeus condemns and for which he punished Heracles (274–279); the punishment, slavery to a woman, is not shameful since it came from Zeus (250–251), yet Heracles in vengeance for his shame sacked Oechalia, another act of wanton violence. Later it is discovered that Heracles' real motive was Eurytus' refusal to give his daughter to Heracles—hardly a better reason. Further, Heracles kills Lichas, whose innocence is emphasized (773), in much the same manner as he killed Iphitus. All this rebounds on Heracles, not as arbitrary supernatural intervention, but in the natural and inexorable pattern of the universe, *Dikê*.[34] Sophocles does not even hint at the apotheosis itself because it is no part of his story; Heracles is from the beginning the mighty hero, son of Zeus, yet even he, as a mortal, is brought low by a robe woven by the Erinyes (1051–1052), the agents of *Dikê*. The action of the drama is concerned not with Heracles' elevation to godhood but with his subjection to *Dikê*. The human aspect of Heracles' nature is portrayed through the action and the principal characters; but Heracles' divinity is evoked not by the action but by the presence of his almost worshipful believers, the chorus of Trachinian women.

33. Cf. Bowra, *Sophoclean Tragedy*, 116–161, especially 132–138 and 159–160.

34. These conclusions on the operation of *Dikê* in the play are substantially Kitto's (*Poiesis*, 154–191, especially 158–160, 167, 175–176, and 185–188). See also Lloyd-Jones (*Justice*, 128 and 199n151) and Easterling (*BICS* 15 [1968], 67–68); but compare Winnington-Ingram (*Sophocles*, 89 and 212–215).

CHAPTER 6

Electra

A superficial examination of *Electra* reveals a play that is far less condemnatory than Euripides', certainly not an unmitigated censure of the crime of matricide. Yet Sophocles portrays Electra as an unflagging accomplice to her brother in the slaying of their mother. The universal human difficulty of reconciling the horror of such an action with Sophocles' apparent failure to insist upon punishment for the deed is in large measure responsible for the controversy that surrounds the interpretation of this play. It is easy to agree, as nearly all the critics do, that Sophocles emphasizes the figure of Electra heavily. The disagreement arises over the nature of her character and the emphasis, or lack of it, that the structure of the drama places upon the matricide.

These two components have become interdependent in most interpretations of the play. If Sophocles wants us to respect and even admire Electra, as one view has it, then he naturally deflects attention from the matricide. Electra is a noble figure, heroically dedicated to a task of filial piety, and a warm and loving sister to Orestes. By strength of will she endures the trials a hero must suffer, to triumph justly over her enemies and, with the gods' blessing, to begin a new life of peace and joy. Sophocles glosses over the matricide, approving it almost in passing, and ignores the Furies; he makes us concentrate upon the doers rather than upon the deed.[1] If, on the other hand, one perceives the horror of the matricide as the chief theme of the play, Electra's character must include deceit, a desire for vengeance, and the emotional ability to assist in murdering her mother. By means of a

1. The leading proponents of this view are Bowra (*Sophoclean Tragedy*, 260), Whitman, who maintains that Electra discovers divinity within herself (*Sophocles*, 171), Maddalena (*Sofocle*, 207–209), and Musurillo (*Light and Darkness*, 106–107), perhaps Electra's most ardent admirer.

hundred hints—references to the death of Agamemnon and to the Furies, bitterly ironic uses of deception, and a subtle but compelling delineation of Clytemnestra's natural maternal feelings—Sophocles surrounds the matricide with horror. Electra perforce becomes an unpleasant and even despicable figure. Degraded by her years of grief and hatred, governed wholly by her emotions, she commits crimes more heinous than her mother's.[2]

Readers who are uncomfortable at these extremes, and yet attracted by some of their explanations, have tended to compromise by agreeing to a mixture of horror and righteousness. The slaying of Clytemnestra and Aegisthus was just, a necessary and divinely sanctioned punishment. One of those necessary deaths was, however, matricide. Such an act cannot be ignored or even glossed over by anyone possessed of ordinary human feelings, and Sophocles therefore carefully maintains a grim atmosphere throughout the play. It follows naturally from this interpretation that Electra's character is caught in the middle between heroism and brutality. She stubbornly endures and does what must be done—what is right—but her personality suffers in consequence, as she herself admits. Although the "evils" that she must accomplish are technically just, they weaken her moral fiber and leave her at the end embittered and vindictive. We respect her and sympathize with her, but we do not like her. Thus Electra retains her official stature as a Tragic Hero, but the poet also acknowledges the corruptive effect of unnatural behavior, however necessary it may be, on even the noblest of mortals.[3]

In all this controversy the chorus stand unnoticed except in passing. They are the least problematic of Sophoclean choruses and, perhaps for that very reason, one of the least discussed.[4] It is generally agreed that they

2. Cf. Sheppard (*CR* 41 [1927], 2–9), Gellie (*Sophocles*, 106–130), and Minadeo (*C&M* 28 [1967], 114–142). In his commentary (especially 11 and 213–214) on the play, Kells attempts to show that Orestes is a selfish and amoral killer and that Electra becomes a raving lunatic subject to hallucinations.

3. See especially Friis Johansen's eloquent summary of this view (*C&M* 25 [1964], 31–32). The notion that Electra is not a "stainless heroine" is also accepted by those who deny that any sense of horror or foreboding is associated with the matricide, for example, Kamerbeek in his commentary (19–20), and even Alexanderson (*C&M* 27 [1966], 98), who vigorously opposes much of Friis Johansen's argument. Linforth too finds that her sufferings have made Electra "harsh" ("Electra's Day," 119).

4. Even Kirkwood in his chapter on the chorus (*Sophoclean Drama*, 181–214) says only that they fall into his category of choruses "devoted" and "attached" to a principal. Cf. Whitman (*Sophocles*, 164): "The chorus, plying its usual task of mitigating all emotion, good or bad. . . ."

represent ordinary women with the usual human instinct for caution and reasonableness, in contrast to Electra's heroic stature and capacity for suffering, and that they rebuke her emotional excesses, attempt to persuade all parties to yield to moderation, and in general serve as an effective foil to Electra's character.[5]

The chorus' identity is admittedly vague, in that they seem to be merely a group of local women. Their entrance, like that of the Trachinian women, has not been prepared by any of the other characters, nor do they identify themselves when they arrive. Once again, the absence of the visual aspect of Greek drama forces us to look ahead to the rest of the play for the answers to questions the audience would never need to ask: what do these women look like, and where do they come from? The richness or poverty of their costume would clearly define their social status, or at least show whether they are slaves or nobility, and its style would probably also indicate their relative age and marital status.[6] The place of their entry, either parodos or palace, would have some significance for their relation to the house of Atreus.

The second *hypothesis* to the play supposes that the chorus are "maidens," παρθένοι. No one in the play calls them such, only γυναῖκες (254, 1098, 1398), but that does not mean they are married women, for the girls of Trachis are also called γυναῖκες.[7] In the parodos and also at many subsequent places they call Electra παῖ (121, their first words) and τέκνον (154, 174). These vocatives are never in Greek tragedy addressed by anyone to a nonslave elder or even to a contemporary. Furthermore, the chorus once say that they are speaking to Electra "with kind intent, as a true mother would" (233–234), a statement which, although only a comparison, might still sound strange coming from young girls. They must be some years older than Electra, who is herself no longer very young despite her unmarried state, as Clytemnestra reminds us (614). The text provides no reason to suppose that they are beyond middle age, nor is it likely that Sophocles would give them an elderly appearance to no purpose. The text is also silent about their marital status, which suggests either that it is wholly irrelevant or, more probably, that it would naturally be deduced

5. Only Errandonea (*El coro de la Electra;* cf. *Sófocles* [1958], 127–164, *Sófocles* [1970], 143–174) differs markedly from these opinions, so much so that he believes the chorus reprimand Electra's failure to act and, by the tenacity of their will, drive her to the matricide.

6. See above, chapter 5, on the parodos of *Trachiniae.*

7. Jebb makes the chorus of *Electra* "maidens" in his translation (e.g., of line 129), without giving any justification. Kamerbeek (*ad* 121–250) assumes that γυναῖκες must be married women; cf. Errandonea (*Sófocles* [1958], 131–132).

from their costume and age. They do refer to Electra as "the virgin" (464: ἡ κόρη), probably implying that they are distinct from her in this regard as well as in age.

Electra declares at once their social status: they are noblewomen of Mycenae, γενέθλα γενναίων (129);[8] later she calls them "citizens" (1227: πολίτιδες), although they are of course subject to the house of Atreus (764). If they were seen coming out of the palace, it would probably be assumed that they were closely related to the royal family, for although in reality many noble families might have had "rooms at court" in the Bronze Age palace complexes, the fifth-century playwrights never suggest that anyone other than the immediate family (and, of course, slaves) lives in the royal house. In fact, the chorus are ignorant of proceedings within the palace; they have to ask Electra in order to learn whether Aegisthus is at home or away. From this we may assume that the chorus entered from the parodos: fifteen women richly dressed, mature in bearing, eminently respectable—a sharp contrast to the foreign slaves who emerged from the palace with Aeschylus' Electra.[9]

In both form and content, the parodos (121–250) at once establishes an intimacy between Electra and the chorus. It is an evenly balanced kommos, with Electra and the chorus having an equal share in, rather than alternating, each strophe and antistrophe. This form strongly reinforces the comity and warmth that Electra and the chorus display toward one another. It is readily agreed by most critics that in this parodos the chorus sympathize with Electra on many points, such as the murder of Agamemnon, but in some ways disapprove of her behavior and gently rebuke her excess of grief and stubbornness.[10]

In her entrance anapests, Electra quickly informs the audience of the general mood within Agamemnon's house—no one mourns his death (100f.)—and of her particular circumstances—her home is loathsome and

---

8. In supposing that γενναίων refers only to "disposition," Jebb (ad 128f.) ignores the familial connotation of γενέθλα, which must mean either "family, race, stock" or "offspring," not just "group." If here the women are merely "noble-hearted," the subsequent use of γενέθλα without a genitive at line 226 is puzzling; but if they are "the offspring of noble parents," the phrase ὦ φιλία γενέθλα refers naturally back to the notion of "family, stock." See also Kamerbeek's suggestion (ad 129) that the πατέρων (or τοκέων) after γενναίων in the MSS was originally a gloss.

9. So also Burton, *The Chorus*, 186–187.

10. For example, Woodard (*HSCP* 68 [1964], 179–180): "Electra, they say, engages in shameful polemics and reproaches"; Kells (ad 153ff.): the chorus think her behavior is "excessive and quixotic, therefore hybristic"; Burton (*The Chorus*, 192): the chorus "represent a norm of balance" against Electra's "obsession."

wretched (92f.). She affirms her intent to lament her father's death publicly (109). Thus far the poet has presented no persons or facts to contradict or in any way criticize Electra's statements. Instead, directly after Electra's prayer to the Erinyes for help, Sophocles brings on the chorus of women, who vigorously denounce the murder of Agamemnon (124ff.). This juxtaposition of prayer to deity and entrance of mortal, a device that Sophocles uses elsewhere to great effect,[11] suggests that the chorus will be Electra's helpers in "balancing the counterweight of sorrow" (120). It is possible that the chorus' opening question may contain a tone of criticism: "with what ceaseless lamentation are you ever wasting away . . . ?" (122–123). But the interrogative phrase alone does not imply rebuke; that must come from vocal inflection or dramatic context. It is difficult, however, to achieve the subtle inflections of speech in a song; as for context, the chorus proceed directly to a condemnation of Agamemnon's murder without the slightest hint of criticism of Electra.

The question with which the chorus enter conveys an explanation of their entrance, a sense of public awareness of Electra's outcry, and a feeling of concern for her. The rest of the bipartite strophe establishes a reciprocity of affection and respect between Electra and the chorus (134). They have not come to berate Electra or to scold her, but to provide consolation and relief (130: παραμύθιον). This Electra recognizes and appreciates, but tries politely to refuse (136: ἱκνοῦμαι), for she wants to be allowed to continue immersed in grief.[12] After the nature of the relation between Electra and the chorus has been established in the strophe, the chorus attempt to be a παραμύθιον in the antistrophe. Their first statements show practicality and concern for Electra's well-being: her mourning will not bring her father back to life and is killing her. They are not discussing matters of philosophical principle, nor criticizing Electra's manners, they are asking why she is destroying herself with incurable pain (140).[13] This is the first verbal suggestion that Electra's own situation is not a safe or comfortable

11. *Oed. Tyr.* 924, *El.* 660. Compare also *Aj.* (695, 719) and *Ant.* (1149, 1155), where the prayer for a divine appearance and the subsequent human entrance are part of the joy-before-disaster effect.

12. Jebb renders line 135 as "leave me to rave thus"; Kells (*ad loc.*) claims that ἀλύειν may almost be translated as "be demented." But there is no proof that the word refers to a condition rather than an action, or describes any aspect of behavior other than vocal utterance ("cry aloud," "wail," "lament," etc.).

13. Kells' translation, "you waste yourself . . . upon intractable grief," misses the lexical force of ἀμήχανον ἄλγος and διόλλυσαι. Further, τὰ μέτρια here is not so much "what is reasonable" or "moderation" as the opposite of ἀμήχανον, that is, "what is manageable"; cf. LSJ, *s.v.*

one, that her grief alone is not her entire problem. Surely the audience
would have been awaiting some explanation of Electra's apparently unsuitable costume (191, 452). When Electra replies that it is right to mourn
one's parents forever, that such dedicated sorrow is divine, the chorus do
not argue or deny her statement. Ignoring the principle and concentrating
on the practical, they point out that the burden is not hers alone to bear,
for she has sisters with her in the palace. Further, the chorus know of
Orestes' secret existence and offer the prospect of his glorious and triumphant return.

There is, however, no comfort for Electra in the thought of Orestes' return, for it is an old hope. She informs the audience (164ff.) that she has
been waiting for him, but he hesitates and delays. Now it becomes clear
her situation is unpleasant: she has not been married (surely it is the duty
of her closest relatives—Clytemnestra and Aegisthus—to find a husband
and provide a dowry for her) and she lives in misery (167). Again, the chorus
do not deny Electra's assertions. They offer her the ultimate recourse, to
leave her troubles to the gods. They are suggesting a compromise, that
Electra rely on others to take effective action—namely, Zeus and Orestes
and Hades himself—while she disguises her own anger without wholly ex-
tinguishing it. This is a common and practical attitude of the chorus', for
expediency is often the only means of survival. Time will take care of
everything (179). But, as Electra points out, time has not taken care of
anything thus far; the better part of her time has already passed, yet she is
still unmarried, childless, enduring wretched treatment in her own murdered father's home.

For the third time the poet leaves Electra's assertions unrefuted. This
time the chorus do not try to offer another comforting vision of the future.
Instead Sophocles conjures up the hideous spectre of the past, the scene of
gore that led directly to Electra's dreary present. It is only after Electra, in
response to the chorus, cries out against Aegisthus and Clytemnestra,
curses them with the vengeance of Zeus, that the chorus try to hush her
(213–220). Their admonition to speak no further has a tone of urgency
and suggests conspirators' fear of being overheard; they issue the same
warning when they see Chrysothemis coming out of the house later (324).
They do not say that Electra's behavior is "abnormal" or "hubristic," [14] but
that it is dangerous. By not keeping silent, by openly defying the ruling
powers, she has got herself into terrible trouble. Electra does not deny

14. Kells, *ad* 153, 213, 221.

their assessment; indeed, she says that she is well aware of what she is doing (222), but that she has no alternative to rejecting the "serviceable [i.e., expedient] word."

In their response, with its twenty-one successive long syllables contrasting with the preceding rhythms, the chorus voice a wholly personal plea that Electra not make her own life more miserable than is necessary (233–235). The intensely personal basis of their plea, likening their concern to that of a true mother, provides a suitable introduction to Electra's final statement of moral dedication and religious belief: it can never be right to neglect one's dead parents; if their slayers go unpunished, neither society nor religion can endure. The poet has made this both the climax and the end of the parodos, for it stands unchallenged. Instead of continuing the lyric dialogue with its attempts at mollifying Electra's determination, the chorus yield, in the iambic trimeters of rational discourse (251–253), to Electra's uncompromising principles. Accepting her idealism as right, they agree that she shall lead and they shall follow.

By making the parodos an evenly balanced kommos with equal division of the stanzas, the poet has introduced the chorus as a group of mature and practical women who converse with Electra nearly as with an equal. The duet form enhances the intimacy of their maternal affection for Electra and of her fond regard for their friendship. Some modern critics seem to believe that the chorus are concerned about either the propriety of her lack of "moderation" or its psychological effects upon her inner being. These critics assume that Sophocles was presenting Electra's mourning as a piece of neurotic self-indulgence, the morbid ruminations of a spinster traumatized in childhood by her father's death. Even those who in the end generally assert the necessity of Electra's deeds perceive a destructive element within her, an irrational compulsion that prevents her from controlling her emotions.[15] But not once do the chorus suggest that Electra's troubles are psychological or involve the contravention of a philosophical principle of "moderation is best." All the miseries mentioned in the parodos are physical: because Electra dares to defy the ruling powers she is unwed, meanly clothed, and ill fed. These are the conditions the motherly chorus are trying to assuage. This is not a crowd of starry-eyed idealists or frenzied partisans, but fifteen sensible and concerned adults whom Electra persuades to her view of the right way to proceed.

15. Cf. Kamerbeek, *ad* 222; Linforth, "Electra's Day," 115–116; Burton, *The Chorus*, 191–196.

The play began with a conspiracy of men coming from abroad; the parodos initiates a conspiracy of women at home. When Electra graciously responds to the chorus' submission (254–255) and then sets forth the details of her life that were hinted at in the parodos, the women of Mycenae neither question nor comment upon her assertions. Instead they appear to ignore them completely by changing the subject to the question of Aegisthus' whereabouts (310–311). The brief dialogue between Electra and the chorus-leader (310–316), with its emphatic repetition of the fact that he is out of the house and the consequent assumption that they may speak more freely, greatly increases the air of secrecy and danger that was beginning to gather in the parodos. At line 316 we are not sure what the chorus are up to—at least, we probably have not been expecting an abrupt change of subject. But when they ask for news of Electra's brother, the conspiratorial nature of this scene becomes apparent. They have twice mentioned their hope for the eventual and triumphant return of Orestes, but now their tone is one of immediate concern. The implication is obvious that they accept without question Electra's description of the wrongs she suffers within the house and that they see Orestes as the champion who should and will return to right those wrongs. When Electra complains of his delays, they do not criticize her impatience but again try to cheer her with their optimistic faith that good will win out in the end (322). Electra shares their faith to some extent; it is the only thing that has kept her alive all this time (323). The chorus' act of suddenly warning Electra to silence at the appearance of Chrysothemis reinforces the secretive mood of the scene, which ends on a note of complete agreement among the conspirators.

With the entrance of Chrysothemis, the chorus' role changes from that of interlocutor to that of intermediary. Chrysothemis embodies the advice that the chorus were giving Electra in the parodos: she recognizes the dangers of open opposition to power and by keeping silence ensures her own personal safety. Electra, who was intense but polite when she answered the motherly chorus on the same subject, now displays a passionate anger toward her collaborating sister. At this point (369–371) the chorus intervene to mediate, not because it is the inescapable fate of choruses to mediate,[16] but because the poet chose to have them intervene. He has given the chorus-leader's initial words a sharp and urgent tone. Her curt admonition against anger, μηδὲν πρὸς ὀργὴν, is so clipped that it does not even contain the imperative verb form, much less a polite subjunctive or inter-

16. Cf., for example, Kamerbeek, *ad loc.*

rogative; and the following phrase, πρὸς θεῶν, has more the urgency of "for God's sake!" than merely "I beg you!" [17] We cannot tell precisely from the text whether the chorus-leader is meant to address Electra or Chrysothemis, but it seems likely that at first she speaks about anger to Electra; when she says that there is something to be gained from each of their views, "if you would learn to profit by her words, and she by yours," she is probably meant to turn or gesture from one character to the other.

The effect is to reinforce our perception of the chorus as practical, level-headed, and mature. They criticize not the substance but the anger of Electra's accusations against Chrysothemis; their attitude is positive in that they seek to advance a common purpose by advising the two to "make use of" each other's advice. Depending on the position of the characters onstage, the dramatic effect could be that of a mother stopping a growing quarrel between two sisters, coming between them to propose a compromise. The chorus-leader does, in fact, achieve mediation: Chrysothemis responds to her about Electra, then Electra speaks directly to Chrysothemis, both somewhat pettishly, and soon they are engaged in dialogue, although not in agreement. By creating a triangular pattern of dialogue, the chorus function to unite the two characters rather than isolate or separate them, and thus to maintain the pace of the action.

This exchange leads directly to the advancement of the conspiracy, in which the chorus are also instrumental. Directly after Electra's proposal to Chrysothemis to discard Clytemnestra's offerings and substitute their own, the chorus-leader asserts the piety of Electra's request and fondly but firmly (σὺ δέ . . . ὦ φίλη) urges Chrysothemis to comply with it (464–465). It is significant that Chrysothemis, while expressing agreement with Electra's arguments, seems actually to address her response (466–471) to the chorus rather than to Electra. There is no indication of her speaking directly to Electra, although she may include her as one of the φίλαι when she asks them all not to tell Clytemnestra about this act of defiance (469). The poet has used the chorus in another triangular pattern of dialogue to reinforce and extend the sense of the united conspiracy of women.

The dream that Chrysothemis reports generates action and argument, but no interpretation by the principals save a general sense of fear and the belief expressed by Electra that it was sent by Agamemnon. With the departure of Chrysothemis, the women of the chorus expound to Electra the

---

17. As Jebb translates it. Compare, for example, the urgent tone of *Phil.* 1185, *Aj.* 371, *Oed. Tyr.* 1037.

portent's significance, in the first stasimon of this play. The vehemence of their opening statement in the strophe—"unless I am an insane prophet" (472)—is matched by the conclusion of the antistrophe—"else there is no validity at all in any dreams or oracles." It is impossible, inconceivable to them that the dream could portend anything but approaching retribution for Clytemnestra and Aegisthus. The chorus offer to Electra what they see as the clear indication that the delays are over and help is actually on the way. It suits the mood of the conspiracy that they do not bid Electra to take hope, but say instead that they themselves take hope from the omen, implying that they are as deeply affected as she by everything that is happening. And in their view, a great deal is happening. Agamemnon is showing his concern, both as father and as king of the Hellenes (482–483); the murder weapon itself is conscious of the foul deeds (484–487); and the Erinyes, whose aid Electra invoked just before the parodos, have posted an ambush (488ff.).

The mention of the Fury here and previously (112, 276) is supposed by some to have the effect of foreshadowing the results of Electra's revenge, of reminding the audience that the Furies will pursue Orestes as the matricide. Each of the references, however, occurs in a sexual context where the emphasis is on the unholy mixture of marriage and murder. The first reference is general, to the Furies as those "who have an eye for unjust deaths, for illicit unions" (113–114). In the next, Clytemnestra is specified, and the fact that she dares, "fearing no Fury," to cohabit with a man so vilely stained by blood-guilt (275: μιάστορι). Now in this song the chorus dwell at greater length on the foul and polluted coupling that has provoked the Fury's attack.[18] If the poet had made the chorus and Electra speak of the Furies solely as avengers of kindred blood, we might perhaps think of an Aeschylean pursuit of Orestes yet to come. Here, however, attention is being drawn to the sexual perversion of the lovers that began for them with the killing of Agamemnon but still continues in the present. If one is reminded of anything Aeschylean here, it is of Clytemnestra's perverted pleasure in the titillation of seeing the corpses of Agamemnon and Cassandra lying together (*Agam.* 1447). When in the epode the chorus look

18. The γάρ of line 492 implies the cause-and-effect relationship between them. See also Winnington-Ingram on the Furies and adultery (*Sophocles*, 231–232). On the sexual imagery of the passage, see Segal (*TAPA* 97 [1966], 494–495). The Erinyes in Sophocles are not portrayed as punishing only murder or adultery as here, but are also expected to avenge the prevention of burial (*Aj.* 1390, *Ant.* 1075); and Ajax even expects them to wipe out the entire Greek army in retribution for the slight to his honor (*Aj.* 837, 843).

back to the chariot race of Pelops as the source of all the house's troubles, they are not speaking simply of a general family curse that may continue to bring trouble. In that contest Pelops obtained his marriage with Hippodameia by treachery and murder; it is the curse engendered by that blood-stained marriage that has eventually produced this new horrid union.[19]

The conspiratorial atmosphere is suddenly shattered as Clytemnestra bursts forth upon the scene. Her entrance seems to have been intended to startle, for it is sudden and wholly unprepared. She does not even bother to identify herself, yet there could be no doubt about who this richly dressed and angry woman is who proceeds at once to lambaste Electra, nor any question about the motivation of her entrance, since both the chorus and Chrysothemis have entered unsummoned in response to Electra's lamentings. During the ensuing confrontation between Electra and Clytemnestra, the chorus are wholly silent except for lines 610–611, when the chorus-leader remarks that she sees that Electra is angry, but no longer sees any concern on her part to have justice ($\delta i \kappa \eta$) on her side. In view of their previous support of the righteousness of Electra's cause, it seems a bit strange for the chorus to criticize her speech here as lacking concern for justice. True, Electra's last words (608–609) are a stinging personal insult; they would account for the chorus' remarking on her anger, but otherwise everything she says has already been approved by the chorus—especially the notions that Clytemnestra's adultery is hideous, that she treats Electra shamefully, and that Orestes should return to punish her.

If we accept the lines as they stand, without emendation or re-attribution, there are three possible interpretations. First, it has been suggested that the chorus are not referring to Electra at all, but to Clytemnestra, who has become so upset during Electra's speech that she is making angry gestures by the end of it.[20] This would be a novel situation, for we have no other Sophoclean instances in which anyone, chorus or character, can be shown to ignore entirely a lengthy speech and to refer instead to an action taking place during the speech, unless to report an arrival or departure; even then, there is usually some transitional reference to what has just been said (e.g., *Tr.* 813–814, *El.* 1322–1323). Nor should we accept without question the assumption, often made but wholly unproven, that char-

19. The apparent irrelevance of the epode leads Gellie to suggest that Clytemnestra has already entered, so that the chorus are restricted to general remarks about disaster (*Sophocles*, 113); but the marriage of Pelops is especially relevant in this context.

20. Kamerbeek and Kells, *ad loc.*, both follow this view. Cf. Dawe's objections and emendation in his review of Kamerbeek's commentary (*Gnomon* 48 [1976], 228–234), 232, *ad loc.*

acters or chorus might indulge in elaborate mime or gestures during another's speech. That sort of "upstaging" distracts the audience's attention from the speaker's words, and we have no reason to believe that the Greek playwrights would have been any more likely to allow it than are modern ones, especially during such an important speech as Electra's defense against Clytemnestra.

If we disallow the possibility of otherwise unrecorded action or gestures, we must ask how the audience, assuming the remarks to refer to Electra, would have interpreted them in the instant. The lines might have been heard as direct criticism of Electra's arguments, but that, as everyone agrees, would be a noticeable contrast to the chorus' previous statements and thus probably surprising enough to raise the audience's expectations about the change in the chorus' attitude. After all, for them to turn around and criticize Electra in the hostile presence of Clytemnestra, whose behavior they have just been damning, is a form of betrayal. Yet no explanation of their supposed defection is ever presented by the poet; they continue to sympathize with Electra's plight and to insist upon divine vengeance (823–825). Perhaps Sophocles has deviated from his usual careful technique and allowed a dramatic inconsistency here that serves no evident dramatic purpose. But before accepting that view, it is worth asking why, if the chorus are really questioning Electra's righteousness, Clytemnestra does not pick up their use of the word δίκη (610) and fling it back in the usual Sophoclean manner, for she ignores that crucial word entirely and fastens instead upon the notion of φροντίς (611, 612). This suggests a third interpretation, that φροντίς and not δίκη is the most significant word in the chorus' remark, and that δίκη would not have been heard as "justice" but as something more mundane and particular. Δίκη can mean "judgment" or "punishment," and since the chorus have hitherto been worried about Electra's well-being, it would not be surprising if they should say that she seems to have lost all concern (φροντίς) for whether she is behaving prudently or is courting punishment by this outburst in front of Clytemnestra.[21]

One other proposed solution should also be considered: to take the lines

---

21. On the archaic usage of δίκη in connection with "property law and economic behavior," see M. Gagarin, "*Dike* in Archaic Greek Thought" (*CP* 69 [1974], 186–197). The phrase εἰ δὲ σὺν δίκῃ ξύνεστι is, as Jebb notes, "an unusual pleonasm"; certainly one might expect a more specific verb than ξύνεστι, such as "speak," "argue," "accuse" (cf. 1041). It is very tempting to emend the problem away, as does Dawe (*Gnomon* 48 [1976], 232).

away from the chorus and assign them instead to Clytemnestra.[22] It is a tempting proposition, for it would create a vivid contrast with the surrounding scenes in which the chorus help to create a triangular pattern of conversation. Here the chorus, who are known to oppose Clytemnestra, keep silent throughout the entire confrontation. Further, Clytemnestra's arrogance and the isolation of Electra would be enhanced by Clytemnestra's turning and speaking to the chorus about Electra instead of replying to her at once. Elsewhere Sophocles does use the device of thus isolating and spotlighting the hero, but not after a long speech in an *agon* such as this one. A possible parallel may be sought from *Ajax* 1091, where, after Menelaus' lengthy tirade against Teucer, the chorus-leader briefly admonishes Menelaus; then Teucer, instead of replying to Menelaus, turns to the chorus and speaks to them about what Menelaus has just said. There is also another instance, at *Phil.* 1348ff.: Neoptolemus has just predicted the benefits that Philoctetes would receive from going to Troy and begged him to cooperate. Philoctetes does not reply directly, but speaks for a while as if to himself about Neoptolemus' plea (1350: "What shall I do? How can I refuse him?"). Still, in the absence of more convincing arguments, these examples alone are not sufficient to confirm the proposed re-attribution of the lines.

Whichever interpretation we place on the chorus' words, the fact remains that they are unusually quiet in this scene as compared with the preceding ones, in which they have been continuously involved. They never address Clytemnestra directly, and they only speak twice more in her presence. When the Paedagogus enters and inquires whether he has reached the house of Aegisthus and Clytemnestra, the brief unadorned phrases with which the chorus reply (662, 665: "this is it, you are correct"; "yes indeed, this is she") may suggest their aloofness from the words and actions of the queen. Their curtness may also suggest a certain difficulty in accepting without any comment the notion that this is "the house of king Aegisthus" (661) and that Clytemnestra is "his wife." But these restrained and colorless words are certainly the opposite of the fervor of the chorus' final utterance in the scene, for when the long description of Orestes' death is brought to its end, the chorus-leader cries out ($\phi\epsilon\hat{v}$ $\phi\epsilon\hat{v}$) in sorrow for the end of the "race of the ancient rulers" (764–765). This may not be a strong political declaration, but it is rather bold in view of the chorus'

22. Proposed by Lilley (*CQ* 25 [1975], 309–311).

concern for safety, and its directness and spontaneity make a significant contrast to Clytemnestra's indecision over how to receive the news of the death of her son (766–768).

With the departure of Clytemnestra, the chorus become increasingly active participants in the action of the play. Their intimacy with Electra is reaffirmed almost at once in an agitated kommos of two strophic pairs (823–870) that is generally called a consolation and as such is criticized as a failure. But it has more the aspect of agitated conversation than of any formal consolation. We might have expected, after the exit of Clytemnestra and the Paedagogus, that the poet would insert a lyric passage. Instead we get another speech, in which Electra voices her defiance and despair in rational iambic trimeters. Next we might expect the chorus-leader to reply with an iambic couplet, in conversational fashion; but again the poet uses the unexpected to keep the pace of the drama rapid. The chorus burst into a lyric expression of outrage, as they did upon their arrival, and insist, as they also did before, on the rightness of divine vengeance upon the wicked: "How can the Light of the world, by night or by day, fail to expose these horrors?" This expression causes Electra to weep and cry out, so that the chorus, following their already well-established concern for danger, try to muffle her cries.[23]

Electra now rejects their hope of assistance from the supernatural. When they offer the story of Amphiarus as proof of the power of the dead, she proves them wrong: Amphiarus had Alcmeon, but Orestes is dead. So also in the parodos the chorus offered the hope of the gods' eventual assistance (173–184) and Electra countered with the fact that time was running out. If the story of Amphiarus seems a poor and irrelevant consolation, as critics complain, it is because it is not presented as a consolation but as a proof, and as such it is so relevant to the present situation that it proves the opposite of its speakers' intent. So, at the end of the first strophic pair, both the chorus and Electra are left without hope. Only now does the real

---

23. It is important to note that Electra does not begin to mourn lyrically until after the chorus have begun to protest the injustice of Orestes' death. In a flight of imagination the scholiast apparently reasoned in reverse that the chorus must be admonishing Electra and therefore μηδὲν μέγ' αὔσῃς (830) must mean "do not utter an overbold word"; as she has not said a whole word yet, he concluded that she must be making gestures indicating an imminent outburst against the gods. But since Electra has never before shown the slightest inclination to blaspheme, and since μέγα αὔω most likely means "shout a great shout" here as it does everywhere else (cf. Homer, Il. 11.10, 5.101, etc.; Soph., Oed. Tyr. 1260), the scholiast's proposal should not be taken seriously. See, however, contra, Kamerbeek (ad loc.) and Burton (The Chorus, 204).

mourning begin. The chorus sympathize with Electra's sufferings (849, 853), offer their usual practical observation (860: "all mortals must die"), which Electra again shows to be inadequate to the facts of the present situation, yield to her view (864), and finally become so involved in the sorrow that they themselves cry out (867: παπαῖ). The poet has brought even these most hopeful and enduring persons to the nadir of despair, in artful preparation for the intricate "recognition scene" that is about to begin with Chrysothemis' appallingly joyful entrance.

But Sophocles does not choose to bring happiness to Electra just yet, perhaps because he has not yet plunged her into totally unrelieved hopelessness; she still has the support, however shaky, of her sister inside the house. Now the poet dissolves the conspiracy of women, so that Electra appears deprived of all possibility of help. The contrast in dynamic tension between the two Electra-Chrysothemis scenes is in large measure effected by the changed position of the chorus in respect of the two characters. After Electra's speech to Chrysothemis proposing the slaying of Aegisthus, the chorus-leader proffers advice to both sisters, addressing each in turn (990–991), just as she did before (369–371). The admonition that in such troubles forethought is a useful ally (σύμμαχος) to both speaker and hearer is given in lines heavily laden with almost the same dative plural phrases as the earlier advice that each might find profit (κέρδος) from the other's words. And just as before, Chrysothemis responds to the chorus about Electra (992, cf. 372) and then tries to persuade her sister to the cautious way of inaction and silence. At this point, however, the dramatic patterns of the earlier scene are entirely reversed: it is now Chrysothemis instead of Electra who persuades the chorus to her point of view; the chorus bid Electra to act with Chrysothemis' caution (1015: πρόνοια) where once they commended Electra's pious action to Chrysothemis (464: εὐσέβεια); finally, where once Chrysothemis agreed without hesitation to the chorus' opinion, now Electra completely ignores the chorus and defies her sister. With Chrysothemis' exit, the scene ends in discord instead of the former conspiratorial harmony.

Before, the chorus were used to unite the two sisters; now their failure serves to emphasize the rift between the characters. We may suppose that when Electra ignores the chorus' direct address to her, an uncommon occurrence in Sophocles, her behavior is a significant part of the dramatic effect, especially since the poet has so carefully established intimacy between Electra and the chorus. This is not to say that the chorus turn against Electra or separate themselves from her as Chrysothemis does.

Their admonition of caution issues naturally from the practicality that they have consistently advocated. Neither they nor Chrysothemis in any way criticize the moral or political aspects of Electra's proposal; their only complaint is that she refuses to value expediency as highly as they do. Although we may have the feeling that the chorus would not physically help Electra do what she proposes, any faint notion we might have that they may abandon her is negated by the ode in praise of her devotion sung directly after Chrysothemis goes off into the house.

In this second stasimon (1058–1097), the chorus seem to have made a decision, for they confirm the moral validity of Electra's values as against those of Chrysothemis, and indeed they actually condemn, albeit mildly and briefly, Chrysothemis' desertion. The characteristically indignant tone of the first stanza, where they call the birds who care for their parents (i.e., Electra) φρονιμωτάτους in contrast to Chrysothemis' recent use of φρονεῖν (1056), the implication that those who neglect their parents (i.e., Chrysothemis) will suffer for it (1065: δαρὸν οὐκ ἀπόνητοι), and the statement that Electra has been betrayed (1074: πρόδοτος)—all these must have been heard as criticism of Chrysothemis' final departure. The women may have agreed with her prudence, but not with her withdrawal; they come down firmly on Electra's side and praise her devotion unreservedly for the rest of the song.[24]

The chorus' fervent wish in the antistrophe that Electra's piety may be rewarded by exaltation over her enemies is answered by the entrance of Orestes (who is surely recognizable to the audience), as Clytemnestra's insidious prayer was answered by the entrance of the Paedagogus. This action begins a succession of heavily ironic contrasts, both verbal and structural, between the earlier Clytemnestra-Paedagogus scene and the present Electra-Orestes scene. Clytemnestra closed her prayer for her own triumph with the statement that "all is evident to the sons of Zeus"; the chorus end their prayer for Electra's triumph with praise of her "piety toward Zeus." The Paedagogus addressed his first words to the chorus, asking for "the house of King [τυράννου] Aegisthus" and they then referred him to Clytemnestra; now Orestes also addresses the chorus, but asks only for "the place where Aegisthus lives" (1101), and this time they refer him to Electra. The parallels continue through the scene, as the Paedagogus'

---

24. Kells' proposed addition of a negative at line 1087, to make the chorus call Electra "*not* wise, but nevertheless good," is not wholly unsuitable; but neither is it necessary, since the chorus seem to have given up the idea that Electra is "unwise." In fact, never again during the rest of the play do they urge prudence or caution upon the heroine.

speech describing the false death is matched by Electra's speech mourning the false death, and the kommos of sorrow following Clytemnestra's departure is replaced by a duet of joy.

Within the parallel structures of the two scenes, the chorus perform contrasting functions, just as they did in the two Chrysothemis scenes. Whereas in the earlier scene they had no communication whatsoever with Clytemnestra, here the poet has carefully woven them into the fabric of the action. It is the chorus-leader, and not Electra herself, who confirms Electra's identity for Orestes, as she tries to alleviate Electra's sorrow with the thought that all mortals shall die someday (1171–1173).[25] This is more than a merely conventional consolation; Electra has, after all, just expressed the desire to die now and so be free of sorrow. Then, almost at the point of the recognition, the poet draws attention to the chorus by making Orestes remark their presence and Electra assure him of their allegiance (1203–1204). And only a moment after she has acknowledged that the man before her is truly Orestes (1224), she presents him to the chorus, calling them "dearest ladies" and "compatriots" (1227). To this introduction the chorus-leader responds that not only do they see him, but tears of joy have sprung to their eyes at this good fortune (1230–1231).[26] Such a strongly emotional response by the chorus indicates that the audience is not to perceive Electra's imminent lyric rejoicing as being "excessive" or "hysterical" (as some do), since she can hardly be said to exceed the point of tears, which the chorus have already reached.

In this manner the poet draws the chorus into the joy, and hence the subsequent plot, from the start. The rejoicing that we naturally expect to follow the revelation does not retard the pace with static lyric; nor are we offered the significant contrast between Electra's emotional lyrics and

25. It is not a question of defining the precise moment that Orestes recognizes Electra, and, of course, the notion that the recognition does not occur until these lines is absurd (cf. Kamerbeek, *ad* 1117). The sole reason for the naming of Electra here is to make the *audience* absolutely certain that Orestes must have recognized her by the time he begins to speak. If the poet had not named Electra at this point, he would have had to make Orestes say at once that he recognizes her; otherwise, during the next forty lines the audience might wonder whether or when he has managed to identify her.

26. Curiously, in line 1230 the chorus-leader uses both the singular and the plural of the first person: ὁρῶμεν and μοι. Kaimio (*Chorus of Greek Drama*, 162n2) seems to ignore this, suggesting only that the plural "reflects the second person plural used by Electra in 1228" (ὁρᾶτ'). Although the mixture of persons here tends perhaps to contradict the view that the chorus-leader's "immediately expressed sensory perceptions" are always in the first person singular, it does confirm the observation that the chorus-leader "can be said to speak as an individual" without, of course, differing from the rest of the chorus (161).

Orestes' cool, cautious iambics that some critics seem to perceive. Certainly there is a metrical contrast, although Electra's lyrics also have a touch of iambic trimeter (1235, 1256), and certainly Electra savors the present joy while Orestes worries about the present danger. Still, the polarity of the scene is reduced by the third party to it, the chorus. Even if they do remain silent throughout the entire recognition sequence, because of their initial weeping the spectator cannot forget for a single moment their presence at and participation in the reunion.[27] The rejoicing is more that of a group than of a pair, and Orestes' fears of being overheard serve more to maintain dramatic tension than merely to set off Electra's alleged emotionalism; it has, we must remember, been indisputably established that Electra can be overheard from within and that Clytemnestra can appear without warning at any moment.

If the chorus have remained silent during the preceding episode, their next brief song (1384–1397) informs us that they no longer seem to feel a need for cautious restraint. Rather, they thoroughly approve both the plotting to which they have just been privy and its acknowledged goal, the killing of Clytemnestra by deceit. Again, the placing of iambic trimeter lines in the middle and end of each of these two short stanzas probably modifies the lyricism and prevents any slackening of the suspense and anticipation. The series of metaphors that the chorus use here to describe the entry of the avengers is particularly indicative of their approval of the vengeance. The deadly god of war, they say, is advancing, the inescapable hounds (i.e., Furies) who relentlessly hunt down wicked villainy have entered the house; Orestes, the advocate of the dead (1392: ἀρωγός, as in *Il.* 18.502), is formally led into his father's ancestral home by Hermes himself. There is nothing in their words to suggest that this is a deed of personal vengeance. The women speak only in general societal terms: this is an act of war, to punish those who have committed all manner of crimes (1387: κακῶν πανουργημάτων) and to restore the rightful heir to his patrimony.[28] The

---

27. If, as few do nowadays, we read φίλαι at 1281 instead of φίλε, Electra is again drawing the chorus in as a third party to the scene. Further, the scholiast asserts at 1322 that some give "these" lines to the chorus; if we join Dawe (*Studies on the Text*, 198, *ad loc.*) in giving all of 1322–1325 to the chorus, then they are apparently accepting and entering upon the great deception. Cf. David Bain (*Actors and Audience* [Oxford, 1977], 80n3), who prefers giving only 1322–1323a to the chorus.

28. The chorus' initial assertion in the ode, that "Ares is advancing, breathing invincible death," obviously echoes Pindar, *Pyth.* 11.35–37, and Aeschylus, *Choëph.* 938. But Ares is not "the god of destructive force, of bloodshed, . . . the lust of murder personified" (Kamerbeek, *ad* 1385). In Athens he was the god only of organized warfare between armed warriors;

potential objection that deceit must be used to accomplish these worthy ends is answered by the sanction of the god Hermes.

Having committed the chorus to approval of the coming murder of Clytemnestra, Sophocles then uses them to effect the substitution of a dialogue scene for the customary messenger's speech reporting the death within. The only possibly comparable device in Sophocles appears in *Ajax*, where the hero himself announces and in a way describes his imminent death and so precludes the need for an eyewitness report. The resultant scene in *Electra* is conspicuous for its artful twists in the patterns of both movement and speech. Electra's startling return has a threefold function. First, it maintains the dramatic tension by continuing the apprehension of danger; Electra has come to guard against Aegisthus' apparently impending return (1402–1403). Further, her immediate reappearance makes a material connection between the visible action and the action within, so that there is a sense of factual description here as contrasted with *Agamemnon*, where the chorus guess and wonder in ignorance. Finally, Electra's return has removed her from the presence of the action, so that she takes no physical part at all in the murder, and has joined her with the sympathetic and approving chorus at this crucial moment in the drama.

Metrically this kommos is far more a dialogue than a lyric passage. Of the twenty-four lines in the first stanza, only nine can be said to be in truly lyric portions (1407–1408, 1413–1414, 1417–1421—of which 1420 is an iambic trimeter), the rest being iambic trimeters. The dramatic effect is therefore one of rapidity and rationality rather than the slower pace and heightened emotions of regular lyric. In this context the chorus voice their own judgment of the matricide as the retribution that they have desired and awaited throughout the play.[29] At this moment, the very end of the

---

cf. Farnell, *Cults* V, 396ff. In Sophocles, too, "Ares" always signifies the mythical figure of the god himself or, by extension, war and battle between armed combatants: *El.* 96; *Oed. Col.* 1046, 1065, 1391, 1679; *Ant.* 126, 139, 952, 970; *Aj.* 614, 1196. There are three places where the word is used in a symbolic sense: *El.* 1242 (even women may sometimes have a "warlike" spirit), *Oed. Tyr.* 190 (the plague is a "bronzeless Ares"), *Aj.* 254 (death by public stoning, λιθόλευστον Ἄρη). For Ares as a savior, see *Aj.* 706 and *Tr.* 653.

29. Not only are these lyric lines embedded in an iambic trimeter context, but the goriest of them is itself an iambic trimeter (1420: "blood flows for blood, drained from the [slayers]"—Jebb). It was probably meant to be delivered in a less lyric, therefore less emotional, mode than fully lyric lines. On the Sophoclean theme of the dead killing the living, see Kitto, *Form and Meaning*, 93; and with this passage in *Electra* compare *Oed. Col.* 621–623 where, in his famous speech on Time, Oedipus asserts that his buried, sleeping corpse shall someday drink the warm, fresh blood of Thebans.

strophe, Orestes and Pylades come out of the house, an ironically (some might say melodramatically) well-timed and striking entrance. The chorus' announcement of the entrance, made in iambic trimeters (1422–1423), is actually the beginning of the responding antistrophe, in which the poet weaves Orestes into the dramatic pattern by expanding the pattern from the chorus and one actor, with cries offstage, to the chorus and two actors onstage. We cannot tell at what point the audience began to perceive the passage's true nature as an antistrophe rather than merely dialogue, but the precisely repeated pattern of the antilabe and lyric portions, and (if we assume with most editors lacunae after 1427 and 1429) of the number of full iambic lines per speaker, is so clearly deliberate that the poet must have expected the audience to recognize it. Perhaps we should therefore presume that some "background" music was played during the nonlyric portions of such stanzas, not enough to eradicate the iambic patterns but sufficient to suggest the unity of strophe and antistrophe and to distinguish these iambics from the nonresponding passages of iambic trimeter dialogue that are sometimes inserted between lyric stanzas (as probably at *Oed. Tyr.* 669–677).

The chorus have described the killing in terms that suggest their approval, but now with Orestes' entrance they state it unequivocally: the act was a sacrifice to Ares and they find no fault with it.[30] But it would seem that they step beyond simple passive approval and actively throw themselves into the deception. If lines 1428–1429, 1433–1434, and 1437–1441 are, as most editors agree, correctly attributed to the chorus, then these women warn of Aegisthus' approach, order the men to rush inside, and then advise Electra to deceive Aegisthus with soothing words. All this is compressed into the antistrophe of a kommos that must be considered unique, for Sophocles at any rate, in its devices, metrical arrangements, and frantic activity.

The end comes swiftly, signaled as usual by a brief anapestic system preceding the exit of the chorus. Few critics, however, have any high regard for the chorus' closing words here (1508–1510). Many perceive a tone of ruthless exultation in the congratulatory statement, in the notion that worthy aims have been accomplished and freedom attained, a tone that does not sound well at all to the delicate ear of modern sensibility. Therefore they call it a mere tag ending that may be ignored in the context of the

---

30. Accepting ψέγειν for λέγειν at 1423; see Kamerbeek, *ad loc.*, and Dawe's review of Kamerbeek (*Gnomon* 48 [1976], 233–234).

whole play, or a deliberately ironic or even ominous hint dropped by the poet lest the audience should be tempted to believe the literal meaning of the chorus' words. If we refrain from the Gordian-knot method of solving the passage's problems by excising it altogether,[31] we must consider its fitness and relevance to the chorus' character both in the present scene and in the play as a whole.

It is widely and probably correctly believed that Electra is alone in front of the house with the chorus at the very end. Certainly the postulated withdrawal of the men and the corpse at line 1507, probably on the *ekkyklema*, has been more than adequately prepared for by the verbal sidestepping between Aegisthus and Orestes (1491ff., 1501ff.); and the chorus' initial vocative (1508: ὦ σπέρμ' ᾿Ατρέως) could reasonably be addressed to a single person. If this is indeed the situation, its effect is to isolate Electra from the corpse of Clytemnestra and to remove her physically from the scene of the killing. At the moment of Aegisthus' death, which does not actually occur within the play but is surely assumed to be occurring, she is once again outside and supported by the entirely approving chorus. With or without, but especially with, this arrangement of persons on the scene, the chorus' final words are entirely in keeping with their role in the preceding scenes: at last all has turned out well for Electra, as they have predicted and prayed for throughout the play.

Their statement that she has at last through great effort emerged from the sufferings of the past, from the troubles that have plagued her as Atreus' descendant,[32] into the freedom of the present harks back to their fervent prayer at lines 1090–1097 that the past be overcome and Electra emerge into the better future that she deserves because of what she has endured and dared through her piety. There is no word or phrase in these final lines that in any way connotes rejoicing, exultation, or ghoulish delight. It is hard to see how the passage could by itself offend the taste of any era, for it is a restrained expression of relief from trouble, an assurance given that the worst is over. It is the idea of the killing of Aegisthus

31. Dawe (*Studies on the Text*, 203–204) favors deleting at least 1505–1510 and has serious doubts also about the authenticity of preceding lines. But the chief argument is still only a matter of taste: the lines "hardly seem to flow from the well-spring of Sophoclean genius."

32. Aegisthus has just referred to the troubles of the past (1498), which are also those of the present and future—for Aegisthus, as Orestes says (1499). There is little reason to think the audience heard this as a hint of the Furies' pursuit of Orestes; Aegisthus speaks of the ills of the *Pelopidae*, a term much more applicable to him and his ill-gotten, bloodstained marriage than to Orestes, an *Atreides*.

and Clytemnestra as welcome relief from trouble that offends twentieth-century sensibilities; but for the chorus to express any other idea at this late point in the play would be so contrary to the pattern of their behavior that the audience would be left questioning not simply the meaning of the play but the reason for the chorus' unexpected and unexplained change of mind.

Once again, and finally, we can say that the chorus of this play do have a distinct character and that the poet does maintain them consistently in that character; no choral passages can be shown to be out-of-character utterances. The women of the chorus are always the noblewomen of Mycenae, not merely γυναῖκες but πολίτιδες. Probably some years older than Electra, perhaps even by a generation, they are nevertheless not "old women" in the sense that the chorus of *Oedipus Coloneus* are "old men." They are matrons of the community, the imaginary baronesses of the legendary Heroic Age, although their societal role does not seem to differ much from that of the upper-class wives of classical Athens, who probably held the important priestesshoods and set the standards for respectable female behavior. The poet has given them the personality of warmhearted, kindly women (they actually weep for joy at the fraternal reunion) who are also reasonable and practical, as is evinced by their concern for Electra's well-being and their advocacy of prudence, forethought, and the value of compliance rather than defiance when necessary to survive and attain eventual success in a worthy cause. Thus they are not foolish or hysterical, not starry-eyed romantics, nor yet blindly vengeful and bloodthirsty like the chorus of Euripides' *Ion*. Nor, on the other hand, can their commonsense approach be construed as timidity or cowardice, since their utterances contain recurrent tones of spirited indignation at wickedness and an irrepressible confidence in the righteous order of the universe; despair is almost unknown to them. Moreover, no criticism of their behavior is ever voiced by any character or implied by any action concerning them. This rather persuasive combination of positive characteristics and absence of censure, either explicit or implied, suggests that the audience was supposed to see them as good, sensible, respectable women, probably closer to the ideal rather than the average woman.

Sophocles has used this choral persona most patently to elucidate important aspects of Electra's conduct. The chorus also have another, less obvious function in the drama, but we shall consider this one first because it has considerable significance for the audience's assessment of Electra's character. That the chorus are intimate with and fond of Electra, and that the warm attachment is reciprocal, is early established by the exchanges of terms of endearment and politenesses (Electra actually apologizes to the chorus, 254–257), and even more emphatically by the structure of the play. The parodos and subsequent episode between Electra and the chorus are entirely different in tone from the comparable scenes in *Trachiniae*, where the chorus lecture Deianeira in an ode, and then speak only two lines to her (178–179) before the Messenger arrives. *Electra* contains two more such kommoi, in which the chorus share the heroine's most intense emotions: when Electra hears the news of Orestes' alleged death and again during the death of Clytemnestra. The chorus are also drawn into the recognition scene by Electra herself (1203–1204) and share her deep joy. It is through this relation between the chorus and Electra that we see her as a normal, decent woman, fond of her friends, treating them respectfully as equals in rank, and highly regarded, indeed loved, by them in turn.

From the moment of their entrance, the chorus support the righteousness of Electra's cause in words that are at least as vehement as hers. We may take further notice, however, of the method by which Sophocles reinforces the chorus' statements of support. There is a clearly perceptible progression in the chorus' dedication to Electra's way of doing things. At first they do object gently to her method of avenging her father by keeping his memory alive to irritate the murderers, not because of its impropriety or unattractiveness but because of the serious discomfort it causes the murderers to inflict on her. But when she has expounded her reasons and principles, especially the religious ones (245–250), they agree to her method without reservation (251–253). Next, when a larger question arises, not of discomfort but of mortal danger, the chorus counsel caution and then support Chrysothemis' objection—which is only to placing oneself in deadly peril without hope of success. But after they witness Electra rejecting Chrysothemis and accusing her of dishonor, the chorus seem themselves to have been persuaded, as they praise Electra's contemplated action and condemn Chrysothemis' desertion. After this, they join in the action of the plot almost as much as Electra does. Indeed, the only way in which Electra is more active than the chorus is in entering the house with Orestes—and she quickly returns without actually having done anything. She does, of course, deceive Aegisthus, but then she has been advised to do so by the chorus. Thus by the end of the play these sensible, admirable women are with Electra in every aspect—in emotions, in principles, and in action—so that her behavior is not that of one aberrant person but of sixteen persons. If, as some would claim, Electra is filled with hatred, so are they; if she is neurotically obsessed with the death of Agamemnon and the sexual behavior of Clytemnestra, they are even more so! In fact, they serve to show Electra as a woman who is not harsh, cruel, or even unreasonably stubborn.

In addition to their role in providing a context for Electra's demeanor, the chorus are the medium by which the poet introduces and answers the religious problems raised by the action. The principals occasionally pray to or swear by the gods, but Apollo is the only one of whom they make serious mention. But the chorus frequently assert an unwavering belief that numerous supernatural beings are concerned for and will assist in the punishment of Aegisthus and Clytemnestra: Zeus (162, 175, 823, 1063), Time (179: χρόνος . . . θεός), Hades (184), Dikê (475), the dead (who have power to affect the living, 482–483, 839–841, 1066ff., 1419), an Erinys (491), the Sun (824), Themis (1064), Ares (1385), and Hermes (1395). This is not to imply that the chorus' utterances in this play have the overtones of religious ritual that they seem to have in *Trachiniae*. Nevertheless, by far the largest number of religious asseverations in the play have been placed in the mouths of these women of impeccable character; and no one offers them any contradictions.

In the same manner the poet deals with the political implications of the action through the chorus. In their initial kommos it is they, and not Electra, who bring up the subject of Orestes (160–163) and insist that "the famous land of Mycenae will receive him as his father's heir" (162: εὐπατρίδαν). Soon they again express their desire for Orestes' return (317–318, 322) and speak of Agamemnon as the Lord of the Hellenes (483; they have already cursed his murderers). When Orestes' death is reported, the first response comes not from his mother but from the chorus, who cry out in sorrow for "the race of ancient rulers" (764–765); when he does arrive, the poet makes Electra present him at once to the chorus of πολίτιδες (1227). Moreover, they describe the killing of Clytemnestra as an act of war (1385: Ares) rather than a matricide or murder; at the critical moment in the killing of Clytemnestra when she cries out to her son to pity her (1410–1411, the only reference to matricide in the play) and Electra responds that she did not pity her son or his father, the chorus immediately cry out for the city and the family, as one and the same, that their past troubles are at last coming to an end.[33] While the death of Aegisthus occurs

33. 1413: ὦ πόλις, ὦ γενεά. As Jebb also notes, *ad loc.*, these words express the chorus' belief that "the cause of the house is that of the city. They hail the approaching deliverance of

offstage, they address Electra in formal fashion for the first time, speaking of freedom obtained at last.

The women who utter these opinions are not dependents or connections of the family, but outsiders. Sophocles has emphasized the fact that Aegisthus and Clytemnestra do not permit Electra to go outside the gates of the palace, lest her complaints should be heard by outsiders and prove embarrassing to the royal couple. She has "escaped" now only because Aegisthus is away (310–311, [329], 516–518, 638–642). Clearly they have good reason to restrict her movements and to fear the rebelliousness among the citizens which Aegisthus implies at lines 1458–1463, for Electra is an object of sympathy and admiration to those outside the palace, represented in the members of the chorus. If Sophocles had made this a chorus of men, he would have had to deal with questions of political morality, of revolution, of the relationship between ruler and subject or between citizen and state. In consequence, the focus of the play would very likely be shifted from Electra's behavior to the males as the true body politic. Therefore, Sophocles has made the chorus women who, filling the office of the many allegorical female figures from Roma to Columbia, symbolize the spirit of the nation without implying any actual participation of women in the political reality of the state. It is the function of these Mycenaean women to display, as representatives of the people of the land, the emotional response of those people: the conviction that Electra's actions are right and just, approved by society and the gods.

Mycenae from the tyrants." For further discussion of the vital emendation of σε to σοι, see Kamerbeek, *ad loc*.

CHAPTER 7

Electra and Judgment

It is hardly necessary to rehearse all the particulars of plot and situation that seem to vindicate Electra's action, many of which have already been noted, or all the citations of the poet's attempts to condemn Electra that are quickly refuted when examined within their dramatic context.[1] There does not appear to be any character or incident in the play of sufficient gravity to counterbalance the dramatic weight of the chorus' approval; nonetheless, a brief look at some that critics cite will show additional uses both of the chorus and of the same dramatic technique that the poet uses with the chorus: a progression in the intensity of effect that eventually becomes overwhelmingly convincing.

If the poet were seeking to create some ambiguity in the audience's attitude toward Electra by offsetting the effect of the chorus' support, perhaps the likeliest way would be to induce some sympathy for Electra's victims, a group that could include every other character in the play (except perhaps the Paedagogus), depending on one's point of view. Poor Chrysothemis, for example, is opposed to and afraid of Clytemnestra and Aegisthus and concerned for her sister's welfare, yet she receives nothing but scorn and abuse from Electra. But she is introduced as a coward and a collaborator (332–340, 357–362); when she does assist in a pious act, her last words before leaving are a request for secrecy that is motivated entirely by fear (468–471). In her speech against Electra's proposal that they kill Aegisthus themselves, she dwells solely on the danger of the act. In her stichomythia with Electra, she answers Electra's every argument with the same fear of danger (1042: "even Justice is injurious"). Finally, she goes back inside

---

1. For summaries of Sophocles' sympathetic presentation of Electra's actions, see especially Whitman (*Sophocles*, 153–171), Alexanderson's analysis of Friis Johansen (*C&M* 27 [1966], 79–98), and Lloyd-Jones' review of Kells' commentary (*CR* 25 [1975], 10–12).

after twice predicting that Electra will "praise" her words (1044, 1057), presumably after she has incurred the suffering that Chrysothemis so greatly fears. There is nothing pitiable here, even for the kindly and sensible women of the chorus. They disapprove of her behavior, without even mentioning her by name, and then she disappears from the play forever, to be replaced by Orestes, who does join his sister in the desperate task she proposed.

The rather fanciful notion of some critics that Electra deliberately and cunningly deceives Chrysothemis by proposing only that they kill Aegisthus when she really also plans to kill Clytemnestra arises out of the documentary fallacy and ignores entirely the presence and function of the chorus.[2] Electra is not a living person but a fictive creation; she does not have hidden motives that the audience must cleverly divine. If she is thinking something other than what she is saying, the poet must convey that fact to us verbally. The only hint alleged, however, is her use of the plural "enemies" (979: τοῖσιν ἐχθροῖς) when she cites the praises that the citizens will utter for "the two sisters . . . who, when their enemies were well established, without heed for their own lives came forward to administer death [to the enemies]." Surely Sophocles could have given us a bit more help by using the dual instead of the plural, since he so carefully maintains the "two sisters" in the dual and later has the chorus speak of a "double Erinys" (1081). Ajax's hotly debated "deception speech" is a pack of bald-faced lies compared to this one. And what of the chorus? Does Electra also deceive them? Evidently not, since they seem to imply that she is aiming at overpowering both Aegisthus and Clytemnestra, if they are the "double Erinys." But in that case the audience must assume that the chorus perceive the deception, say nothing specific about it to either sister, and apparently include it in the general approval of Electra's piety that their subsequent ode expresses, although they still do not mention it. It is far more reasonable to suppose that Sophocles makes Electra propose the attack on Aegisthus because he wants her to meet and reject arguments about personal danger and the rightness of self-preservation. If she proposed to kill Clytemnestra as well, it would be very strange if neither Chrysothemis nor the chorus discussed the rightness of the matricide; but if they did, the moral issue would surely eclipse the personal one and the structure of the scene and the characters, and especially of the choral ode, would have to be entirely revised—in fact, it would be quite a different play.

2. This interpretation is elaborated by Friis Johansen (C&M 25 [1964], 21–22), and wholeheartedly supported by Kamerbeek (ad 957).

Aegisthus qualifies physically as a "victim," but hardly a sympathetic one. What little we do hear of him is bad: he joins Clytemnestra in reviling and threatening Electra (300), and her ultimate punishment is said to be delayed only by his absence (379ff., 627). Directly upon his arrival he speaks with an arrogance that falls little short of cruelty, since he does not merely find relief in Orestes' death but takes deliberate pleasure in the unhappiness it must cause Electra. The insolence and contempt conveyed by the repeated use of the second person pronoun in his address to Electra, "You there, I mean you, yes, you, who used to be so bold" (1445: σέ τοι, σὲ κρίνω, ναὶ σέ), recall the imperious Creon's first words to Antigone when she is brought in by the guard as the newly discovered culprit (441: σὲ δή, σὲ . . .). When Aegisthus goes on to say that she can tell the news best since she cares most about it (1445–1446), and then that in affirming Orestes' death she has spoken an unwontedly "joyful greeting" (Jebb's phrase), we may assume the poet is presenting Aegisthus as cruel, since he has already shown, through her speech over the urn, how wretchedly unhappy Electra would be if Orestes really had died, and therefore how deeply Aegisthus' barbs would penetrate.

Perhaps, as some aver, the democratic audience would have reacted hostilely to Electra when she begs Orestes not to permit Aegisthus to speak in his own defense (1483ff.). She is not, however, asking that he be denied the right to speak, but the right to "spin out" his words (1484: μηκύνειν) so as to postpone his execution. The fifth century allowed the right to speak in one's own defense, yet it also saw a danger in the persuasive but unscrupulous speaker, such as Sophocles portrays in Odysseus of *Philoctetes* and Aristophanes indicts in *Clouds*. In the few lines that Sophocles has chosen to allow him, Aegisthus does not debate the morality of vengeance or defend (or repent of) his own actions, but mocks and delays Orestes with clever retorts.[3] In fact, we may presume that Sophocles does not want Aegisthus to make the long speech that would naturally be expected from a newly introduced character, but would obviously spoil the pace here, and

---

3. Cf. 1501: πολλ᾽ ἀντιφωνεῖς. If Sophocles had wanted the audience to be indignant on behalf of Aegisthus, he could most easily have made him supplicate Orestes. The fifth century would certainly not readily accept the killing of a suppliant. Aegisthus' failure to seek Orestes' mercy may seem like romantic defiance to modern spirits, but in Sophocles' day, when the ransoming of prisoners of war was fully acceptable, it may just as well have seemed arrogant folly. And what possible purpose can Aegisthus' "after you, Alphonse" routine have other than to show him as the coward he has been called, attempting to stall Orestes or perhaps even to escape? To remove that notion, Sophocles had only to give to Orestes instead of to his "victim" the initiative in suggesting that the order of precedence has significance.

he therefore creates Electra's interruption precisely to cover and explain the omission. Finally, Electra is supposed to be ordering Aegisthus' corpse thrown to the "birds and dogs" when she asks that after death he be handed over to those "from whom such as he should have burial" (1487; Jebb's translation). We are supposedly meant to recall the unburied bodies of *Ajax* and *Antigone* and so to condemn Electra's request as brutal and impious, or at least ominous.[4] Yet the crime of the Atreidae and of Creon was not that they failed to bury, but that they deliberately prevented others from burying. Electra would not be required to bury Aegisthus, who is after all a traitor (and only a first cousin once removed), but she does not in any way forbid others to do so. There is no suggestion that anyone else would want to bury him either—certainly not the chorus, who represent the people of Mycenae. If Electra's phrase is designed to make the audience think of Aegisthus as "a feast for birds and dogs," it does not at all imply that Electra is the cause, but rather that no one in the land would object.

Clytemnestra remains the most likely instrument by which the poet could demonstrate how Electra has been emotionally and morally damaged by her sufferings. No matter how many crimes Clytemnestra has committed, it is still the crime of matricide that Electra plots with her brother. Most critics maintain, to a greater or lesser extent, that the poet intended certain aspects of Electra's conduct toward her mother to show how unnatural and injurious heroic behavior must necessarily be; such is the stuff of tragedy. In order to accomplish this intent, however, the poet must portray Clytemnestra to some small degree as a maternal figure so that she may serve as a background against which we can clearly see the abnormalities of Electra's behavior as a daughter. The first undisputed example of Clytemnestra's maternal feeling occurs in her first speech (516ff.), in which she defends the murder of Agamemnon as her vengeance for his slaying of their daughter at Aulis. But she is quite willing to let Menelaus kill *his* children, nor does she question the fact that someone's child should be sacrificed, only asking, "Why *my* child rather than someone else's?"

Clytemnestra shows no such "affection" for her living children. She prays for a prosperous life with only those of her children who cause no

---

4. On whether Electra is supposed to mean "birds and dogs," see especially Bowra (*Sophoclean Tragedy*, 255), Alexanderson (*C&M* 27 [1966], 94), Kamerbeek (*ad* 1487), and Winnington-Ingram (*Sophocles*, 230*n*45). The question is not what Electra means, but what the audience is meant to hear; and that would as well be "his other relatives," or "anyone who cares to pick up the body."

trouble (652–653), and even the compliant Chrysothemis says that she herself will suffer if her mother learns of her disobedience (470–471). That the absent Orestes' situation is far more unpleasant is gradually revealed in the early part of the play. First we hear the Paedagogus' statement that he carried away the young Orestes and thus saved his life (12–13). Then Orestes says that the news of his death will be a "pleasing report" to the royal couple (56). Next Electra gives a direct description of Clytemnestra's reaction to rumors of Orestes' return: raving (294: ἐμμανής), she howls (299: ὑλακτεῖ) at Electra for having "stolen Orestes from my hands and carried him away to safety" (296). Soon Electra herself says that she saved Orestes' life (321), and later she speaks directly to Clytemnestra about Orestes, who "barely escaped your hands" (601).[5] Up to the moment of the Paedagogus' entrance, there have been no fewer than four statements that Clytemnestra intended to kill Orestes, one of which she herself is reported to have made, and two more statements that his death now would be a welcome relief for her. Not one of these is in any way contradicted by any of the characters, least of all by Clytemnestra, who never even mentions her son's name onstage. Instead, the poet has gradually built up the impression of Clytemnestra's deadly intent toward Orestes, an impression which is climaxed by the inferences meant to be drawn from her evasive prayer: she is praying for her son's death (644ff.).

At the same time, the facts of Clytemnestra's maternal relation to her daughter are consecutively revealed. First we learn that Electra is treated as a slave rather than a royal offspring (165, 189–192). Still worse, she must watch her mother celebrate the anniversary of her father's death and must keep her grief to herself (285–286), for her mother reviles her, even hates her (289: μίσημα), curses her (291: "may you die horribly," κακῶς ὄλοιο), and threatens her (298); then Aegisthus joins in (300). Electra's situation grows even worse, as Chrysothemis brings the news that, as soon as Aegisthus comes home, they will send Electra away to a prison outside

---

5. The use of "hands" here cannot possibly have the ambiguous import that Kells insists on in his comments, *ad* 296. Among other reasons, "to come into the hands of" regularly means danger, especially in Homer and Xenophon; conversely, "to escape the hands of" implies escape from danger, of which Euripides, *El.* 28, is a startling example: μήτηρ νιν ἐξέσωσεν Αἰγίσθου χερός. In addition, the verb reportedly used by Clytemnestra, ὑπεκτίθεμαι, always means "convey to a place of safety" in the sense of "away from the danger of war." This interpretation of "hands" is reinforced by the verb σώζω, used of Orestes' rescue; in connection with persons it always means "to save from death." We may also note that ὑλακτέω (299) is commonly used of animals' howling.

the land (379–382, in words that suggest the entombment of the living Antigone).

Next comes the actual confrontation between Electra and her mother, in which Electra, with a speech of rebuttal that is nearly twice as long as her mother's, refutes Clytemnestra's points and brings up several more, especially her neglect of her own legitimate children. Clytemnestra makes no answer except that Electra is insulting her mother (613), much as Creon uses his fatherhood, instead of reason, to answer his son (*Ant.* 726–727, 742). Finally, Clytemnestra herself threatens Electra with punishment when Aegisthus returns (626–627)—and we have just been told what that means!

If ever a mother were given a chance to display maternal feeling, to redeem herself for past acts against her child, Sophocles gave Clytemnestra that chance in the narrative of her son's death at the Olympic chariot race. The dramatic effect of this speech is to show that Clytemnestra behaves utterly unlike a Greek mother. It is the description of a valiant and glorious young man, who won every prize at the games, engaged in a heroic contest, was nearly victorious over champions of many other cities, then died in a particularly horrible manner: caught in the reins, dashed up and down by the horses' hooves, and so mangled that his corpse was unrecognizable. His glory makes his death the more horrible: the people who saw "bewailed the young man who, having done such deeds, came to such a terrible end" (750–751). For a fifth-century Athenian, this would be an ideal son and sufficient justification for his mother's existence. Yet Clytemnestra's first remark is the question whether it is a blessing or a terrible thing but still a gain. Then she says that it is grievous to save one's own life by one's own misfortunes (766–768). Finally, she declares that a mother, even if suffering ill from a child, never hates her own child—but we have already heard that she hates Electra (289).

The possibility that the audience is meant to hear these sentiments sympathetically, as expressions of genuine maternal feeling, is considerably weakened both by the order of the words of her first remark (766–767: εὐτυχῆ . . . δεινά . . . κέρδη) and by the actual facts of her previous behavior. Furthermore, her subsequent speech (773ff.) contains not one single word about this son's incredible glory, not a word about his hideous fate. To her, he is only a threat, and his death is a welcome relief. Even Aeschylus' haughty Clytemnestra displays more maternal feeling (*Choëph.* 691–699). It is likely that, far from redeeming herself in this scene,

Clytemnestra is condemning herself out of her own mouth. The poet has heavily underscored his point by making Electra refer to Orestes' pitiable death, which his own mother does not mourn (788–789, 804–807, esp. ὧδ' ὀλωλότα), and bewail his horrible end, alone in a strange land without even a proper funeral (86off.). This contrast between what Clytemnestra ought to feel and what little she actually says, between Electra's grief for Orestes' death and Clytemnestra's lack of it, continues to be emphasized in Electra's lament over the funerary urn, in the repetition that Electra saved Orestes' life (1131), in the effect of Electra's appearance on Orestes (1181, 1187–1188), and in the added fact that Clytemnestra physically abuses Electra (1196).

Against the cumulative effect of all these unmotherly statements and incidents, all revealed gradually and with increasing intensity, never denied but stressed and stressed again, one can set pitifully few examples of Electra's unfilial behavior. Her admission to her mother that her own behavior is "unseemly" (616ff.) has been taken as proof that she is scarred by her experiences. But it may just as well show her self-awareness and freedom from delusion. She has already displayed a similar perception of her own conduct in the context of propriety by apologizing to the chorus in much the same words that she uses to her mother (254ff.). If the poet had omitted these passages, it is very likely that the Athenian audience would have perceived Electra as too self-important and defiant for a "decent" woman. Instead, these objections are vitiated by her agreeing that her conduct would be improper under normal circumstances and by her yielding, fully and effusively, all initiative to the recognized male authority, Orestes, as soon as he arrives (1301–1306, 1318–1321). Unlike Antigone or Deianeira, Electra never performs any action; it is hard to see how the poet could have made her less "improper" and still have given her enough strength to come outside the palace against her mother's wish.

In the end, the only substantial accusation against Electra is brought forward in the form of her second cry during the killing of Clytemnestra, "strike if you can a second blow!" (1415). If such violence seems unbecoming in a woman, it is wild and vicious in a daughter. But the initial offensiveness of the phrase is greatly mitigated in two ways. First, Clytemnestra has continuously been portrayed as threatening Electra with physical violence; by now, according to the plot, Electra's only choice is to see her mother destroyed or be destroyed by her. (It may be argued that she need only destroy Aegisthus, but Sophocles has carefully insisted that Clytemnestra struck down Agamemnon—could she not easily kill Electra herself?) Furthermore, it is particularly suitable at this precise point in the carefully orchestrated dialogue sequence that portrays the unseen but overheard death of Clytemnestra. Instead of employing the usual eyewitness report after the fact, the poet presents to the audience each step in this action as it occurs within the house, through the utterances of persons both onstage and off. Clytemnestra is attacked and calls to her lover for help (1409); then she perceives the attacker is her son and cries out to him, but he still advances while Electra and the chorus voice the reasons why he will not stop. He strikes Clytemnestra, and she cries out. What is Electra expected to do at this point—burst into tears? Dash inside and beg the brute to stop? Sophocles makes her declare, consistently with her conduct so far, that she approves the deed even when confronted by its reality and simultaneously uses her words to exhibit the figure of Orestes raising his arm for the second, killing blow. Then, instead of having someone remark that the queen is indeed now dead, he has Electra remind us that Aegisthus is still very much alive, so that there is no pause in the pace of the action.[6] Most important, Electra's reaction to the killing of her mother occurs in the presence of the chorus. If, as seems likely, the Mycenaean women were costumed as well-to-do women of Clytemnestra's age, the poet kept continuously before the audience's eyes the spectacle of an intimate relation between Electra and a group of motherly women (cf. 234), forcing the spectator to compare their mutual respect and affection with Clytemnestra's appallingly nonmaternal conduct toward her children.

We are left with the fact that the poet establishes an atmosphere of sympathy for Electra at the beginning of the play and then sustains and reinforces it without pause or regression. Nor does the heroine's demeanor

---

6. The delivery of Electra's lines is important; with the well-timed gesture and vocal tremor of a good actor, the poet could easily prevent the audience from hearing the words as in any way bloodthirsty. Kamerbeek (ad 1415) does not adequately refute Linforth's ingenious suggestion ("far-fetched idea") that Electra is directing her words not to Orestes but to Clytemnestra, that $\pi\alpha\hat{\iota}\sigma\sigma\nu$ . . . $\delta\iota\pi\lambda\hat{\eta}\nu$ does not mean "strike a second blow" but "strike a blow in return" ("Electra's Day," 109 and n5). The not uncommon interpretation, that Electra is bitterly mocking Clytemnestra in her death throes, returns to the notion that "the old rancor" is always festering in Electra's soul, oozing out here and elsewhere. Friis Johansen (C&M 25 [1964], 26) is obviously correct in assuming that Sophocles has modeled the scene on the killing of Agamemnon and Cassandra, but not that the audience is meant to perceive the scenes as equal in moral significance. Sophocles is contrasting his scene with Aeschylus' in numerous ways, especially in the use of the chorus, who are so confused in the *Agamemnon*, so certain here. On Sophocles' comparable technique of alluding to specific passages in Homer in order then to make a deliberate contrast, see Kirkwood, "Homer and Sophocles' *Ajax*," esp. 58ff. and 70.

provide any evidential reason for the original spectators to dislike or mistrust her.[7] There is nothing subtle or psychological here. Sophocles relentlessly manipulates his audience into agreeing that Electra's actions are, under the circumstances, not only justifiable, but even inevitable. This conclusion, however, raises the question of why the good and pious poet wrote a play in which a matricide is portrayed without censure or punishment. But if we are to reach any answer other than "because he chose to," we should rather ask, "why Electra?" That question involves the additional difficulty of the uncertain chronological relation between Sophocles' and Euripides' *Electras*. If we suppose Sophocles' play to precede Euripides', the previous tradition about the figure of Electra is sparse. She does not appear under that name in Homer, although Aelian (*Var. Hist.* 4.26) reports that Xanthus claimed that she was really Laodice. Electra might have figured in Stesichorus' *Oresteia;* still, the title of the work suggests that she was a minor figure, that Orestes was the central character. Pindar omits her entirely from his brief narrative of the tale of Orestes in the *Eleventh Pythian*. When at last she does appear in Aeschylus' *Choëphoroi*, she plays only a minor part. The play is named not for her but for the chorus; she prays with Orestes for vengeance, but takes no part in any physical action, least of all the killings; she ceases speaking at line 509, is dismissed around line 579, and vanishes forever. The rest of the story is entirely Orestes'. Until Sophocles, then, we see only Orestes as the center of attention. Why did he lift Electra to such prominence?

It is not unreasonable to speculate that perhaps Aeschylus introduced the figure of Electra into the action for dramatic purposes,[8] and subsequently questions arose, at least in literary and philosophical circles, as to

---

7. Opponents of this view have not yet given up hope of discovering the Aeschylean Furies lurking in the corners of the play, ready to pursue Orestes to Athens. But the Furies of the *Oresteia* are allegorical figures whose participation in the story was probably invented by Aeschylus for his own dramatic purposes. Despite Jebb's ingenious reconstruction (xxi), from the scholia on Eur., *Or.* 268, of the Furies in Stesichorus' plot, there is no proof of their appearance in the pre-Aeschylean tradition about Orestes; certainly Homer omits them from the story. As Winnington-Ingram observes (*Sophocles*, 206–207), Aeschylus made them "a great symbol of tragic process"; but we have no evidence that Sophocles felt obliged to use either the same interpretation or the same symbols as Aeschylus. The story of Electra need not contain the Furies in every literary version. The lowest level of Dante's Hell was frozen over, but this is seldom reflected in later literary (or religious) practice.

8. Xanthus' etymology of Electra's name, as cited by Aelian (*Var. Hist.* 4.26: ἀλέκτρα, "unmarried"), suggests the dramatic reason for inventing her as a character. Some character is wanted as a liaison between Orestes and the palace, one intimate enough to effect a recognition. A brother would be impossible, unless some reason could be found for his failure to take

her involvement in such a crime. A son avenging his father's death and re-
gaining his rightful heritage might be acquitted of matricide, but what of a
woman? If a daughter should actively desire and assist in the murder of her
mother, even though she did not actually strike the deathblow, would she
not be doubly censured and despised, both for the deed itself and for being
unnaturally bold for a woman? The familiar belief that women, being
inferior to men, must properly be passive, obedient, silent, and uncon-
cerned with higher matters of justice and honor is expressed with considerable frequency in the fifth century, not only by Pericles (Thuc. 2.45) but
also by numerous characters in both Euripides' and Sophocles' plays (e.g.,
Ajax, Creon, Ismene, Chrysothemis). In this case Sophocles has shown
how, contrary to conventional notions, a woman, a daughter, could be involved in such a crime yet not be a monster. And if Euripides' play is the
earlier one, it would tend to confirm this view, for Euripides' Electra is
monstrous. The Dioscuroi blame Apollo, but Euripides blames Electra,
presenting her as stubborn, selfish, vain, and utterly unprincipled, obsessed with clothes, sex, and status. She sneers at her husband and at the
old man, she pushes in and dominates the plotting of stratagems. Oblivi-
ous of piety, and of the sanctity of sacrifice and hospitality, she finally goads
Orestes into killing his mother against his better judgment. Euripides'
Orestes, hardly an admirable man, is nevertheless a man—he realizes the
difference between right and wrong—but the clever and aggressive woman
is utterly without honor or decency.

Thus there may have been a "contemporary tradition" that immediately
preceded Sophocles' *Electra,* a common opinion that a sister who would
encourage her brother to matricide, who would act so aggressively, must
summarily be condemned as despicable and criminal. If this is the case,
perhaps Sophocles has deliberately set out to portray another possible
view, that of a "decent" woman forced by circumstances into such a crime,
which, if those circumstances are carefully examined, would not be judged
a crime. This uncomplicated interpretation also has considerable validity
for the other extant Sophoclean plays, of which *Oedipus Tyrannus* is a particularly apt example. There, too, Sophocles presents a version of a dread-

---

on the vengeance himself. The "old nurse" character had already been used by Homer for
Odysseus and may well have become a trite device. A sister would suit well, and could be
invented without straining historical fact. But to be old enough to recognize Orestes and yet
still living in her father's house, she would have to be unmarried. Thence the notion that she
was treated in a servile fashion, since her guardians have neglected to arrange a marriage for
her even though she is a princess.

ful act in which the doer of terrible deeds is not inherently a wicked person. Oedipus has committed both patricide and incest with his mother, yet at the end we do not condemn him as a villain; even the "tragic flaw" notion has been laid to rest by most scholars nowadays. If in a previous or current popular version of the story Oedipus was considered "guilty,"[9] then Sophocles was working with a story that is far more shocking than Electra's, for he presents before the audience's very eyes a mother and a son behaving as wife and husband, addressing each other as such, using terms of endearment. Yet we see them both as "decent" persons, and we do not expect the father's Furies to pursue Oedipus.

There are more parallels. In *Trachiniae*, Deianeira—who kills her husband, Heracles, the savior of Greece—is presented as an innocent, entirely nonaggressive woman. Again the immediately preceding versions of the story are lost, but the poet's dramatic insistence on her innocence suggests that she may elsewhere have been portrayed as a murderer. Nor are murder and incest the only crimes that Sophocles treats. Antigone might well once have been adjudged an unnatural and aggressive woman who committed treason. In all these cases Sophocles is showing spectacular crimes committed under reasonable, humanly understandable circumstances, such as ignorance, desperation, or moral conviction. The perpetrators are therefore not inherently or even temporarily wicked and are not to be condemned. To do so would be a serious misjudgment on the audience's part, and the poet prevents it dramatically. The theme of human beings' misjudging others from ignorance, haste, or prejudice, from failure to examine the circumstances, may be found in all of Sophocles' plays. Creon wrongly accuses Teiresias and Ismene, Oedipus does the same to Creon and Teiresias, Heracles to Deianeira.

Sophocles is admonishing his audience: never judge an accused person only on the repute of the crime, never judge in ignorance, never judge solely on the basis of traditional standards; seek to examine all the circumstances, to understand all the intent. He has sounded this warning in every extant play, whether he presents dramatically an action that has been traditionally or popularly labeled criminal for us to perceive in a new and different manner, as in *Electra, Trachiniae, Oedipus Tyrannus,* and *Antigone;* or whether he presents a misjudgment, trial, and correction of error as

9. Cf. Winnington-Ingram's speculation (*JHS* 91 [1971], 134) that in the second stasimon of *Oed. Tyr.* the poet is presenting an earlier, perhaps Aeschylean, version in which the hero was manifestly culpable and brought about his own downfall, a version that Sophocles goes on to counter with his own.

part of the plot of the drama. *Ajax* is an example of the latter: the Atreidae label Ajax a traitor, but Odysseus displays true understanding. The complex story of *Philoctetes* shows a narrow-minded Odysseus seeing Philoctetes only as a stubborn obstacle to the army's victory, while Philoctetes judges the value of the army's ultimate goal only in terms of the leaders' misdeeds against him, and Neoptolemus must pick his way between them. And the chorus of *Oedipus Coloneus* condemn Oedipus solely on the name of his crimes, but, when they have heard the full explanation, accept him as guiltless.

Such an admonition on human justice would have been particularly relevant to the Athens of the later fifth century. It was an era of primitive jurisprudence: no rules of evidence, no cross-examination, no learned judge to instruct the jury on the meaning of the law, no time for the jurors to discuss and deliberate among themselves before voting. Yet the people were rendering many judgments in the law courts and the assembly. Famous cases of possible misjudgment by the people have come down to us: the punishment of Melos, the hasty condemnation of the generals after Arginusae, and later the condemnation of Socrates. In a society where judgment is not restricted to the few who are trained to it, where the many must exercise it over a range of matters from criminal trials to foreign policy, there is bound to be continuing debate over principles of justice, not only as a topic of philosophical contention but as an immediate and vital part of daily affairs. In a society that accepted the dramatic poet as a teacher whose duty it was, according to Aristophanes' Euripides in the *Frogs* (1009–1010), to make the citizens better, it is more than likely that the poet would often return to the subject of judgment.

It is easy to observe from Sophocles' plays that as an artist he was fascinated by the nature of human greatness and the role of the hero in society. Yet surely he only offered these great figures to his audience to wonder at, not to imitate. Certainly he was deeply convinced of the functioning of *Dikê*, the natural force of divine justice and cosmic order. He seems, however, to present this force as an immutable fact of the universe. If he is teaching the concept of *Dikê* as an ideology, what advice for improvement does he offer, aside from the fact that those who transgress the divine laws of the universe, whether deliberately or accidentally, are eventually punished? That is more a reassurance of the existence of order than an instruction. But human justice, personal and public, is seldom perfect or incapable of improvement; and every Athenian could profit from the lessons that could so easily be learned from Sophocles' dramatic instruction.

CHAPTER 8

Conclusion:
The Choral Character

It has often been assumed that the tragic chorus were largely a traditional element, a convention that the Athenian playwright had to cope with, a special lyrical instrument that could be dramatically useful in a restricted, chiefly emotional, capacity but that was not an integral part of the dramatic mechanism of action and character. This assumption underlies a great deal of the criticism and neglect to which the Sophoclean choruses have been subjected. If this really was the case, however, we should naturally expect the poet to have treated the choruses in a traditional or conventional manner by creating the choral personae with a different set of dramatic techniques from those he used to create the principal characters. If, further, he treated the chorus as a conventional role—that is, if whatever characters they were accorded were always intended to fulfill simply a conventional dramatic function, such as Horace's pious advisors of the good or Müller's average people continuously misunderstanding the great—then we should further expect that the characters of all the choruses would be, within the naturally demarcated categories of age, sex, and social position, fairly similar if not virtually indistinguishable. And given these two conditions, we might also expect that the choruses' lyrical emotional function would regularly eclipse, or at least outshine, their technical importance to the action of the story.

In the preceding chapters the detailed analyses of the Sophoclean choruses from the point of view of the original audience have attempted to demonstrate how unfulfilled these expectations are, how, in fact, the choruses of all of Sophocles' extant tragedies exhibit recognizable and distinctive dramatic characters. Their personae are as extensively developed as those of many of the principals, and they have been so individualized that some vividly contrast with others of the same human type—the Theban lords of *Oedipus Tyrannus* and *Antigone* are as different as the Odysseuses of *Ajax* and *Philoctetes*, or as the mariticides Deianeira and Clytemnestra. This conclusion, that all Sophoclean choruses have carefully delineated and maintained dramatic characters, does not result from anachronistic assumptions or excessive psychologizing but proceeds inexorably from the observation that in each play Sophocles has used the same fundamental dramatic devices and principles to delineate the chorus' character that he uses for the principals' characters. If the application of a particular technique to a principal produces a certain effect of "characterization" in the audience's mind, then we must presume that the use of that same technique on the chorus would have produced a similar effect on the audience's perception of the chorus. A brief comparison of Sophocles' use of some important techniques of characterization for principals with their use for choruses should confirm the essential sameness of his dramatic treatment of the two elements.

   The first step that Sophocles takes in presenting a new character to the audience is to establish the character's identity, provide a reasonable motive for the initial appearance, and secure a natural place for the character in the rest of the plot. Two of these may be done simultaneously, or they may be strung out in sequence, but all three must be done within a fairly short time so that the audience does not waste attention wondering how a character belongs in the play. Sophocles is particularly adept at quickly working his characters into the plot. Even such minor functionaries as informants and messengers often receive an extra bit of motivation (like the Messenger from Creon in *Antigone* who is sent into the house to keep an eye on Eurydice and presumably returns to announce her death), and some are also worked into the story beforehand, like the Shepherd of Laius in *Oedipus Tyrannus*. Nowhere in Sophocles' plays do we find a character's appearance and participation in the story so weakly motivated as those of Euripides' Aegeus in *Medea*, whose mechanical function in the drama Euripides covers with only the flimsiest shreds of characterization and motivation. It is far more reasonable that Oedipus and Antigone should see a man coming toward them on the road through Colonus (*Oed. Col.* 29)— and that he should turn out to be familiar with the area and go to fetch the residents (78), who in turn send him on to fetch Theseus (297)—than that the king of Athens, hitherto unmentioned, should just happen to be passing through Corinth on his way from Delphi to Troezen and turn up in front of Medea's house at a critical moment without any previous announcement and then engage her in a discussion about oracles with no reference at all to their guest-host relation.

Sophocles always uses at least two of four specific devices to establish the identity and initial motivation of a principal (and often also of a minor): a statement by others some little time prior to the character's initial appearance (e.g., *Oed. Tyr.* 69ff.; *Aj.* 720ff., 804), a straightforward arrival announcement (*Oed. Tyr.* 78–79; *Ant.* 1180–1182; *Aj.* 1042–1045), the character's own first statements (*Oed. Tyr.* 1–8), or statements by others in conversations with the character (*Aj.* 210–212). Whatever combination is used, if it does not also provide a reasonable place in the coming plot for the new arrival, then the poet immediately supplies further statements or conversation. Of the seven extant choruses, five have received the same treatment in this regard as any Sophoclean principal. In both *Oedipus Tyrannus* and *Oedipus Coloneus* the chorus' arrival has been carefully prepared beforehand, and in the latter their arrival is also announced by Antigone. The contents of both parodoi make it immediately clear that these are no mere onlookers but persons of consequence whose arrival is a response to the present dramatic situation, and their immediately subsequent conversations with the principals reconfirm their place in the plot. In *Philoctetes*, *Ajax*, and *Electra*, there is no preparation for the chorus' entrance, but when they enter they immediately identify themselves, and their initial conversations with principals during the parodoi confirm their identity and motivation. By the end of the parodos, and during the following conversation with a principal in the latter two plays, the poet has established their right to a continuing place in the action: as Neoptolemus' subordinate but enterprising accomplices, as Tecmessa's associates—who differ somewhat from her in their viewpoints and concerns—in restoring Ajax to his former self, as Electra's sympathetic but practical allies in resistance. The arrival of the Mycenaean noblewomen in response to Electra's complaints may seem to have the least motivation, but in fact it turns out to have an additional dramatic function, since it establishes the fact that Electra can be overheard from within, thus providing an explanation for some later entrances and statements by Chrysothemis, Clytemnestra, and the Paedagogus; and it also demonstrates the public response to Electra's plaints that Clytemnestra and Aegisthus fear.

The other two choruses appear to be somewhat less carefully introduced. There is no preparatory mention of the chorus in *Antigone*, unless we count Antigone's remark that Creon is coming to deliver his edict "to those who do not know it" (33), and when they arrive they do not identify themselves as a "specially convened council of elders" until after they have finished their parodos. As soon as Creon arrives, however, he identifies their position as selected royalists. In Creon's speech and the dialogue following it, the poet implants the chorus in the action as the men from whom the king will expect support in everything he does but who are hardly enthusiastic about his actions. Thus the chorus' identification has not been neglected but only postponed, and the postponement has, as we have seen, the effect of maintaining the dramatic tension by keeping the audience in doubt about the citizens' reaction to Antigone's deed until after it is actually done.

The Trachinian maidens also arrive without any precursory mention of their position and do not identify themselves or their status, although their manner toward Deianeira in the parodos makes it clear that they are both native and nonservile. Deianeira's speech then identifies them as maidens and, toward the end, friends, but the audience hears no more specific reference to their status or place in the plot. Sophocles presents a motive for their arrival, which is briefly mentioned—they have heard of Deianeira's unhappiness—but in comparison with his other plays this chorus certainly have the weakest excuse for arriving and hardly any more for staying around. Before using this as a criticism of Sophocles' choral technique, however, we must observe that all the participants in the beginning of *Trachiniae* are treated in the same way. In contrast to every other Sophoclean prologue, Deianeira offers no reason at all for coming out of the house to talk to her servant, who is given no recognizable character and is not even specifically addressed by the principal. There is no indication in the text that this female slave is the same person as the old woman who later reports Deianeira's suicide; neither of them says anything that suggests the specific character of "Old Nurse," so that even if the two roles were originally one, the poet has not made the fact dramatically significant. Then Hyllus enters without giving any explanation whatever for his arrival. He belongs to the house, of course (unlike Aegeus), but he apparently just happens to be coming home from somewhere and by the merest chance meets his mother outside the door.

This combination of entrances is entirely without Sophoclean precedent; no other prologue has so little dramatic motivation of action and character. Far from being treated in an offhand manner, the chorus of Trachinian maidens are the only persons thus far in the play who have been given a reason for their movements, and they certainly have been more im-

mediately characterized than either Hyllus or the Slave. The apparent
weakness of the chorus' dramatic right to further participation, which is
not nearly as weak as the Slave's, seems actually to contribute to their characterization as emotionally distant from Deianeira, an aspect which would
be lost if they were woven more tightly into the story, by being summoned
by Deianeira or by being members of the household.

Sophocles' further task in presenting a new persona is to create relations
between this new character and the other characters of the drama, whether
they are relations that are supposed to have been established before the action of the dramatic moment or new ones that come into existence before
the audience's eyes. Sometimes he establishes the nature of a pre-existing
relation by informing the audience about it before the two characters meet
onstage, as with Electra and Clytemnestra, or Philoctetes and Odysseus,
or Oedipus and Polyneices, but most commonly he reveals the pre-existing
relation during the course of the first meeting of the characters. The content of their remarks to each other is, of course, the chief device for displaying their attitudes toward each other, but the contrast between the use
of long speeches and the use of dialogue at these meetings is so noticeable
and so consistent that it strongly suggests that the poet deliberately employed it as a device to enhance the dramatic effect of what the characters
are saying to each other. Those principals who are meant to be seen as
having already been on intimate terms with each other first meet onstage in
conversational dialogue, whereas those who are shown as having had a
more impersonal, distant, or even hostile relation first approach each other
with long opposing speeches.

The openings of several plays, however, are apparently exceptional in
that they present some intimate pre-existing relations by both speeches and
dialogue. But these exceptions are the natural result of the prologue's dramatic task, for it must present the characters' identities and relations, together with all the necessary information about time, place, and circumstances of the story, and must do it all fairly quickly. It would seem that
some speeches of more than conversational length would need to be mixed
with the dialogue just to get all the information out in a suitably compact
form. Certainly it can be said that the only three prologues in which at least
one character delivers a speech of more than forty lines involve talk between a principal and a minor whose personal relation, whether new or
pre-existing, is not at present dramatically significant: Oedipus and the
priest of Zeus in *Oedipus Tyrannus*, Deianeira and the Slave in *Trachiniae*,
Orestes and the Paedagogus in *Electra*. The other openings involve prin-

cipals whose relations are going to be important to the drama, and these are largely conversational, with some speeches mixed in that provide extensive information but never exceed about twenty lines.

After the openings of the plays, Sophocles' practice with the principals whose relations have not been described is invariable. Cool, or at least nonintimate, prior relations are revealed in first encounters that begin with lengthy speeches: Creon and Haimon, Electra and Chrysothemis, Antigone and Creon. In contrast, the first dialogue between Oedipus and Creon sounds like a conversation between old friends—as indeed it is— with no single utterance longer than four lines, even though a great deal of information is being delivered. So also Deianeira and her son make no speeches at each other, although the brevity of their conversation probably diminishes the sense of their intimacy. Oedipus and his daughter Ismene do exchange long speeches during their first encounter, but the speeches are preceded by a dialogue that includes seven lines of antilabe and are followed by a long, largely stichomythic dialogue, so that the effect is that of a conversation between intimates. It is especially striking that Sophocles uses a kommos to present two pairs of characters as familiars: Oedipus and Iocasta in *Tyrannus,* Oedipus and Antigone in *Coloneus* (where the initial conversation is interrupted by the Stranger but is then resumed lyrically during the parodos). We may suppose the dramatic effect of such a lyric introduction between principals was to heighten the sense of long-standing emotional bonds, since nonintimate principals never engage in kommoi together. The bond of intimacy may later be seen to dissolve during a kommos—as with Oedipus and Creon, or Ajax and Tecmessa—but lyric dialogue between principals seems restricted to those who have been or are becoming intimates.

Sophocles uses this same distinction of types of utterance to establish pre-existing relations, about which the audience has not otherwise been informed, between chorus and principal. Either kommoi (whether epirrhematic or fully lyric) or iambic conversation between chorus-leader and principal always occur at the first meeting in the play of the chorus and a familiar of long standing. Neoptolemus' veterans confer with their leader in a kommatic parodos; Ajax's men summon their commander, but when his wife unexpectedly comes out instead, their kommos with her reveals a long association marked by mutual respect and a common devotion to Ajax. Sophocles may also be seeking such an effect when he makes the chorus of *Ajax* recognize Teucer's voice just before he arrives and then has the leader converse with Teucer in antilabe as soon as he arrives (974–991) instead of having Tecmessa make a brief speech (which would slow the pace of the action at this point). So also the extent of the Mycenaean women's prior acquaintance with Electra is not specified in the text, but the general impression of familiarity must be enhanced by the fully lyrical kommos in which they immediately engage her.

When, however, the chorus first encounter a principal with whom they are on less familiar terms, they never engage in a kommos or any immediate iambic conversation. Creon's statements to the chorus of *Antigone* might suggest that he is supposed to have some previous acquaintance with the chorus, since he has chosen them in particular, but there is no dramatic sense of intimacy, since the chorus enter alone and sing an ode and then Creon comes on to deliver a lengthy speech to them. Exactly the same pattern occurs in *Oedipus Tyrannus*, where the chorus enter alone with an ode and then Oedipus speaks at length to them, and here also there is no sense of any close personal relation between Oedipus and the chorus, although their political association will be developed very quickly as the scene continues. When *Antigone*'s chorus first meet the heroine, they recognize her, exclaiming in anapests as she is brought in, but they do not speak to her at all in the two hundred lines during which she is onstage. Perhaps the most obvious use of this technique is in *Trachiniae*, where the chorus arrive and address Deianeira not in a kommos but in an ode, to which Deianeira then replies in a single speech of thirty-six lines. This sequence does not seem to differ significantly in its effect from a pair of long speeches that two actors deliver to each other: whatever previous relation they have is largely formal and undemonstrative.

The chorus, like the actors, are also involved in the creation of new associations and attitudes, and they develop new relations—some insignificant, but others that are both extensive and important—in the same way the actors do, through conversation and confrontation, addressing characters and being spoken to in return. Contrary to popular assumptions, Sophoclean choruses' remarks are so seldom ignored by the principals that when they are it may be assumed to have a noticeable effect. Neoptolemus' men get involved with Philoctetes to the point of a kommos and also have a brief exchange with Odysseus. Not only do the chorus of *Ajax* have extensive relations with Ajax, Tecmessa, and Teucer, but the poet also has them change their previous opinion of Odysseus when they actually see him for the first time in the play. In *Oedipus Tyrannus*, they converse with Creon and Iocasta as well as with the hero; and in *Coloneus*, they become involved with everybody else, even including Polyneices. In those cases where a relation between the chorus and a certain principal is noticeably absent, we have seen obvious dramatic effects: the timorous Theban Elders' reticence during Antigone's first appearance, the overawed and despairing Trachinian maidens' silence in the presence of the dying Heracles, the Mycenaean women's conspiratorial reticence during the scenes with Clytemnestra and Aegisthus.

In the establishing of personal relations and associations, Sophocles practices the same dramatic economy on the chorus as on the principals, by not presenting confrontations between chorus and actor that are unnecessary, either because we already know how they feel or because they are simply dramatically irrelevant. There is no need for the audience to hear the chorus actually conversing with Teiresias, or Orestes, any more than to hear Tecmessa with Agamemnon, or Clytemnestra with Aegisthus. What relevance would a conversation between Eurydice and the chorus, or between Polyneices and Ismene, have to the themes and actions of the plays as they now stand? It is no more valid to argue that because some choruses do not have a relation with a certain character or do not actively participate in certain parts of the play, the chorus must be viewed as always having less dramatic significance than actors, than it is to argue that because Tecmessa does not speak to anyone during the last third of *Ajax*, Sophocles always considered women of less dramatic importance than men and had them make their contributions to the action early in the play.

Identification, motivation, and the establishment of relations between characters all produce initial effects of characterization, which a playwright must then sustain by the most fundamental of all dramatic devices, the attribution to a character of a sequence of consistent statements and actions. No one would deny that Sophocles always does this for his principals; it has been the task of the preceding chapters to examine also the many ways in which Sophocles has made every choral statement consistent with the attitudes and mannerisms that the chorus have displayed in all their previous utterances. Critics have often claimed that choral behavior is inconsistent largely because they tend to have conceived different standards of consistency for principals and chorus. Every effort is made to interpret a principal's statement, no matter how unsuitable or unpalatable it may seem at first reading, as integral with and significant for the characterization of the role and the themes of the drama. Many attempts, for example, have been made to show how Antigone's last defense of her actions (904–912) really does suit her character, and those who are not convinced would excise the passage entirely rather than allow it as inconsistent.

Yet choral statements presented in the same fundamental dramatic manner as the actors' are often interpreted as gross inconsistencies, especially if they are delivered in lyric passages. One of the most spectacular examples of this is the notion that in the final antistrophe of the second stasimon of *Oedipus Tyrannus* the chorus are praying to Zeus to make the old oracles about Laius come true so that religion will not perish, a startling contradiction to their earlier loyalty to and confidence in Oedipus even in the face of Teiresias' dire accusations. Those who attempt to explain away this contradiction generally argue that the chorus do not intend to have any harm come to Oedipus, but that they are just not intelligent enough to realize the possible consequences of what they are asking. This view of the chorus as foolishly shortsighted is thoroughly inconsistent with their previous sensible and logical character, whereas the syntax will just as easily, indeed, more readily, support the view that the chorus, reasoning things through as they have been doing all through the play, are now stating that they will no longer go to the famous oracular shrines if those shrines are going to give false oracles and are asking Zeus to stop them from promulgating any further inaccurate predictions, since one set of oracles has just been proven invalid and religion has suffered a setback as a result.

Consistency of utterance is obviously a basic aspect of characterization, but what characters do not say can sometimes be almost as important as what they do say if they fail to comment upon something that other characters are discussing. A certain selectivity is a part of character. When Sophocles makes Clytemnestra utterly ignore the heroic circumstances of her son's death that are reported at great length, but then makes Electra speak of them after her mother's departure, we may presume he expected the audience to note the omission and judge the extent of Clytemnestra's maternal feeling accordingly. So, too, Odysseus' failure to make any mention of Philoctetes' piteous condition, though everyone else comments sympathetically upon it, is a significant part of his characterization, and the exquisite ironies of *Oedipus Tyrannus* are constructed largely upon what information Oedipus chooses as a basis for drawing conclusions and what he ignores or discards. When, therefore, Sophocles makes the chorus of *Antigone* ignore the moral and political issues that are raised by Antigone and Haimon, and has them instead discuss only the danger of disobedience, he must intend the audience to note this omission and to perceive the chorus accordingly. When the chorus of *Tyrannus* finally join in Oedipus' concern for personal matters, their previous refusal to consider anything but civic difficulties contributes greatly to the irony of their joy-before-disaster ode.

By using all these methods of characterization for the actors' roles, Sophocles has created dramatic figures that, although not complex enough by present-day standards to be considered "realistic," are nevertheless reasonable and acceptable to the audience within the fifth-century dramatic illusion. Moreover, he commonly uses these techniques on the minor characters as well as on the principals, so that they also become figures of interest to the audience; modern readers are especially fond of the Guard in *Antigone*, or the Paedagogus in *Electra*. But minor characters, however interesting their appearances may be, somehow seem to lack the depth, the intensity of character, that Sophocles gives to his principals—it is impossible to imagine the Guard and the Paedagogus as major characters in a play. It might therefore be supposed that although the same techniques of characterization are used on both principals and chorus, the chorus remain in approximately the same dramatic position as a minor character, interesting at times but always patently subordinate to the major personae in importance, interest, and depth.

The differences in characterization, however, between major and minor personae are reasonably attributable to Sophocles' methods of presenting the whole of a character. Although all the immediately relevant aspects of a principal's character are presented at first appearance, further aspects that are important to the development of theme and plot are often revealed more gradually, in later confrontations and actions, during the course of which the person may even undergo a change of attitude or behavior; thus the full character is treated as a "dynamic" role rather than a "static" one. Sophocles uses this technique frequently for principal characters who must be onstage for a major portion of the play, so that they remain an active part of the creation of dramatic tension rather than becoming merely experiencers of the plot, whereas those characters whose participation is limited to a scene or two must naturally have their dramatic character fully developed within a relatively short time. Oedipus in *Tyrannus*, for example, or Neoptolemus, or Creon in *Antigone* are presented dynamically, with aspects of their characters being introduced or reinforced by degrees through the actions of the plot, in contrast to more statically presented characters such as Theseus or Teucer. The role of Odysseus in *Ajax* or *Philoctetes* is an example of the most static treatment, for his character is completely delineated at the opening of the play, so that when he returns much later his behavior is immediately comprehensible to the audience.

Sophocles likewise reveals his choral characters far more dynamically than his minor ones. Of course, not all choruses are presented as dynamically as, say, the character of Oedipus the king, but neither are all of the principals. Antigone's is not a static character, but it is certainly treated less dynamically than Creon's, surely because a fully dynamic treatment of her is not necessary to Sophocles' dramatic purpose. The chorus of a tragedy are onstage throughout most of the play, so it is only natural that Sophocles has presented the fullness of their characters gradually, and sometimes even put them through changes of attitude, especially to create the tension of the joy-before-disaster effect. He tests the piety and logic of the Theban Lords of *Oedipus Tyrannus* as they face the revelations first of Teiresias and then of Iocasta, until finally they succumb to the lure of fantasy and speculation; the Theban Elders of *Antigone*, on the other hand, finally mingle their self-concern with civic concern, though too late. Electra's practical friends, always supporting the validity of her cause, are gradually won over to the validity of her methods and acts; and Ajax's men, always firm in their loyalty, nevertheless go through changes of mood and even, in the end, change their minds about their lord's old enemy, Odysseus. In their devotion to their mission, Neoptolemus' soldiers' independence and increasing participation in the deception lead gradually to a confrontation with their commander. The Elders of Colonus make a decision early in the play and then adhere to it without change, but their devotion to the land, their attachment to Oedipus, and their participation in the action increase all the way to the end of the play. Least dynamic of all is the character of the Trachinian maidens, who stay much the same through the first half of the play, until Deianeira's suicide, at which point they undergo a shock, but do not change except by falling silent in the face of the terrible events. With the slight exception of Deianeira, however, the other characters are treated in a similar fashion. Deianeira's initial character receives some further definition in her meeting with Iole, but in her decision to send the robe and then to kill herself there is little sense of additional characterization or change of attitude. Hyllus shows temporary anger, and Heracles raves in pain, and both change their opinion when they learn the truth about Deianeira, but otherwise their characters are as statically treated as the chorus'.

Nevertheless, there are aspects of the choral component of tragedy that seem to place inherent restrictions on the ability of a chorus to function, in a manner comparable to the actors, as a fully integrated character of the drama. Since they are a group, they cannot move about with anything like the freedom that the actors enjoy; hence, their continued presence throughout the play is a physical rather than dramatic necessity. Nor can they deliver speeches; instead, they sing long songs or utter brief iambic remarks through the mouth of their leader. Their group and lyric aspects make their physical behavior so different from the actors' that the audience, it may be argued, would be likely to perceive the chorus' character as less "real" than the actors' and would more readily expect their songs to be independent lyric units than expressions of personality.

Far from setting the chorus apart, however, as less "natural" in their behavior, the lyric mode is the most natural and acceptable form of expression for a group. Although Greek tragedy is certainly "conventional" in comparison to modern "realistic" drama, there is a set of basic human appearances and behaviors in "real life" required to sustain the dramatic illusion of tragedy—as Aristotle observed, Achilles' pursuit of Hector would be ludicrous in a play, because the others (including, presumably, the chorus) would have to stand around watching instead of joining the chase (*Poetics* 1460a13–16). It would be as unnatural, even ludicrous, for a group of persons to speak a series of statements in unison as it would for actors to walk in on their hands. But in real life, singing is a common way for several persons to utter the same words simultaneously, a phenomenon that would be especially acceptable in a society in which choral song was clearly an important part of religious and festal life. Indeed, singing is the only natural mode of utterance for a group, and within the dramatic context it seems no more unacceptable or anomalous than the notion that members of a family speak to each other in iambic trimeters.

No one suspects that the principals' character seemed to the audience to fade a little when they sang, that they became more a lyric instrument and less a character in the drama; nor is there any reason to suspect it of choral songs. A song is always a dramatic performance, whether it is part of a play or performed independently for an audience, and the singer takes on, however briefly, some personality from the words and tone of the song (in the extreme, the singers of popular ballads become the objects of their listeners' romantic devotion). Within a Greek tragedy, the choral ode can be the technical equivalent of an actor's monologue or soliloquy, a group monologue. We accept the concept of the actor's soliloquy because talking to oneself is a recognizable human phenomenon, and a group talking to itself or among itself is an equally recognizable phenomenon that fits easily into the limits of dramatically natural behavior.

Sophocles' choral odes also perform the same mechanical tasks in communication and temporal progression that the actors' speeches do. If other characters are present during an ode, one always responds to the song as if to a speech, unless the scene is immediately interrupted by a new entrance. Dramatic time passes during choral odes just as it does during speeches and episodes. Instead of perceiving the odes as interludes that create a "timeless lyrical world," the audience was accustomed to hearing them describe offstage action, both past (as in the parodos of *Antigone*) and, through speculation and imagination, present (as in the battle scene of *Oedipus Coloneus*). Descriptions of past events commonly occur, of course, in messengers' speeches or in principals' narratives of their own past; descriptions by actors of current offstage actions are not long or common in Sophocles, but Aeschylus provides a memorable example in Clytemnestra's speculations on the sack of Troy (*Agamemnon* 321–340). An audience accustomed to finding mechanical immediacy in choral lyrics would probably look for it in every ode and listen with the expectation that the action is moving forward during the song just as it does during an actor's speech, so that the dramatic mood would naturally be one of progress rather than suspension.

Nor does the lyric mode limit the content of the song so as to affect the characterization of the singers. It is true that new facts vital to the plot are never conveyed in lyrics, probably because the details might be obscured by the musical delivery, but this does not imply that the content of lyrics must always be strictly emotional and reflective and can never contain reasoning and argument, as some seem to infer. On the contrary, Sophoclean choruses can and do reason, argue, and come to decisions in the course of a song when it is suitable to the persona to do so, most prominently in *Oedipus Tyrannus*. Aeschylus' Eumenides, Dale's prime example of the restricted chorus, fail to argue their case rationally not because they are "the Chorus" but because they are the inherently irrational "Furies."

This is not to deny the emotional impact and poetic splendor of so many of Sophocles' odes, but rather to say that, however beautiful his odes may be, they are also always dramatic. There is no evidence to enable one to assume that Sophocles' audience expected his odes to be occasionally undramatic. Because some odes can be removed from their play and still be impressive performances, one cannot say that they are therefore less dramatic within their play than are utterances that cannot be removed, any more than one can say it about Hamlet's famous soliloquy or Falstaff's speech on honor. In fact, we have seen that the contrary is true, that the emotionalism of an ode reinforces its dramatic value rather than detracting from it. The last ode that Ajax's soldiers sing, at the depth of their despair, is necessary to demonstrate the terrible situation in which their commander has left them and to finish building the tension before the final climactic confrontation with the power of the army. The "ode on Man" in *Antigone* is an extremely important statement of attitudes that both defines the chorus' character and prepares for their ambivalent response to Antigone. The Colonean Elders' ode on the beauties of their land establishes their personal commitment to Oedipus and marks the change in his status from beggared wayfarer to honored guest and compatriot.

But when the chorus are not singing, their group nature prevents them from all speaking as the actors do, and their size prevents them from making the frequent entrances and exits that the actors are allowed. These physical restrictions are probably the source of many critics' assumption that the chorus-leader's interventions in the iambic dialogue are not likely to be as significant or dramatically functional as an actor's, especially in the couplets that are presumed "to mark the end of a major speech." It can as well be said, however, that those couplets do not come after a long speech, as a sort of cap, but rather between two speeches or between a long speech and an immediately subsequent passage of dialogue. Pairs of long speeches, unrelieved by the intervention of a third party, are extremely rare in Sophocles and occur only in a few exceptionally tense confrontations such as between Teiresias and Creon or Clytemnestra and Electra; even in the latter, the two long speeches are separated by a brief dialogue between the two actors (552–557). It seems obvious that Sophocles has inserted the chorus-leader's remarks, which cause at least one of the actors to shift the direction of his address, in order to break up the structural monotony of the duologue by creating triangular patterns of speech. Since there is no reason to think that the chorus-leader stood far apart from the chorus, we may assume that on the many occasions when the chorus-leader did speak the attention of both actors and audience was drawn to the presence of the entire group, rather than that the remarks were scarcely noticed by the audience. Thus the much-admired *Dreigespräch* effect, which seems so rare if one considers only the actors, is actually the common speech pattern of Sophoclean episodes.

Still, the chorus-leader never gives long speeches, and this restriction suggests that the chorus-leader's technical importance in the episodes is subordinate to the actors'. But by keeping these iambic remarks fairly short, Sophocles keeps the chorus-leader in the group. It is not natural for a member of a group to make a long speech to another individual, on behalf of and in the presence of the group, without some of the group's other members' giving voice to additional statements. A chorus-leader who spoke at great length would become an individual separate from the group, and the silent chorus would be reduced to mere extras, a crowd of spectators perhaps murmuring an occasional "hear, hear." Rather than set up the chorus-leader as a character, when Sophocles wants an extensive conversation between the chorus and a principal, he uses the kommos to create the effect of the pressure of an entire group talking to or, most commonly, arguing with a single person, an effect greatly different in its intensity from that of two individuals speaking together in front of onlookers.

It is this continued insistence on the chorus' identity as a group, a plurality that speaks with complete unity of thought and feeling, that gives them their most important functions in Sophocles' dramas. Each of his extant choruses represents a group of persons not otherwise portrayed in the play, who are not distinguished as "historical" characters, such as the Erinyes or the daughters of Danaus, but who are a part of society that is deeply involved in the action and its outcome. Such groups and their viewpoints are represented in later, nonchoral Western drama by subordinate characters or allegorical figures, but none of Sophocles' choruses could be adequately replaced by minor characters, along the lines of, say, "Blogo of Salamis, sergeant to Ajax" or "Hieria, a maiden of the district," or "Palaios and Gerontides, two gentlemen of Colonus." By introducing instead the dramatic equivalent of whole segments of society, Sophocles has greatly expanded plots which without the chorus would be essentially narrow, personal tales of individuals or families. Sophocles' kings have subjects that must be ruled, his warrior-heroes have troops that must be commanded.

The specific human character with which the poet has endowed each group has a vital part in conveying the themes of the play. Neoptolemus' soldiers epitomize the defects of followers who justify any action on the grounds of expedience; Ajax's endangered soldiers, on the other hand, show the hero's failure in his leadership of these loyal, honest men. The civically responsible Thebans of *Oedipus Tyrannus* display the functions of a responsible king; in the cautious and compromising Thebans of *Antigone* we see the sort of citizens who acquiesce to tyranny; the reverent and virtuous old men of Colonus show us the heroism of decent, ordinary human beings. The young girls of Trachis, besides demonstrating Deianeira's guiltlessness, present the heroic and divine aspects of Heracles the man; the sensible and compassionate Mycenaean noblewomen of *Electra* present their country's approval of the destruction of usurpers by the rightful heirs. These are only a few of the major dramatic impressions that are created by the choruses. Their presence, their statements, their actions are necessary to display the full public and political consequences of the principals' behavior. The dramatic character of the Sophoclean chorus has an integral and insuppressible role in Sophoclean tragedy.

Selected Bibliography

All references to ancient authors are to the edition of the *Oxford Classical Texts,* unless otherwise noted. A parenthetical note distinguishes editions and commentaries from other works by the editor.

Abbreviations

AJP / *American Journal of Philology*
AntCl / *L'Antiquité Classique*
BICS / *Bulletin of the Institute of Classical Studies of the University of London*
C&M / *Classica et Mediaevalia*
CalSCA / *California Studies in Classical Antiquity*
CF / *Classical Folia*
CJ / *Classical Journal*
CP / *Classical Philology*
CQ / *Classical Quarterly*
CR / *Classical Review*
CW / *Classical World*
G&R / *Greece and Rome*
GRBS / *Greek, Roman, and Byzantine Studies*
HSCP / *Harvard Studies in Classical Philology*

ICS / *Illinois Classical Studies*
JHS / *Journal of Hellenic Studies*
LSJ / Liddell, Scott, Jones, and McKenzie. *A Greek-English Lexicon.* Oxford, 1940.
PCPhS / *Proceedings of the Cambridge Philological Society*
REG / *Revue des Études Grecques*
RFIC / *Rivista di Filologia e di Istruzione Classica*
RhM / *Rheinisches Museum für Philologie*
TAPA / *Transactions of the American Philological Association*
WS / *Wiener Studien*
YCS / *Yale Classical Studies*

Adams, Sinclair M. *Sophocles, the Playwright.* Toronto, 1957.
Alexanderson, Bengt. "On Sophocles' *Electra*," *C&M* 27 (1966), 79–98.
———. "Die Stellung des Chors in der Antigone," *Eranos* 66 (1966), 85–105.

Avery, Harry C. "Heracles, Philoctetes, Neoptolemus," *Hermes* 93 (1965), 279–297.

Bain, David. "Audience Address in Greek Tragedy," *CQ* 25 (1975), 13–25.

Die Bauformen der griechischen Tragödie, ed. W. Jens. Munich, 1971.

Benardete, Seth. "A Reading of Sophocles' *Antigone*," *Interpretation* 5 (1975), 148–196.

Bers, Victor. "The Perjured Chorus in Sophocles' *Philoctetes*," *Hermes* 109 (1981), 500–504.

Beye, Charles Rowan. "Sophocles' *Philoctetes* and the Homeric Embassy," *TAPA* 101 (1970), 63–75.

Bona, Giacomo. "ΥΨΙΠΟΛΙΣ e ΑΠΟΛΙΣ: Nel primo stasimo dell'*Antigone*," *RFIC* 99 (1971), 129–148.

Bongie, Elizabeth B. "The Daughter of Oedipus," in *Serta Turyniana: Studies in Honor of Alexander Turyn* (Urbana [Ill.], 1974), 239–267.

Bowra, C. Maurice. *Sophoclean Tragedy*. Oxford, 1944.

Brown, Sylvia G. "A Contextual Analysis of Tragic Meter: The Anapest," in *Ancient and Modern: Essays in Honor of Gerald F. Else* (Ann Arbor, 1977), 45–77.

Burian, Peter. "Suppliant and Saviour: Oedipus at Colonus," *Phoenix* 28 (1974), 408–429.

———. "Supplication and Hero Cult in Sophocles' *Ajax*," *GRBS* 13 (1972), 151–156.

Burton, R. W. B. *The Chorus in Sophocles' Tragedies*. Oxford, 1980.

Byl, Simon. "Lamentations sur la vieillesse dans la tragédie grecque," in *Le monde grec . . . Hommages à Claire Préaux* (Brussels, 1975), 130–139.

Calder, William M. III. "The Entrance of Athena in *Ajax*," *CP* 60 (1965), 114–116.

———. "Once More: The Entrance and Exit of Athena in *Ajax*," *CF* 28 (1974), 59–61.

———. "Sophoclean Apologia: *Philoctetes*," *GRBS* 12 (1971), 153–174.

———. "Sophokles' Political Tragedy, *Antigone*," *GRBS* 9 (1968), 389–407.

Capps, Edward. "The Greek Stage according to the Extant Dramas," *TAPA* 22 (1891), 5–80.

Coleman, Robert. "The Role of the Chorus in Sophocles' *Antigone*," *PCPhS* 18 (1972), 4–27.

Cook, Albert. "The Patterning of Effect in Sophocles' *Philoctetes*," *Arethusa* 1 (1968), 82–93.

Dain, Alphonse and Paul Mazon (edition). *Sofocle*. 2d ed.: Paris, 1965.

Dale, A. M. *Collected Papers*. Cambridge, 1969.

———. *The Lyric Metres of Greek Drama*. 2d ed.: Cambridge, 1968.

———. *Metrical Analyses of Tragic Choruses*. Fasc. 1: *Dactylo-Epitrite*. London, 1971.

Davidson, J. F. "The Parodos of Sophocles' *Ajax*," *BICS* 22 (1975), 163–177.

———. "Sophocles, *Ajax* 192–200," *Mnemosyne* 29 (1976), 129–135.

Dawe, Roger D. (edition). *Sophocles Tragoediae*. Leipzig, 1975 and 1979.

——— (commentary). *Sophocles: Oedipus Rex*. Cambridge, 1982.

———. *Studies on the Text of Sophocles*. Leiden, 1973 and 1978.

Earp, F. R. *The Style of Sophocles*. Cambridge, 1944.

Easterling, P. E. (commentary). *Sophocles: Trachiniae*. Cambridge, 1982.

———. "Oedipus and Polyneices," *PCPhS* 13 (1967), 1–13.

———. "*Philoctetes* and Modern Criticism," *ICS* 3 (1978), 27–39.

———. "The Second Stasimon of *Antigone*," in *Dionysiaca* (Cambridge, 1978), 141–158.

———. "Sophocles' *Trachiniae*," *BICS* 15 (1968), 58–69.

Ehrenberg, Victor. *Sophocles and Pericles*. Oxford, 1954.

Ellendt, Fridericus. *Lexicon Sophocleum*, ed. H. Genthe. Berlin, 1872.

Else, Gerald F. *The Madness of Antigone*. Heidelberg, 1976.

Errandonea, Ignacio, S.I. *El coro de la Electra de Sófocles*. La Plata, 1968.

———. *Sófocles: Investigaciones sobre la estructura dramática de sus siete tragedias y sobre la personalidad de sus coros*. Madrid, 1958.

———. *Sófocles y la personalidad de sus coros: Estudio de dramática constructiva*. Madrid, 1970.

Farnell, L. R. *The Cults of the Greek States*. Oxford, 1907.

Ferguson, John. "Ambiguity in Ajax," *Dionisio* 44/1–2 (1970), 12–29.

Finley, John H., Jr. "Politics and Early Attic Tragedy," *HSCP* 71 (1966), 1–13.

Fitton, J. W. "Greek Dance," *CQ* 23 (1973), 254–274.

Fowler, B. Hughes. "Plot and Prosody in Sophocles' *Antigone*," *C&M* 28 (1967), 143–171.

Friis Johansen, Holger, "Die *Elektra* des Sophokles: Versuch einer neuen Deutung," *C&M* 25 (1964), 8–32.

———. "Sophocles 1939–1959," *Lustrum* 8 (1962), 94–288.

Fritz, Kurt von. *Antike und moderne Tragödie*. Berlin, 1962.

Gellie, G. H. *Sophocles: A Reading*. Carlton (Victoria, Australia), 1972.

Goheen, Robert F. *The Imagery of Sophocles' Antigone: A Study of Poetic Language and Structure*. Princeton, 1951.

Haldane, J. A. "A Paean in the *Philoctetes*," *CQ* 13 (1963), 53–56.

Hamilton, Richard. "Neoptolemos' Story in the *Philoctetes*," *AJP* 96 (1975), 131–137.

Harsh, Philip Whaley. "The Role of the Bow in the *Philoctetes* of Sophocles," *AJP* 81 (1960), 408–414.

Henderson, L. D. J. "Sophocles *Trachiniae* 878–92 and a Principle of Paul Maas," *Maia* 28 (1976), 19–24.

Henry, Alan S. "Sophocles *Philoctetes* 849–54," *CP* 68 (1973), 61–62.

Hester, D. A. "Very Much the Safest Plan or, Last Words in Sophocles," *Antichthon* 8 (1973), 8–13.

Hinds, A. E. "The Prophecy of Helenus in Sophocles' *Philoctetes*," *CQ* 17 (1967), 169–180.

Hoey, Thomas. "Sun Symbolism in the Parodos of the *Trachiniae*," *Arethusa* 5 (1972), 133–154.

Huxley, George. "Thersites in Sophokles, *Philoktetes* 445," *GRBS* 8 (1967), 33–34.

Jebb, Richard C. (commentaries). *Sophocles: The Plays and Fragments. I: Oedipus Tyrannus* (Cambridge, 1893). *II: Oedipus Coloneus* (1899). *III: Antigone* (1900).

IV: Philoctetes (1902). *V: Trachiniae* (1892). *VI: Electra* (1894). *VII: Ajax* (1896).

Kaimio, Maarit. *The Chorus of Greek Drama within the Light of the Person and Number Used.* Helsinki, 1970.

Kamerbeek, J. C. (commentaries). *The Plays of Sophocles. I: Ajax* (Leiden, 1963). *II: Trachiniae* (1959). *III: Antigone* (1978). *IV: Oedipus Tyrannus* (1967). *V: Electra* (1974). *VI: Philoctetes* (1980). *VII: Oedipus Coloneus* (1984).

Kells, J. H. (commentary). *Sophocles: Electra.* Cambridge, 1973.

Kirkwood, Gordon. "Homer and Sophocles' *Ajax*," in *Classical Drama and Its Influence: Essays Presented to H. D. F. Kitto* (New York, 1965), 51–70.

———. *A Study of Sophoclean Drama.* Ithaca (N.Y.), 1958.

Kitto, H. D. F. *Form and Meaning in Drama.* 2d ed.: London, 1964.

———. *Greek Tragedy.* 3d ed.: London, 1961.

———. *Poiesis.* Berkeley, 1966.

———. *Sophocles, Dramatist and Philosopher.* London, 1958.

Klimpe, Peter. *Die 'Electra' des Sophokles und Euripides' 'Iphigenia bei den Taurern.'* Göppingen, 1970.

Knox, Bernard M. W. "The *Ajax* of Sophocles," *HSCP* 65 (1961), 1–37.

———. "The Date of the *Oedipus Tyrannus* of Sophocles," *AJP* 77 (1956), 133–147.

———. *The Heroic Temper: Studies in Sophoclean Tragedy.* Berkeley, 1966.

———. *Oedipus at Thebes.* New Haven, 1957.

Korzeniewski, Dietmar. "Interpretationen zu Sophokleischen Chorliedern," *RhM* 104 (1961), 193–201.

———. "Zum Verhältnis von Wort und Metrum in Sophokleischen Chorliedern," *RhM* 105 (1962), 142–152.

Kranz, Walther. *Stasimon: Untersuchungen zu Form und Gehalt der griechischen Tragödie.* Berlin, 1933.

Lawler, Lillian B. *The Dance of the Ancient Greek Theatre.* Iowa City, 1964.

Leinieks, Valdis. "Aias and the Day of Wrath," *CJ* 69 (1974), 193–201.

Lesky, Albin. "Zwei Sophokles-Interpretationen," *Hermes* 80 (1952), 91–106.

Lilley, D. J. "Sophocles, *Electra* 610–11," *CQ* 25 (1975), 309–311.

Linforth, Ivan M. "Antigone and Creon," in *University of California Publications in Classical Philology* 15, no. 5 (1961), 183–260.

———. "Electra's Day in the Tragedy of Sophocles," in *University of California Publications in Classical Philology* 19, no. 2 (1963), 89–126.

———. "Philoctetes: The Play and the Man," in *University of California Publications in Classical Philology* 15, no. 3 (1956), 95–156.

———. "Religion and Drama in *Oedipus at Colonus*," in *University of California Publications in Classical Philology* 14, no. 4 (1951), 75–191.

———. "Three Scenes in Sophocles' *Ajax*," in *University of California Publications in Classical Philology* 15, no. 1 (1954), 1–28.

Lloyd-Jones, Hugh. *The Justice of Zeus.* Berkeley, 1971.

———. "Notes on Sophocles' *Trachiniae*," *YCS* 22 (1972), 263–270.

Long, A. "Poisonous Growths in *Trachiniae*," *GRBS* 8 (1967), 275–278.

Longo, Oddone. *Commento linguistico alle Trachinie di Sofocle.* Padua, 1968.

Maas, Paul. *Greek Metre*, trans. H. Lloyd-Jones. Oxford, 1962.

MacKinnon, J. Kenneth. "Heracles' Intention in the Second Request of Hyllus. *Trach.* 1216–51," *CQ* 21 (1971), 33–41.

Macro, Anthony. "Sophocles' *Trachiniai*, 112–121," *AJP* 94 (1973), 1–3.

Maddalena, Antonio. *Sofocle.* 2d ed.: Turin, 1959.

Margon, Joseph. "The Death of Antigone," *CalSCA* 3 (1970) 177–183.

———. "Sophocles, *Antigone* 1108–12," *CP* 65 (1970), 105–107.

McCall, Marsh. "The *Trachiniae:* Structure, Focus, and Herakles," *AJP* 93 (1972), 142–163.

McDevitt, A. S. "Dramatic Imagery in the Parodos of *Oedipus Tyrannus*," *WS* 4 (1970), 28–38.

———. "The Dramatic Integration of the Chorus in *Oedipus Tyrannus*," *C&M* 30 (1969), 78–101.

———. "The Nightingale and the Olive: Remarks on the First Stasimon of *Oedipus Coloneus*," in *Antidosis: Festschrift für Walther Kraus* (Vienna, 1972), 227–237.

———. "Sophocles' *Electra* 495–7," *RhM* 117 (1974), 181–182.

———. "Sophocles' Praise of Man in the *Antigone*," *Ramus* 1 (1972), 152–164.

Meridor, R. "Sophocles *O.C.* 217," *CQ* 22 (1972), 229–230.

Minadeo, Richard W. "Plot, Theme, and Meaning in Sophocles' *Electra*," *C&M* 28 (1967), 114–142.

Moore, John. "The Dissembling Speech of Ajax," *YCS* 25 (1977), 47–68.

Müller, Gerhard (commentary). *Sophokles: Antigone.* Heidelberg, 1967.

———. "Chor und Handlung bei den griechischen Tragikern," in *Sophokles* (Darmstadt, 1967), 212–238.

———. "Das zweite Stasimon des König Oedipus," *Hermes* 95 (1967), 269–291.

Murray, Robert D., Jr. "Thought and Structure in Sophoclean Tragedy," in *Sophocles* (Englewood Cliffs, 1966), 23–28.

Musurillo, Herbert. "Fortune's Wheel: The Symbolism of Sophocles' *Women of Trachis*," *TAPA* 92 (1961), 372–383.

———. *The Light and the Darkness: Studies in the Dramatic Poetry of Sophocles.* Leiden, 1967.

Newiger, Hans-Joachim. "Hofmannsthals *Elektra* und die griechische Tragödie," *Arcadia* 4 (1969), 138–163.

Parlavantza-Friedrich, Ursula. *Täuschungsszenen in den Tragödien des Sophokles.* Berlin, 1969.

Pastrana Riol, A. "Pensamiento y función del coro en el primer estásimo de la Antígona de Sófocles (vv. 332–375)," *Helmantica* 20 (1969), 193–265.

Pearson, A. C. (edition). *Sophoclis Fabulae.* Oxford, 1924.

Perrotta, Gennaro. *Sofocle.* Messina/Milan, 1935.

Pickard-Cambridge, A. W. *Dithyramb, Tragedy and Comedy.* 2d ed.: Oxford, 1962.

———. *The Dramatic Festivals of Athens.* 2d ed.: Oxford, 1968.

Plescia, Joseph. *The Oath and Perjury in Ancient Greece.* Tallahassee (Fla.), 1970.

Podlecki, Anthony J. "The Power of the Word in Sophocles' *Philoctetes*," *GRBS* 7 (1966), 233–250.

Poe, Joe Park. *Heroism and Divine Justice in Sophocles' 'Philoctetes'.* Leiden, 1974.

Pohlsander, H. A. *Metrical Studies in the Lyrics of Sophocles.* Leiden, 1964.

Popp, Hansjürgen. "Das Amoibaion," in *Bauformen* (Munich, 1971), 221–275.

Pötscher, W. "Sophokles, Oedipus Tyrannos 1524–1530," *Emerita* 38 (1970), 149–161.

Pozzi, Dora C. "A Note on δυσχείρωμα," *HSCP* 75 (1971), 63–67.

Prudhommeau, Germaine. *La danse grecque antique.* Paris, 1965.

Raven, D. S. "Metrical Developments in Sophocles' Lyrics," *AJP* 86 (1965), 225–239.

Reinhardt, Karl. *Sophokles.* 3d ed.: Frankfurt, 1947.

Robinson, David B. "Topics in Sophocles' *Philoctetes*," *CQ* 19 (1969), 34–56.

Rode, Jürgen. "Das Chorlied," in *Bauformen* (Munich, 1971), 85–116.

Ronnet, Gilberte. "Reflexions sur la date des deux *Électres*," *REG* 83 (1970), 309–332.

———. *Sophocle, poète tragique.* Paris, 1969.

Rosivach, Vincent J. "Ajax' Intended Victims," *CW* 69 (1975), 201–202.

———. "Sophocles' *Ajax*," *CJ* 72 (1976–1977), 47–61.

Sansone, David. "The Third Stasimon of the *Oedipus Tyrannus*," *CP* 70 (1975), 110–117.

Schlesinger, Eilhard. "Erhaltung im Untergang: Sophokles' *Aias* als 'pathetische' Tragödie," *Poetica* 3 (1970), 359–387.

———. "Die Intrige im Aufbau von Sophokles' *Philoktet*," *RhM* 111 (1968), 97–156.

Schmidt, Jens-Uwe. *Sophokles-Philoktet: Eine Strukturanalyse.* Heidelberg, 1973.

Schwinge, Ernst-Richard. "Die Rolle des Chors in der sophokleischen *Antigone*," *Gymnasium* 78 (1971), 294–321.

———. *Die Stellung der Trachinierinnen im Werk des Sophokles.* Göttingen, 1962.

Seale, David. "The Element of Surprise in Sophocles' *Philoctetes*," *BICS* 19 (1972), 94–102.

Segal, Charles. "The *Electra* of Sophocles," *TAPA* 97 (1966), 473–545.

———. "The Hydra's Nursling: Image and Action in the *Trachiniae*," *AntCl* 44 (1975), 612–617.

———. "Sophocles' *Trachiniae:* Myth, Poetry, and Heroic Values," *YCS* 25 (1977), 99–158.

———. *Tragedy and Civilization: An Interpretation of Sophocles.* Cambridge (Mass.), 1981.

Seidensticker, Bernd. "Beziehungen zwischen den beiden Oidipusdramen des Sophokles," *Hermes* 100 (1972), 255–274.

———. "Die Stichomythie," in *Bauformen* (Munich, 1971), 183–220.

Sheppard, J. T. "*Electra:* A Defence of Sophocles," *CR* 41 (1927), 2–9.

Shucard, Stephen C. "Some Developments in Sophocles' Late Plays of Intrigue," *CJ* 69 (1973–1974), 133–138.

Sicherl, M. "The Tragic Issue in Sophocles' *Ajax*," *YCS* 25 (1977), 67–98.

Simpson, Michael. "Sophocles' Ajax: His Madness and Transformation," *Arethusa* 2 (1969), 88–103.

Sophocles: A Collection of Critical Essays, ed. Thomas Woodard. Englewood Cliffs (N.J.), 1966.

Sophokles, ed. Hans Diller. Darmstadt, 1967.

Stanford, W. B. (commentary). *Sophocles, Ajax.* London, 1963.

Stinton, T. C. W. "Notes on Greek Tragedy, I," *JHS* 96 (1976), 121–145.

———. "The Riddle at Colonus," *GRBS* 17 (1976), 323–328.

Taplin, Oliver. "Significant Actions in Sophocles' *Philoctetes*," *GRBS* 12 (1971), 25–44.

———. *The Stagecraft of Aeschylus: The Dramatic Use of Exits and Entrances in Greek Tragedy.* Oxford, 1977.

Torrance, R. M. "Sophocles: Some Bearings," *HSCP* 69 (1965), 269–327.

Tyler, James. "Sophocles' *Ajax* and Sophoclean Plot Construction," *AJP* 95 (1974), 24–42.

Valk, M. van der. "Remarques sur Sophocle, *Trachiniennes,* 497–530," *REG* 80 (1967), 113–129.

Vellacott, P. H. "The Chorus in *Oedipus Tyrannos*," *G&R* 14 (1967), 109–125.

Vögler, Armin. *Vergleichende Studien zur sophokleischen und euripideischen Elektra.* Heidelberg, 1967.

Waldock, A. J. A. *Sophocles the Dramatist.* Cambridge, 1966.

Webster, T. B. L. (commentary). *Sophocles: Philoctetes.* Cambridge, 1970.

———. *The Greek Chorus.* London, 1970.

———. *An Introduction to Sophocles.* 2d ed.: London, 1969.

Whitman, Cedric H. *Homer and the Heroic Tradition.* Cambridge (Mass.), 1958.

———. *Sophocles: A Study of Heroic Humanism.* Cambridge (Mass.), 1951.

Wigodsky, Michael M. "The Salvation of Ajax," *Hermes* 90 (1962), 149–158.

Wilamowitz-Möllendorf, Tycho von. *Die Dramatische Technik des Sophokles.* Berlin, 1917.

Winnington-Ingram, R. P. "The *Electra* of Sophocles: Prolegomena to an Interpretation," *PCPhS* 3 (1954–1955), 20–26.

———. "The Second Stasimon of the *Oedipus Tyrannus*," *JHS* 91 (1971), 119–135.

———. *Sophocles: An Interpretation.* Cambridge, 1980.

———. "Tragica," *BICS* 16 (1969), 44–54.

Woodard, Thomas M. "*Electra* by Sophocles: The Dialectical Design," *HSCP* 68 (1964), 163–205.

———. "*Electra* by Sophocles: The Dialectical Design (Part II)," *HSCP* 70 (1965), 195–233.

Zielinski, Thaddeus. "De Sophoclis Fabula Ignota," *Eos* 27 (1924), 59–73.

Ziobro, William J. "The Entrance and Exit of Athena in the *Ajax*," *CF* 26 (1972), 122–128.

———. "Where Was Antigone?" *AJP* 92 (1971), 81–85.

Index